IDEOLOGY AND CHANGE

The Transformation of the Caribbean Left

PERRY MARS

WAYNE STATE UNIVERSITY PRESS   Detroit

Published by The Press University of the West Indies
1A Aqueduct Flats Mona
Kingston 7 Jamaica
ISBN 976-640-057-1

Published simultaneously in the United States of America by
Wayne State University Press
Detroit, Michigan, 48201

ISBN 976-640-057-1 (The Press UWI)
ISBN 0-8143-2768-0 (Wayne State University Press, cloth)
ISBN 0-8143-2769-9 (Wayne State University Press, pbk.)

06 05 04 03   6 5 4 3

Library of Congress Catalog Card Number 97-62548
A publication in the African American Life Series

CATALOGUING IN PUBLICATION DATA

Mars, Perry
    p. cm
    Includes bibliographical references.
    ISBN 976-640-057-1 (The Press UWI)

    1. Caribbean Area – Politics and government. 2. Communist parties –
    Caribbean area. 3. Right and left (political science).
    4. Caribbean area – History. I. Title.F2175.M38 1998
    972976 dc-20

Set in 9.5/13pt Trident
Cover and book design by Robert Harris

This book has been printed on acid-free paper

IDEOLOGY
AND
CHANGE

African American Life Series

A complete listing of the books in this series
can be found online at http://wsupress.wayne.edu.

Series Editors

Melba Joyce Boyd
Department of Africana Studies, Wayne State University

Ronald Brown
Department of Political Science, Wayne State University

This book is dedicated to my mother Midget and Sister Dorry
who defied the odds and raised so many of us in the extended family

Contents

List of Tables

List of Figures

Abbreviations

ABB	African Blood Brotherhood
ACLM	Antigua Caribbean Liberation Movement
AFLCIO	American Federation of Labour and Congress of Industrial Organizations
ALCAN	Aluminum Company of Canada
ALCOA	Aluminum Company of America
ASCRIA	African Society for Cultural Relations with Independent Africa
BLP	Barbados Labour Party
CBI	Caribbean Basin Initiative
CCC	Caribbean Council of Churches
CLAC	Civil Liberties Action Committee
COMECON	Communist Economic Union
COSSABO	Conference of Shop Stewards and Branch Officers
DLM	Dominica Liberation Movement
DLP	Dominica Labour Party
EPZ	Export Processing Zones
FSLN	Frente Sandinista para la Liberación Nacional
GAWU	Guyana Agricultural Workers Union
GHRA	Guyana Human Rights Association
GIWU	Guyana Industrial Workers Union
GTUM	Guyana Trade Union Movement
GUARD	Guyana Association for Reform and Democracy
GULP	Grenada United Labour Party
GUMP	Guyana United Muslim Party
ICFTU	International Confederation of Free Trade Unions
JEWEL	Joint Endeavour for Welfare, Education and Labour
JLP	Jamaica Labour Party

JPL	Jamaica Progressive League
KKK	Ku Klux Klan
LP	Liberation Party
MAP	Movement for the Assemblies of People
MBPM	Maurice Bishop Patriotic Movement
MND	Movement for a New Dominica
MNU	Movement for National Unity
MONALI	Movement for National Liberation
MPCA	Manpower Citizens Association
NAACIE	National Association of Agricultural, Commercial and Industrial Employees
NBM	New Beginning Movement
NIEO	New International Economic Order
NJAC	National Joint Action Committee
NJM	New Jewel Movement
NLM	National Liberation Movement
NNP	New National Party
NUFF	National United Freedom Fighters
NIEO	New International Economic Order
OAS	Organization of American States
ONR	Organization for National Reconstruction
OREL	Organization for Revolutionary Education and Liberation
OWTU	Oilfields Workers Trade Union
PAC	Political Affairs Commission
PCD	Patriotic Coalition for Democracy
PLP	Progressive Labour Party
PNC	People's National Congress
PNP	People's National Party
PPM	People's Popular Movement
PPP	People's Political Party
PPP	People's Progressive Party
PRG	People's Revolutionary Government
PSU	Public Service Union
PTWU	Post and Telegraph Workers Union
PYO	Progressive Youth Organization
RMC	Revolutionary Military Council
RSS	Regional Security System
SWP	Socialist Workers Party
UF	United Force
ULF	United Labour Force

UNC	United National Congress
UNITA	National Union for the Total Liberation of Angola
URO	United Revolutionary Organization
VLD	Vanguard of Liberation and Democracy
WFTU	World Federation of Trade Unions
WIIP	West Indian Independence Party
WLL	Working Liberation League
WPA	Working People's Alliance
WPB	Workers Party of Barbados
WPJ	Workers' Party of Jamaica
WPVP	Working People's Vanguard Party
YULIMO	Youth Liberation Movement

Preface

This book is about what could be called the heart of Caribbean politics. First, it seeks to address issues involving the impassioned and often unrequited commitments of dedicated individuals in the pursuit of noble political ideals, ideologies and causes for which many among them seem prepared to give their lives. Secondly, it indicates the central significance, however controversial this might be, of particular groups that have frequently been forced into political and social marginalization, notwithstanding their indelible and pivotal contributions to democratic political developments in Caribbean and other peripheral capitalist societies. Thirdly, it focuses on a critical political constituency comprising both the well educated middle class elements and the politically conscious working people who together constitute what could be termed the nerve center of Caribbean political culture.

By characterizing the role of the Caribbean Left as embracing such a potentially wide range of considerations, we presuppose a rather broad definition of the Left to include reformist politics at the one end of the political-ideological spectrum, and radical and revolutionary political movements and activities at the other. The Left, therefore, represents a varied array of agencies which challenge established precepts of the international and domestic status quo, and seek to initiate change or relevant alternatives to the prevailing class structure within the established political system. In the Caribbean context, the Left originated from specific inchoate forces, groupings and movements specialized in the articulation of what is sometimes termed a "culture of resistance" that is historically rooted in the slavery and indentureship periods throughout the region. Defined in this way, the Caribbean Left becomes all the more impressive, since their role propels its members into positions of historical prominence in the highly contested terrain that is Caribbean politics. Indeed, much of the heated international political controversies, tensions and conflicts that characterized the cold war era was often most violently played out on Caribbean soil where the contest between Left and Right seemed to have edged out all other political considerations.

The intensity of the contest for power between Left and Right has momentous implications for the shape of Caribbean democracy and the prospects for social transformation. After decades of struggle towards these ends the Caribbean Left became significantly transformed through periodic capitulations to persistent external and internal destabilizing pressures. These periodic capitulations are discerned here as "rightward shifts" by which the most radicalized or revolutionary of the Caribbean Left ended up becoming mainstream reformist groupings, or totally decimated by the experience, while at the same time the promised fundamental democratic transformations envisioned by the more radicalized elements failed to materialize. At the same time the intense Right-Left struggles have led to a kind of zero-sum conception of Caribbean politics in which political conflict and instability became imbedded in the very definition of democratic political participation and culture in these parts.

Most significantly, the modal expression of this conflict dimension of Caribbean political culture is the frequent interaction between the politicized general strike and ethno-political rivalries often culminating in massive riots and other dimensions of political violence. It is the persistent reduction of Caribbean politics to the fundamentalist dimension of ethnic and racial hostilities that has often led to something akin to a crisis of Caribbean democracy which consistently relegates the Caribbean Left to a largely marginalized existence. Even when the Left engages in the most benign forms of protest and resistance available within Caribbean political culture, of which political ridicule, rumour mongering, propaganda, and street corner meetings are the most prominent examples, these varying "everyday forms of resistance", to paraphrase James C. Scott, more often than not invite the most extreme and violent forms of repressive responses from ostensibly democratic regimes in the region.

The main argument of this book is that the transformation of the Caribbean Left is due largely to circumstances over which they had little control. Relentless pressures towards ideological conformity stemming from the international capitalist environment, coupled with the consequential elitist and factional tendencies on the part of the Left leadership as a whole, would seem to be the most significant sources of the debacle. Other competing explanations for the Left's predicament – about inherent flaws in and irrelevance of the Marxist ideology which influenced significant sections of the movement, or the defeat or dismantling of the socialist model on a world scale – would seem to pale comparatively alongside explanations associated with the problems inherent in world capitalism itself. The Caribbean experience has indeed demonstrated that, contrary to the more orthodox Marxist predictions, the capitalist system has not exhausted its potential for ascendancy, and that the socialist project adopted by the Left was consequently premature.

On the other hand, the Caribbean experience has largely demonstrated the relevance of Gramscian Marxist insights; in particular suggesting a more flexible interpretation of class relations and political conflict involving (a) a significant determining role for political and ideological commitments as compared with that of blind economistic forces in advancing Leftist causes and movements, (b) an understanding of the nature of political choice and change in the context of understanding tradition and continuity in the political process, (c) the usually critical role of intellectuals compared with that of the proletarian classes in initiating struggle towards social and political transformations – and (d) an understanding of the distinction between "organic" and "conjunctural" movements which facilitates appreciation of why the Left in the Caribbean and third world contexts tend to be usually temporal, transient and unstable.

Beyond examination of the competing explanations for the decline of the Caribbean Left, this book briefly attempts to evaluate their capacity for resurgence, given the possibility that, with the end of the cold war, a relaxation of foreign destabilizing pressures against the Left would naturally follow; and secondly, that the observed failures of IMF-determined structural adjustment measures to stimulate the promised economic development, and eventually arrest or reverse the economic deprivations and lumpenization affecting the greater proportion of the subordinate classes in Caribbean and other third world societies, could lay the foundations for increased political disgruntlement in these parts. The probability that these two circumstances can facilitate the generation of increasing mass demands, and opportunities for the future development of even more radicalized political and social movements for fundamental changes can hardly be disputed.

Although this book is interested in a panoramic view of the Caribbean political landscape the focus here is on the larger territories in the English-speaking Caribbean – in particular Guyana, Jamaica, Trinidad and Tobago and Grenada – where members of the Left have either controlled political power, or have played a most significant, lasting and dynamic role in the mainstream of political life.

Whatever positive contributions could be gleaned from this study are due in no small measure to a variety supportive and helpful people and institutions. First, I wish to acknowledge indebtedness to the many leading personalities associated with the Caribbean Left movement who provided important party documents, or gave some of their valuable time for interviews or discussions on the main issues involved in the series of crises that faced the Left movement in the English-speaking Caribbean between the 1960s and the 1980s. Most prominent among these are the late Cheddi Jagan, Clement Rohee, and Feroze Mohammed of the People's

Progressive Party (PPP); the late Forbes Burnham, Elvin McDavid, and Halim Majeed of the People's National Congress (PNC); Eusi Kwayana of the Working People's Alliance (WPA), and Brindley of the Working People's Vanguard Party (WPVP), all in Guyana; Trevor Munroe of the Workers' Party of Jamaica (WPJ) in Jamaica; George Belle of the Workers Party of Barbados (WPB); Bill Rivière, closely associated with the Left in Dominica; and James Millette, one of the most militant intellectuals and political activists among the Left in Trinidad and Tobago. Special thanks are also due to my wife, Joan, for reading and making valuable comments on various parts of the original manuscript.

I am also grateful to the following of my colleagues for their unwavering support and encouragement over the years: Paul Singh of the University of Guyana, J.E. Greene and the late George Beckford of the University of the West Indies, Rudy Grant of York University, Toronto, and Charles Tilly of the New School of Social Research. For their valuable technical, editorial, and/or research assistance, thanks are due to Norman Dalrymple, Elizabeth Ramlall, Bridget DeFreitas, David Nelson, Judith Allsop, and Ms. Leona Bobb-Semple. My gratitude also extends to the following institutions for allowing me access to their extremely valuable library and archival resources: the Caribbean Research Library of the University of Guyana, the Libraries of the University of the West Indies (UWI), and the Institute of Social and Economic Research at UWI, Mona campus, the library of the Center for the Study of Man and the archives of the Schomberg Center in New York. The following political and labour organizations must also be thanked for providing valuable documents or access to their files: the PPP, the PNC, the WPA, the WPJ; National Association of Agricultural, Commercial and Industrial Employees (NAACIE), the Guyana Trade Union Congress (TUC) and the Federation of Independent Trade Unions (FITUG) of Guyana.

Needless to say the shortcomings of this work are entirely my responsibility.

1

Introduction

The Global

Context

Notwithstanding the significant contributions of the Caribbean Left to the level of political development in the region, very little attempt has so far been made to systematically chronicle and analyse their activities and struggle in this usually neglected part of the world.[1] That the Left have largely been overlooked in Caribbean Social Science is undoubtedly a reflection of their consistent marginalization in Caribbean politics, in as much as the region as a whole is being increasingly marginalized in relation to global political developments and trends.

But this neglect is not the only reason why a book about the Caribbean Left is important. For one thing, their impact in general has been far out of proportion to the numerical size of both their membership and popular constituencies. Secondly, at this critical conjuncture in world developments, the remnants of the Caribbean Left need to critically assess their own strength and weaknesses if they are to escape possible annihilation in the grip of cataclysmic world events. This critical self-examination is all the more necessary following the self-destruction in 1983 of the New Jewel Movement in Grenada which initiated probably the most far reaching socialist experiment in the English-speaking Caribbean up to that time. To avoid repeating this kind of catastrophic possibility, the remaining Caribbean Leftist forces need to understand the basic reasons for their past failures or successes and their prospects of making further contributions to political developments in the region.

The more lasting contributions of the Caribbean Left are reflected in their leadership roles in the attainment of significant constitutional advances, the inculcation of heightened political awareness among the Caribbean masses, the struggle toward political independence, and in crucial instances, the ultimate attainment of state power. We also see their significance in a negative sense, that is, in what could be termed their 'nuisance value', or their relatively disruptive influence on the ruling classes and governing regimes. Indeed, in their efforts toward cultivating the very idea of progress among the Caribbean population, Left political movements have long been the single most effective sources of challenge to the very entrenched and typically conservative political *status quo* throughout the region. At the same time the ruling classes' strenuous efforts to eliminate the Left despite the latter's potential contribution toward political development, have served to call into question the very nature of Caribbean democracy, and the capacity of the Caribbean political system to accommodate critical and creative political inputs.

The objectives of this book are threefold. The first is to examine the contributions of Left political movements and organizations at both theoretical and practical levels. Second, to evaluate the prospects of the Left for making further and perhaps more creative contributions to Caribbean political culture and processes, despite their relatively disadvantageous location within a rather hostile and inhospitable domestic and international environment. It is also our contention that the test of any genuinely democratic political system lies in its capacity to accommodate political deviance and critical challenges to its basic premises and practices. What we are basically interested in, therefore, are (a) the role of the Left, (b) the problems they face, and (c) the strategies they employ toward political change within a largely hazardous political and social universe. The basic changes sought by the Left, prior to the realization of socialist objectives, are usually for some degree of political autonomy, for influencing or setting the national political agenda, and ultimately for the attainment of political power.

This study, therefore, stops short of considerations of questions surrounding the debate about the transition from capitalism to socialism which had been the central concern of much of the existing literature on Leftist politics in these parts.[2] For us, emphasis on the transition to socialism in the Caribbean during the 1970s and 1980s was indeed premature since it failed to address the issue of how the Left, under almost impossible odds against them, and given their location in what is regarded as the backyard of the most powerful hegemonic power in the international political arena, could first be able to obtain and consolidate state power as a necessary precondition for the ultimate realization of their socialist project.

THE ARGUMENT

The main argument of this book is that the entire Leftist project in the Caribbean has been seriously circumscribed by the nature of its political environment, and more fundamentally the class character of its leadership. Thus much of the failure of the Left in attaining their goals is attributable to the inertia imposed on the vulnerable classes by the capitalist system and the attendant limitations of the politically dominant middle classes which invariably lead the Left movements. There is also the anomaly in which the more radical elements of the Caribbean middle classes purport to lead in the interest of the subordinate classes which are often very conservative in ideological orientation. This argument would seem to complement similar theses advocated by a variety of social theorists who assert the essentially problematic nature of middle class political behavior, particularly in peripheral Third World societies such as the Caribbean.[3]

The Caribbean Left became relatively isolated from the international Left movement, not only because of the prospects of United States engineered destabilization but because the Soviet Union and the Eastern bloc communist world displayed very little tangible interest in these rather splintered movements which they regarded as ideologically deficient.[4] The result was a consistent and predictable rightward shift of the organized Left throughout the Caribbean. Ideology definitely gave way to pragmatism, sometimes gradually as for the most part of the post-war years, and sometimes more rapidly as during the more globally problematic period of the 1980s. One of the most significant implications which follow from the foregoing observations is that the apparent inevitability of the rightward shift on the part of the Caribbean Left would seem to make superfluous the massive militarization programs and foreign interventions to put down Leftist movements in the interest of US hemispheric hegemony. In addition, military interventions to protect democracy harbour a fundamental irony; that is, democratic pluralism is ill served by the repression of Leftist politics which has contributed so much to the democratic openings in Caribbean political systems in the first place. In any case, military and state repression of the Caribbean Left tended to be counter-productive in another important sense as well. It usually left untouched or sometimes exacerbated the basic contradictions which fueled the development of Leftist forces in the first instance.

The basic problem with Caribbean democracy is its relative fragility and vulnerability to external intervention and manipulation. Hence, what is democratically possible and within the logic of political pluralism in developed metropolitan states like the United States, is often not tolerable in peripheral states such as in the Caribbean. For example, an organized political campaign for upgrading the position of the poor, the underprivileged and the underdog, and for seeking policy alternatives to the traditional political agenda as characterized say in the Jesse Jackson presidential campaign in the United States in 1988, would in all probability have been destabilized if pursued within Caribbean peripheral states, as happened to the Manley/Peoples' National Party (PNP) electoral campaign in Jamaica which was violently destablized by the United States during the 1970s.[5]

The imperative of US destabilizing interventionism in the Caribbean is historically rooted in precepts like the Monroe Doctrine of 1823, deals like the exchanges of military hardware (in particular destroyers) for air and naval bases in Caribbean territories during World War II, and ideological stances such as the invocation of cold war fears, all aimed against further European incursions into a region that, increasingly over time, had been viewed as an 'American backyard'.[6] The combined effect of these historical circumstances coupled with the US self-asserted quest for global hegemony, has served to establish what could be termed an 'impermissible world context' for Caribbean political movements seeking fundamental changes and transformations of the international or domestic *status quo*. This 'impermissible world context' represents a global regime of consistent hostilities to ideological alternatives and their advocates throughout the region.[7]

Apart from the violence of external destabilization and internal state repression, the Leftist struggles for political power in the Caribbean tended to be largely non-violent. In fact, the overwhelming majority of Caribbean Leftist political organizations and movements, even some of the most orthodox types, openly eschewed the violent approach to political power and change. That the democratic processes involving the contention for power in the region frequently gave rise to varying levels of political violence, had less to do with Leftist ideological rigidity as is often assumed, than with deep-seated social structural problems such as ethnic divisiveness, electoral competition among the mainstream political parties, and more or less spontaneous labour-related disturbances, particularly in the larger multi-racial Caribbean territories such as Guyana, Trinidad and Tobago, and Jamaica. Indeed, most of the Caribbean Left demonstrated a great deal of ideological and political flexibility which enabled them to survive decades of the most deadly onslaughts from the most powerful of opposing political and international forces. The minuscule few which demonstrated tendencies toward ideological rigidity or uncompromising acceptance of the violent road, such as the Working People's Vanguard Party (WPVP) in Guyana, or the National United Freedom Fighters (NUFF) in Trinidad and Tobago, were either quickly exterminated or left to atrophy for lack of any semblance of political legitimacy or popular sympathy and support.[8]

This observation of the relative flexibility of the Caribbean Left helps us not only to understand the possibility of their consistent rightward shift over the years, but momentarily to correct some popular misperceptions that the Leftist movement in the region was only recently forced to change course, ideologically and tactically, following either the Grenada/New Jewel Movement (NJM) fiasco of 1983, or the more recent cataclysmic events in Eastern Europe stemming from the revisionist influences of Glasnost and Perestroika in the Soviet Union. However, far from representing sources of the decline of the Caribbean Left, these incidents have to some extent served as vindication of what was perceived to be the revisionist mood which had long characterized the theory and practice of the mainstream Left in the region.[9] In short, this revisionist mood had for approximately three decades preceded both the Grenada and the continental events, as it was a function of both the peculiar historical development of the Caribbean Left and the severe constraints imposed upon these groups by a generally hostile political and international environment.

The most proximate sources of this rightward shift on the part of the Caribbean Left are, therefore, to be sought among the following closely interdependent factors: (a) continual pressures and hostilities from a typically interventionist international environment, (b) the vulnerability of the essentially middle class political leadership to external interventionist pressures, (c) the susceptibility of the middle class Left leadership to internal sectarian fissures, and the cultivation of elitist and authoritarian tendencies, and (d) the ultimate alienation of the Caribbean masses and subordinate classes from the Left leadership and movement as a whole.

THE APPROACH

Our analysis of the political significance of the Caribbean Left is based on what could be regarded as a modified political economy approach. By this is we perceive the relationship between political and economic factors not as fixed, predetermined or linear as is often assumed by a variety of Marxist and non-Marxist theorists, but rather as a relatively flexible interdependent one in which either the political or the economic instance can become interchangeably dominant depending upon the particular historical circumstances. In the peripheral countries of the Caribbean, political movements are motivated as much, if not more so, by ideological and political factors as by economic conditions. The fact, for example, that some Caribbean economies such as those in Jamaica and Guyana have tended to be in a continuous state of depression between 1980 and 1990 does not necessarily mean that there was a corresponding proliferation of Leftist anti-systemic movements, or a continuous increase in revolutionary activities in these countries during this particular decade. Both the number of Left political organizations and volume of insurrectionary events have tended to fluctuate and vary in both frequency and intensity from time to time in the region as a whole – a variation which does not necessarily seem to depend on the particular level of economic development of the Caribbean country.

A second important aspect of our particular political-economy approach is recognition of the overwhelming impact of international factors and events on national political and economic relationships and activities. As already cogently argued by Modern World Systems and Dependency theorists, and echoed by a particular version of the Caribbean 'Plantation Society' school of thought, this relationship between the international and national affairs is invariably an unequal one in which case the peripheral states, such as those in the Caribbean, occupy a definitely disadvantageous and subordinate position *vis-à-vis* the more dominant metropolitan powers in the international political system.[10] The inevitable globalization of the international capitalist system does not necessarily negate all tendencies towards peripheralization of Third World, including Caribbean societies, but might in some instances intensify the contradictions and conflicts between dominant but foreign dependent classes and the more exploited classes within these societies – a process which Samir Amin characterized as the intrinsic tendency towards polarization of the capitalist system.[11] This polarization could be seen not only in terms of what Amin suggests as the increasing revolutionary potentialities of the oppressed masses in peripheral societies,[12] but equally in terms of the strengthening or reinforcing of the capacity of the domestic ruling classes to defend themselves against possible onslaughts from the awakened exploited and oppressed classes.[13]

This sharpened polarizing tendency of international capitalism allows for the maintenance of the asymmetrical relationship between dominant hegemonic powers and subordinate states in the international political system, the reinforcement of the ideological dominance of the former over the latter, and not surprisingly also, the fostering of counter-hegemonic trends on the part of progressive forces in peripheral capitalist, including Caribbean, societies. However, unlike the more orthodox dependency and world system's theses, the determination of specific political events and trends does not invariably flow one way, from the international to the domestic scene, but can also have its locus within national, political and economic life as well. Thus, Leftist politics in the Caribbean gain much of its inspiration from localized conditions of conflict as well as from international structural inequalities.

In our political economy approach we emphasize class analysis which is crucial for a proper understanding of the derivation and orientation of Leftist movements and politics. However, our concept of class for Caribbean conditions derives as much from superstructural as from structural considerations, in which case racial, political and ideological as much as economic factors play significant roles in the definition and the determination or shaping of the behaviour patterns of the pertinent social classes in the region. It is by now commonplace knowledge that the twin effect of colonialism and international capital is the creation within Caribbean and other peripheral states of unequal and hierarchical relationships in both the production and distribution of resources – a situation out of which serious social conflicts emerge. Leftist politics is definitely a natural response to this seemingly inevitable inegalitarian trend.

The objective of Leftist politics is to correct the imposed structural and superstructural imbalances in the interest of elevating the underdog, the disadvantaged and the dispossessed in the system. This somewhat revised class perspective helps us explain what appears to be a basic contradiction in Caribbean Leftist politics, that is, the situation in which a typically middle class leadership aims at protecting and pursuing typically working class interests. The difficulty posed by this seeming paradox is that the observed relationship between the middle classes and the masses or the working population in the Caribbean and other Third World contexts reflects mutually exclusive or opposed ideological positions, so much so that the middle class leadership of the Left can represent working class interests only to the extent the former are willing to commit what Cabral termed 'class suicide',[14] or as Rodney put it with regard to Caribbean intellectuals, they are able to transcend their 'Babylonian captivity' of privileges and rewards granted by the colonial-capitalist system.[15] Also, the ramifications of this same contradiction for the advancement of the Leftist political movements in the region need to be explained. To do this we need to understand more closely the character of the politically dominant middle classes and the nature of the Left political movements which invariably spring from these sources in the English-speaking Caribbean.

The structure and behaviour patterns of the Caribbean middle classes will be discussed more fully in the next chapter. But suffice it to say at this stage that our conceptualization of 'middle classes' follows that of earlier works as involving a relatively amorphous but highly differentiated social category located in an intermediate position between capital and labour, in the particular political system.[16] In the Caribbean context the concept of middle classes assumes a peculiar significance. First, these classes emerged and developed more out of political than of economic considerations, having been deliberately cultivated by the colonial powers to govern and help maintain the colonially imposed political system.[17] Thus, even though they are intermediary between foreign capital and domestic labour, their political style tends to lean more towards the former than the latter, and consequently becoming more elitist than mass oriented. Secondly, while they are in actuality the politically dominant class, they are at the same time economically dependent on or exploited by an externally located, (absentee) owner-capitalist class; it is no doubt from this kind of status inconsistency that much of middle class radicalism is derived. Thirdly, because of this discrepancy between their political and economic status, middle class dominance becomes extremely fragile and vulnerable particularly to external penetration and control; and fourthly, their sense of vulnerability predisposes these classes to seek alliances with social categories such as race and colour groupings in order to reinforce their power, prestige and legitimacy in the society as a whole.[18] The Caribbean middle classes therefore harbour a high degree of contradictory relations *vis-à-vis* their external and domestic, as well as their economic and political environments.

Yet, notwithstanding the inherent problems and contradictions of the Caribbean middle classes, we do not totally subscribe to the thesis made famous by some foremost Caribbean social theorists that the middle classes as a whole are totally useless, parasitic and intellectually bankrupt.[19] It is conceded here that at some critical moments, particular elements within the middle classes display these negative and self-destructive features, but more significantly the Caribbean middle classes have historically demonstrated a remarkable organizational capability and ingenuity out of which have sprung a wide variety of political parties, social movements and progressive intellectual trends;[20] and it was out of this particular type of creative interlude, in conjunction with the tensions inherent in these classes and Caribbean society as a whole, that Leftist movements and thought emerged and developed. How the same social forces can simultaneously spawn both conservative and radicalized political tendencies is a mark of the peculiar and complex character of the middle classes, an issue to be dealt with more closely in the next chapter.

The Caribbean Left display some specific characteristics. First, while these groups in keeping with Leftist objectives in general pursue fundamental political and economic change at both the national and international levels, their mark of distinction is that they generally tend to restrict their methods principally to the electoral and institutionalized processes while eschewing the more violent alternatives characteristic of their counterparts in much of Central and Latin America. Reliance on the established institutional procedures toward democratic changes has allowed the Caribbean Left the relative freedom to concentrate on ideological or theoretical issues such as the capitalism/socialism debate at the expense of the more immediate concerns of strategy and tactics toward political power. But at the same time this emphasis on theory by the Left leadership has contributed to much of their neglect of the Caribbean masses on whom their survival and development depend. It is also this tendency to absolutize theory in relation to mass work that has got the Caribbean Left into a lot of serious trouble, whether it be the paralytic preoccupation with debate on the merits or demerits of practical involvement which afflicted the New World Movement of the 1960s and Tapia House in the 1970s,[21] or the intoxication of the Coardist Organization for Revolutionary Education and Liberation (OREL) faction with orthodox theoretical commitments which decapitated the New Jewel Movement in Grenada in 1983.[22]

The relative lack of serious concern about the appropriate relationship between theory and practice in the struggle for power and change among the Caribbean Left has impelled the need for this kind of study which focuses on this particular problem; for the success of Leftist political movements and organizations in realizing their basic objectives largely depends on their ability to maintain a proper balance between the two. One factor which might have further contributed to the apparent confusion among much of the Caribbean Left as regards this theory-practice problematic is that the movement has so far failed to develop its own more indigenous vocabulary of discourse. As such, much of the self-concept of the Caribbean Left is rooted in a typically rationalistic type of discourse characteristic of the liberal establishment in North America and the United Kingdom, on the one hand, or deduced from very orthodox Marxist-Leninist tenets on the other. The rather intricate dialectical and epistemological concerns of Western European Marxism and such theoretical trends as post-modernist and post-structuralist discourses, have not yet come home to the Caribbean Left. The closest the Caribbean Left have approximated a localized Leftist discourse is their common advocacy of the anti-colonialist perspectives of Aimé Césaire and Frantz Fanon, and the dependency and plantation society theories of Latin American and Caribbean underdevelopment. This discourse is couched largely in empiricist terms and therefore does not go far enough in grasping the dialectics of strategy and praxis which are indispensable to relatively weak forces struggling against overwhelming and disproportionate odds. That the Caribbean Left invariably find themselves in such a disadvantaged position *vis-à-vis* the more powerful rightist and anti-Left forces linked to international capitalist and hegemonic interests can hardly been denied.

The impact of the Caribbean Left is limited by several factors stemming basically from their political and international environment. How these movements survive, or are accommodated within these inhospitable conditions is to be understood in relation to their capacity for making significant and far-reaching changes in Caribbean political processes. This issue of survival and adaptation is at the very crux of what was earlier observed as the problem of the 'rightward shift' of Leftist forces in Caribbean politics over the years. To understand more fully this rightward shift phenomenon, one has to first understand the limits to change imposed on the Left by these historical and environmental circumstances.

Among these limiting factors are not only the incapacities of middle class leadership but other social structural conditions such as racial cleavages which tend to divide and fragment both the Left political forces and class politics on which they are based. The frequency and variety of internal dissensions and fragmentation affecting the Left in general are largely a reflection of these international and domestic pressures towards a rightward ideological conformity.

The rightward shift is therefore the tendency on the part of the Caribbean Left to be perpetually pressured into accepting these institutionalized limitations. More specifically, the conceptualization of rightward shift entails (a) change of ideological commitments from the more revolutionary positions such as adherence to Marxism-Leninism, towards the more moderate or conservative ideological positions such as nationalism or liberalism, and (b) preference for more piecemeal, gradual or incremental changes instead of the more abrupt and far reaching transformations. The type of impact which the Left forces are capable of, given these rightward limitations, can be better understood in terms of a classificatory scale demonstrating different levels of their involvements and orientations, and characterized by the extent of change envisaged within the political system. For our purpose the Caribbean Left could be classified along three distinct lines, based on their programmatic stances and ideological orientations. These are: (a) Reformist movements which aim at the lower levels of impact or change, or piecemeal and moderate adjustments within the system, (b) Radical movements aiming at the intermediate levels of impact, either gradualist but fundamental, or moderate in ideological orientation but immediate as far as their tactics and strategies are concerned, and (c) Revolutionary movements which tend to be more extreme in their methods and far reaching in their aims as far as socio-economic changes or transformations are concerned. These particular differentiations will be dealt with more closely in chapter 3.

What would seem to be particularly advantageous about the differentiation between Reformist, Radical and Revolutionary Left movements is not only the recognition of the specific stages of shifts from the more Left (that is, revolutionary) to the more Right (that is, reformist) orientations and vice-versa, but also that it enables an understanding of the strategies, alliance possibilities and options available to each type. In addition, this type of Left differentiation gives us an insight into the extent to which each category is prone to use legitimate as opposed to extra-legal approaches to change. In fact, both the nature or type of alliance formation and propensity to use or reject force are crucial yardsticks for the recognition of tendencies toward revolutionism or moderation (that is towards a rightward shift) resulting from particular environmental stimuli within the particular political system.

This classifactory scheme, however, does not necessarily follow the traditional distinction between simply the 'non-Marxist' and 'Marxist' categories. Indeed, it is tempting to suggest that the non-Marxist elements represent the more gradualist and therefore reformist approaches, while the Marxist ones tend to be necessarily more radical or revolutionary. In fact, however, some of the very reformist Left have often claimed to be Marxist (such as the People's National Congress (PNC) under Forbes Burnham in Guyana during the 1970s). Also, some of the radical Left movements such as National Joint Action Committee (NJAC) in Trinidad and Tobago have rejected Marxism, while many of what could be termed revolutionary Left have maintained variable, inconsistent and even contradictory levels of commitment to Marxist ideology and practice over the years; the now defunct Working People's Vanguard Party (WPVP) in Guyana was a case in point. Moreover, particularly since the Grenada fiasco in 1983 and the devastation of Eastern European communism under Glasnost and Perestroika in the Soviet Union during the late 1980s, the Marxist Left in the region have found the need to downplay or camouflage their once strident commitment to Marxist-Leninist internationalism and ideology. This was the case particularly of the Workers' Party of Jamaica (WPJ) during the latter part of the 1980s.[23]

THEORETICAL PERSPECTIVES

To fully understand the reasons for the rightward shift, it is necessary first to understand the structural derivation of the Left movements themselves. In this regard the interplay between international and domestic factors is most important. Our theoretical framework for comprehending the class derivation and social location of Left political forces in the Caribbean is outlined in Figure 1.

Figure 1 is based on our modified political economy perspective of the class derivation of Leftist political movements and organizations in the English-speaking Caribbean. It is suggested here that Caribbean political movements, as perhaps in other peripheral Third World societies, are derived essentially from the middle classes which themselves are located in an intermediary position between the international capitalist classes and the masses and subordinate classes of the domestic population. Whereas the Rightist political forces tend to represent the interest mainly of the commercial stratum of the middle classes and the embryonic national capitalist or big business sector, the Left on the other hand are derived largely from the intellectual stratum which seeks to organize and represent the interest of the subordinate classes in these peripheral political systems. The remaining professional and bureaucratic strata which link the middle classes with the state tend to be randomly distributed in the hierarchy of both Left and Rightist movements. At the same time the political behaviour of both the national state and the indigenous capitalist classes at the periphery are directly influenced, conditioned, and in some cases in the Caribbean, determined by the activities of international capital. Indeed, there is some consensus surrounding the observa-

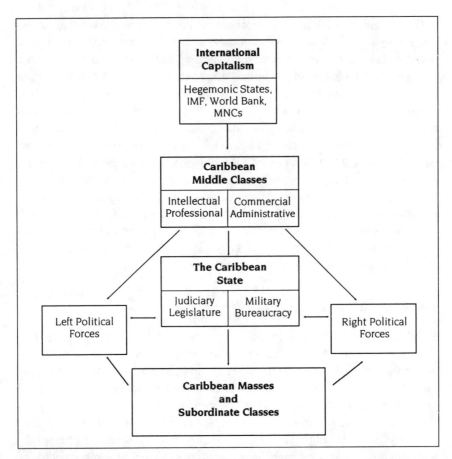

Figure 1 Origins of Left and Right Political Forces in the Anglophone Caribbean

tion that a critical, although not necessarily sole factor explaining the political and economic processes of the Caribbean, and many peripheral societies for that matter, is the dynamic interdependence between capital and labour at both the national and international levels of operation.[24]

On the surface there would appear to be close theoretical affinities between our outline model in Figure 1 and Modern World Systems, Dependency and Hegemonic Stability theories.[25] Such affinities are reflected in the fact that, like these theories, our model discerns the necessary interconnection between international and national capitalist relations. As such it facilitates analysis of the relations between what is perceived to be the dominant centre and the subordinate periphery nations within the international capitalist system. There is, therefore, the presumption in our model of an essentially hierarchical and unequal relationship between the international and national capitalist structures. A variety of political economy literature already exists to demonstrate this kind of inegalitarian, dependency relationship between Caribbean states and Western European or North American metropolitan nations.[26]

More fundamentally, however, our model seeks to go beyond these primary assumptions by its assertion of the relevance of class relations in explaining political behaviour at the national level, although the class structures might themselves have been shaped by international political-economic relations in the first place. The relative neglect of this issue of class struggle in the national political arena is the basis of some of the most insightful Marxist criticism of Modern World Systems and dependency theories.[27] By focusing on class analysis, we return to the internal dynamics of political struggle and change, to counterbalance the almost exclusive preoccupation of both World Systems and Dependency theories with the international sources of both global and national political and economic processes. Whereas also these theories, particularly Hegemonic Stability Theory, emphasize the tendencies toward conformity on the part of subordinate groups and states to the international capitalist system, our model seeks to explain both conformity and change within these two spheres of activity.

Conformity of peripheral states in relation to hegemonic international powers, and domestic political groupings in relation to the established national political institutions, is explainable in terms of several closely related assumptions of our model. The assumption of Hegemonic Stability theory, for example, that the power of the existing hegemon, that is, the United States following World War II, is declining relative to other global powers such as Japan and West Germany tends to overlook the probability that, in consequence, its power stance as against peripheral Third World countries might necessarily increase as a compensatory measure. In short, North/South dominance has naturally replaced East-West or global hegemonic control. What Cheryl Payer termed the "debt trap",[28] and a variety of military and violent destabilization experienced by Caribbean and other Third World states and peoples particularly during the decade of the 1980s, are indeed reflections of this renewed attempt by a globally declining hegemon to reassert its international power and prestige. Accommodation to stringent structural adjustment conditionalities imposed on debt ridden Third World countries by dominant capitalist powers and international lending institutions such as the IMF and World Bank, is therefore a natural Third World and Caribbean response to these kinds of international pressures toward conformity.[29] How then is 'change' to be explained within a model that asserts the pressures toward conformity?

A most important theoretical exposition of the concept of change within conformity is Gramsci's concept of ideological hegemony which suggests that the modern capitalist state is an instrument not only of coercion but more fundamentally of ideological domination which engenders the sometimes submissive sometimes voluntary consent of the subordinate population.[30] Applying the Gramscian concept to the international system, Keohane alludes to the possibility of consent and cooperation between hegemonic powers and subordinate states and peoples in his suggestion that "[h]egemons require deference to enable them to construct a structure of world capitalist order."[31] But at the same time, Keohane goes beyond the 'voluntaristic consent' model of Gramsci, to suggest that the willingness on the part of subordinate states to give consent to the hegemonic superstructure, is dependent on the prospects of receiving material rewards for such consent. As Keohane himself put it: "[h]egemony rests on the subjective awareness by elites in secondary states that they are benefiting, as well as the willingness of the hegemon itself to sacrifice tangible short term benefits for long term tangible gains."[32] It is in the demand of peripheral states and peoples mainly for intangible benefits within the hegemonic capitalist order that, we contend, lies the limits of consent, and therefore the possibilities for ideological deviance, counter-hegemonic struggle and ultimate systemic transformations.

Further, for Gramsci, the role of the traditional intellectual stratum is mainly to transmit this dominant ideology to the masses; and to this extent, at least, intellectuals generally contribute to the perpetuation of the ruling classes.[33] On the other hand, the subordinate classes also have the capacity to produce 'organic' intellectuals who are capable of challenging the *status quo*. For Gramsci, therefore, intellectual work has the capacity not only for buttressing the hegemonic structures, but equally for building counter-hegemonic struggles in the system as well.[34] Also, the organic alliance between the intellectuals and masses is powerful enough to produce what Gramsci calls a 'crisis' of the ruling class' hegemony which can culminate into a revolution.[35] However, although Gramsci's thesis is meant to apply to the more modern and developed capitalist state, with some modification it could equally contribute to our understanding of ideological conformity on the part of the subordinate classes within the weaker peripheral capitalist society (like in the Caribbean) as well. But while the concept of hegemony harbours both coercion and consent as its driving force, it also allows for the possibility of non-economic superstructural factors such as ideology and political movement as being the motive forces of change in modern capitalist societies. The emphasis on superstructural considerations makes Gramsci's theses most relevant to Caribbean and Third World conditions which demonstrate relatively low levels of economic development in the international capitalist system.

The compatibility of Gramsci's perspectives on ideological hegemony with the Caribbean experience is to be viewed at several levels. First, at the international level the relevance of insights drawn from both the Modern World Systems and Hegemonic Stability theories is recognized in the process by which globally hegemonic states and institutions invariably subordinate relatively powerless nations, and entrap them into a fatalistic, disadvantageous relationship which William I. Robinson refers to as a "Faustian bargain"[36] – reflecting a kind of contrived consent to a relationship from which the powerless cannot voluntarily extricate themselves. Secondly, this perspective is exemplified in the fact that Caribbean intellectuals play a key role in the initiation of political changes, while a significant proportion of these educated elite become advocates of the working classes through leadership of trade unions or mass political parties. In addition, ideological radicalization in the Caribbean first came through foreign educated intellectuals and middle class professionals, and these were in the forefront of the decolonization protest movements and advocacies of revolutionary change throughout the region. Finally, Gramscian perspectives are applicable to the Caribbean in the sense that the economic necessity and survival demands of the working and subordinate classes make them relatively conservative (or pragmatic), and therefore vulnerable to absorption within the overwhelmingly powerful capitalist mainstream.

The Caribbean experience, however, suggests also some variations on Gramsci's perspectives. The main variation relates to the fact that the Caribbean ruling middle classes, which are essentially political, perpetuate their rule more through exploitation or manipulation of the weaknesses of the subordinate groups and classes than through the institutionalization of the latter's consent. Secondly, the subordinate classes in Caribbean and other peripheral capitalist societies do not always accept their subordination voluntarily and totally. Indeed, the Gramscian scheme would seem to underestimate the capacity of the subordinate classes to independently resist ideological hegemony imposed from the outside, even though the prospects for success in these efforts might indeed be limited. Decolonization and non-alignment trends, as well as the demand for a New International Economic Order (NIEO) are good examples of this counter-hegemonic defiance coming from the subordinate states and disadvantaged peoples of the world. Thirdly, the Gramscian scheme does not satisfactorily explain the radicalization of sections of the dominant classes themselves, except in the very tautological suggestion that these outcomes often occur historically, or that the ruling classes do not totally control intellectual life.[37] The radicalization of sections of the professional intellectuals in the Caribbean has been a continual process which fuels the creation of Leftist movements and political organizations in these parts. The sources of this intellectual radicalization are varied, and include most prominently, the frequent exposure of members of this group to international standards perceived to be more desirable than domestic conditions, their history of exclusion from crucial positions of political authority since colonial times, the intermittent opening of opportunities for initiating efforts towards fundamental change, and of course their unique capability for articulating the grievances of the subordinate classes in the political system.

However, the radicalization process, whether of the dominant or subordinate classes, or fractions of these classes, would appear to be subordinated to the process of ideological and institutional conformity on the part of these groups, principally because the conformity process is rooted ultimately in structural or economic conditions. Why the hegemonic capitalist ideology is most powerful in attracting the compliance of even the most exploited classes under the system relates to the fact that the content of this ideology holds the promise of both reward and punishment – in that the hegemon controls vast amounts of economic resources which the subordinates want, and massive military resources which the subordinates fear. The demands of the subordinates for economic betterment, or for avoiding war or repressive political violence, puts the hegemonic powers in a good position to demand compliance in return for fulfillment of these objectives. Beyond these typically materialist considerations is the further (however mythical) promise contained in capitalist hegemonic ideology, of future empowerment of the underdog through democratic inclusion in the political process, which tends to enhance the legitimacy of the hegemon in the eyes of the masses and subordinate classes at the periphery.[38] This process of mystification is reinforced by tendencies within the hegemonic ideology, particularly through ideological and propaganda instruments like the media, churches and educational institutions, which seek continually to assert the commonality of interests between the ruling and subordinate classes in the political system.[39]

The constitution of a more or less favourable world environment for Leftist developments at the periphery is, therefore, dependent on (a) the relative availability of access to material and symbolic resources demanded by the subordinate classes and peoples in the system, (b) the extent to which hegemonic powers are willing to use force to ensure conformity to the hegemonic ideology, (c) the level of commitment by intellectuals to counter-hegemonic struggles, and (d) the availability of alternative models of ideological change in the international system. Various combinations of these factors existed at different historical periods to produce different levels of Leftist activism in the Caribbean region. The 1980s and early 1990s, for example, represented a period which combined economic and political destabilization with foreign military interventions, thereby increasing the intensity of environmental hostilities against the Left and making their retreat or eclipse most likely during this period. On the other hand, the 1960s and 1970s would seem to have provided a relatively more facilitating world environment for the Caribbean Left, in terms of both the powerful demonstration effect of anti-systemic and radicalized movements within the hegemonic states themselves (most notably the civil rights and Black Power struggles in the United States, and mass upheavals in France and Germany), the post Vietnam war syndrome in the United States contributing to a reluctance on the part of the hegemon to send further troops abroad, and ultimately, the incorporation of human rights standards and ideological pluralism in the US foreign policy agenda for the 1970s.[40]

SCOPE AND SIGNIFICANCE

A systematic study of the origins and problems of Left political organizations and movements in the Caribbean is important in several respects. First, it can enable the kind of critical self-analysis which aids in the construction of a better political practice in the future. Secondly, it can generate insights into the development of adequate policy measures in the interest of more viable and dynamic institutions which are sufficiently inclusive so as to reflect a genuinely pluralistic democratic political system. These are the more practical concerns; but our interest here equally embraces theoretical considerations as well. How, for example, does political radicalization, from which Leftist forces emerge, take place in the midst of a virtual sea of aggressively conservative interests? What are the implications of our findings for both theory and practice in the pursuit of change on the part of weaker groups within Caribbean and other Third World conditions? These are basic questions which issue from what could be discerned as the agony of Leftist politics in the region particularly during the last two decades of the twentieth century.

It would seem ironic that the international economic, political and ideological factors which helped the creation of the Leftist movements in the Caribbean might themselves unleash the forces which will ultimately contain or perhaps even destroy them. But these are the kinds of contradictions which help to make history both dynamic and interesting. The situation would appear to be even more paradoxical when the very factors which had long been thought to aid progressive movements, such as the current Third World debt crisis which furthers the impoverishment of the popular masses in these parts, would seem to deny the Left forces the very resource basis of their survival, or that reversals in the international communist bloc might in fact contribute to the renewal of Leftism in the region. These are some of the more critical issues to be addressed in the following chapters.

2

Caribbean
Conditions

The Caribbean is a region full of contrasts. Here, visions of an erstwhile playground for the very rich and affluent mingle with the rather uncomfortable realization that the region is typically backward, impoverished and politically unstable. The coexistence here of a complex variety of peoples makes the Caribbean both a colourful cultural amalgam of life, and a kind of hot bed for the dynamic interplay of conflictual forces. Contrast is also apparent in the juxtaposition of relaxing sandy beaches in so-called paradise islands, with the repeated incidents of erupting volancoes and devastating hurricanes.

The English-speaking Caribbean, which is the focus of this study, embraces a wide variety of island formations scattered in the shape of an arc from the Caribbean Sea to the Atlantic Ocean. There are also two mainland territories, the one, Belize, situated in Central America, the other, Guyana, in South America, which are traditionally regarded as intrinsic parts of the English-speaking Caribbean. The diversity which characterizes these territories is evidenced, for example, in their respective geographic and demographic sizes. The smallest islands such as Montserrat and Grenada constitute little over 100 square miles, while the largest is the mainland territory of Guyana, comprising 83,000 square miles. Similarly, population differences are striking between the smaller and larger Caribbean territories, the smallest population being approximately 7,000 people, while the largest is Jamaica with approximately 2.5 million.

Table 2.1   General statistical features of the English-speaking Caribbean

Countries	Statistical Profile					
	Geo. Area Sq. Km.	Population '000	GDP per. capital	Labour Force '000	% Organized Labour	% Unemployed
Antigua	440	64	5.5	30	80	5
Barbados	430	262	5.2	112	32	19
Belize	22,960	220	1.2	51	30	14
Dominica	750	85	1.4	25	25	10
Grenada	340	84	1.5	36	20	26
Guyana	214,970	746	0.4	268	34	n/a
Jamaica	10,990	2,441	1.5	729	25	19
Montserrat	100	13	3.7	5	30	3
St Kitts	360	40	3.2	20	30	25
St Lucia	620	153	1.2	44	20	19
St Vincent	340	113	1.3	67	10	30
Trinidad and Tobago	5,130	1,344	3.0	464	22	22

Source: Central Intelligence Agency, *World Factbook*, 1990, Washington D.C.

The Caribbean is what could be called an artificial product of the exploits and rivalries of warlike European powers ever since Columbus stumbled upon the islands during the late fifteenth and early sixteenth centuries. As such, its connection with the international, political and economic systems is both natural and historical. For good or ill, the political and economic life of Caribbean peoples has been shaped almost entirely by external forces. The English-speaking Caribbean, for example, has developed a political and economic system directly out of British colonial impositions which were later, particularly during the post-colonial period, influenced and controlled by US hegemonic interests.

The political legacy of British colonialism in the Caribbean is the institutionalization of a rather truncated form of Westminster democracy with its inherent tendency to foster autocratic types of rule. Although theoretically it is based on constitutional rule and a parliamentary system of government, in practice Caribbean democracy is controlled by vested interests, particularly those allied to foreign capital.[1] Such vested interests would seem to displace all pretenses to the more egalitarian patterns of democratic political participation or popular representation. More aberrant tendencies originated in the nineteenth century colonial imposition of what was known as Crown Colony Government throughout the

British controlled Caribbean, with the exception of Barbados.[2] Through this system colonial governors were given virtual arbitrary powers over a legislature that was comprised overwhelmingly of nominated as opposed to elected members. By their economic class background and political orientation, these nominated members could be relied on generally to favour British colonial policies.[3]

Economically, the Caribbean territories are almost totally dependent on foreign capital. This economic dependence is further compounded by the monoculture development introduced by colonialism which regarded these territories primarily as sources of raw material to further the development of industries in the British metropole. In this way, sugar became the most lucrative product in the region as a whole. The result of this monocrop dependence is the failure today to develop a more diversified industrial base which could have significant positive implications for overall economic development. It was this external oriented and monocultural dependence on the part of the Caribbean economy that undoubtedly gave rise to the development of what was later referred to as the 'plantation economy'.[4] Through the concept of the 'plantation economy', it is recognized that the Caribbean, since the sixteenth century, became intrinsically immersed within the international capitalist division of labour, a factor which has left a legacy of volatile class and ethnic conflict and economic underdevelopment in the region.[5]

CARIBBEAN CLASS STRUCTURE

The emergence, development and dispersal of class forces in the Caribbean were basically the fruits of European conquest and colonialism which introduced capitalism in the region. Although the primary class divisions were derived from the broad economic distinctions between capital and labour, the nature of the class divisions themselves varied depending on the different historical phases and shifts in the nature of capitalist penetration in the region. Thus beyond the simple capitalist/worker division is a variety of sub-divisions each influenced by different combinations of economic and super-structural factors. At the same time, each sub-division would seem to emphasize different behaviour patterns and potential for inter-class alliances, depending on specific historical and political circumstances. Figure 2 illustrates a somewhat schematic representation of the economic basis of class divisions over different historical phases of capitalist development in the Caribbean.

As viewed from Figure 2, colonial capitalism in its earliest form was exercised through mercantile capital which was responsible for the establishment of slave labour into the Caribbean.[6] At this stage the master/slave division represented the dominant form of class distinction. This set of extremely exploitative class

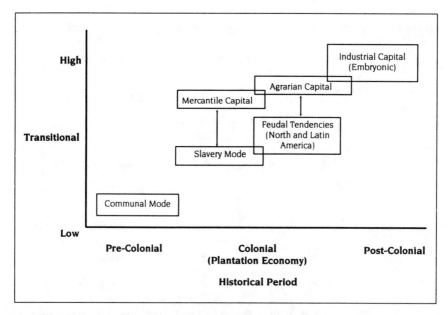

Figure 2 Stages of Capitalist Development in the Caribbean

relations replaced typically communal relations among the pre-colonial indigenous people of the region.

Mercantile capital also introduced the commercial classes which later fostered
the beginnings of both an urban labour force mainly attached to shipping wharves,
and an administrative service sector attached to commercial enterprises to augment the already existing colonial governmental administration. The development of plantation society originating in agrarian capital and slave labour superseded the earlier mercantile form of capitalism during the colonial era. Here,
particularly after slave emancipation in 1834, there was the emergence of an
embryonic working class (mainly a field labour force) tied to the plantation system.
At the same time a semi-peasant class was being formed essentially from those
ex-slaves who created their own 'independent' villages outside the plantation, and
who at the same time augmented their income from part-time employment on
the plantations.[7] It was mainly during the latter phase of the colonial period that
some levels of diversified industrialization were encouraged particularly after the
decline of the plantation system at the turn of the century.[8] Caribbean and other
Third World theorists, for example, testify to the existence of a basic antagonism
between merchant and industrial capital in the region, the former being interested
in the development of the metropole directly at the expense of localized industrialization.[9] Later, industrial capital took the form mainly of investment in mining,

Table 2.2   Breakdown of representative classes in the English-speaking Caribbean

Types of Classes	Differentiations	Descriptions
Expatriate controlling class interests	Capitalist Landlords Church (established)	Traditional ruling classes
Middle classes	Commercial Professionals Intellectuals Administrative	Politically dominant, but economically dispersed classes
Working classes	Urban Proletariat Rural Proletariat Semi-Peasantry Lumpen Proletariat	Subordinate, property-less and powerless classes

and much later in small manufacturing. Mining, particularly in areas such as bauxite and petroleum, became operational in the larger Caribbean territories such as Guyana, Jamaica and Trinidad. In this way, an urbanized or 'proletarian' working class took root, although its numerical size continues to be small in keeping with the very limited scale of industrialization in the region.

The earlier plantation period witnessed the political supremacy of an owning class of planter aristocracy (or plantocracy). Meanwhile, particularly since the plantation system was in decline following emancipation, the British colonial authorities carefully cultivated the emerging middle classes for political control of Caribbean states.[10] Thus, by the time of the British withdrawal and the granting of independence during the 1960s, the local middle classes were firmly entrenched as both the leading and dominant political class in the region.

Caribbean social classes during the post-colonial period are differentiated along the following lines: as Table 2.2 indicates, the upper capitalist classes are represented by typically expatriate owners of plantations and large estates and big (large scale) businessmen. The middle classes are essentially the managerial classes constituting not only professionals and intellectuals but also small scale businessmen, commercial traders and self-employed people. The lower (working or labouring) classes comprise mainly the field and factory workers on plantations, mineworkers, village farmers, casual workers, labourers on wharves, as well as the unemployed potential workers.[11] The relative significance of each of these classes in relation to the Caribbean economy could be gleaned from the nature of the distribution of the labour force along occupational lines. A very large concentration of the Caribbean labour force is in occupations such as agriculture, mining, manufacturing and construction. However, there is also a sizeable proportion of workers in the service industries comprising mainly the commercial and administrative (bureaucratic) sector of the middle classes. By contrast, the proportion of the professional and intellectual elements of the middle classes is minuscule in relation to the total work forces in the Caribbean.

Beyond their basic economic derivations, class relationships in the Caribbean tend also to be based on political and social inequalities. In particular, the relationship between dominant and subordinate classes could be described as both exploitative and oppressive depending on the character and orientation of the particular ruling elite. For example, the conflation of both economic inequalities and cultural domination in either the master/slave relationship during the slavery period, or the near apartheid system practiced by management over workers in plantations, mining and other multinational corporations, such as the bauxite industry during the colonial period, are well known.[12] But what is most peculiar about Caribbean class structure is its tendency to overlap or coincide racial and ethnic categories, thereby adding a great deal of complications to class analysis. The creation and development of the Caribbean middle classes follow in the complex class analytic tradition.

CLASS/RACE DYNAMICS

Perhaps the most peculiar feature of Caribbean political life is the interrelationship between racial or ethnic divisiveness and class categories and formations within Caribbean political systems. The Caribbean was not only a preserve for economic exploitation by metropolitan capitalism but a base for the transportation of different peoples from different parts of the globe to satisfy the labour demands of the plantation economy, particularly after the abolition of slavery in 1834.[13] However, the introduction of different ethnic populations was far from uniform in terms of their spread over the entire Caribbean region. The larger Caribbean territories, for example Guyana, Trinidad and Tobago, and Jamaica received much wider varieties of ethnic groups compared to the smaller islands of the Eastern Caribbean which are, therefore, more ethnically homogeneous. Nevertheless, there is sufficient ethnic or racial variety in the region as a whole to allow for the generalization that ethnic diversity characterizes Caribbean societies. Even in the more racially homogeneous territories where it is difficult to speak of clear cut racial distinctions such as Chinese, East Indians, Portuguese and Africans which characterize the larger territories, there are still significant divisions involving skin colour gradations which operate in a way very similar to ethnic and racial distinctions, particularly when it comes to the pursuit of upward mobility within

Table 2.3   Distribution of ethnic groups in the English-speaking Caribbean

Country	Percentages of Ethnic Groups					
	Africans	East Indians	Native Amerindians	Mixed	Chinese/ Europeans/ Others	Total Population ('000)
Bahamas	85.0	–	–	–	15.0	246
Barbados	80.0	–	–	16.0	4.0	263
Belize	39.7	2.1	9.5	40.7	8.0	220
Guyana	43.0	51.0	4.0	–	2.0	765
Jamaica	76.3	3.4	–	15.1	5.2	2,441
St Lucia	90.3	3.2	–	5.5	0.8	153
Trinidad and Tobago	43.0	40.0	–	14.0	3.0	1,345

Source: Central Intelligence Agency, *The World Factbook*, 1990, Washington D.C.

the political and social systems in the region. Skin colour gradations also overlap class distinctions as is most sharply manifested in situations involving the selection of political party leadership in some cases, notably in Jamaica.[14]

Labour was imported in the Caribbean from different parts of the world, such as Portugal, China, India and some parts of West Africa. East Indian immigrants were the most widely distributed throughout the English-speaking Caribbean. Between 1836 and 1917, for instance, the distribution of East Indian labour to the different Caribbean countries was as follows: Guyana 238,000; Trinidad 145,000; Jamaica 21,500; Grenada 2,570; St Vincent and St Lucia 1,550.[15] The second most widely distributed immigrant population following emancipation were the Chinese who went to such countries as Guyana, Jamaica and Trinidad, with Guyana receiving the largest numbers amounting to about 14,000.[16] Large numbers of Portuguese were also imported into the Caribbean during this time, the great majority of whom, some 30,000, settled in Guyana.[17]

The wide variety of immigrants in conjunction with the already settled white, black, 'coloured', and indigenous population constitute a very complex multi-ethnic universe. The result today is that much of the English-speaking Caribbean is composed of multiple cultural and social tendencies. The racial and ethnic distribution of the Caribbean territories is reflected in Table 2.3.

One of the most significant consequences of this shifting nature of the immigrant labour force was that there developed a strict ethnic division of labour in the Caribbean colonial economy in general. It was this ethnic-based division of labour more than anything else which complicated the process of class relationships and development, and laid the basis for the structural inequalities which today tend to undermine the prospects of political stability and meaningful developmental change. An African semi-peasant population emerged in the rural villages created by groups of ex-slaves and their families in various rural districts where plantation owners were willing to sell portions of bankrupted estates for this purpose. Similar peasant plots were created and developed by the East Indian estate labourers particularly after indentureship was abolished at the turn of the century. The Portuguese and Chinese, the earliest immigrants following emancipation, quickly fled plantation labour and were directly encouraged by the British colonial authorities to seek their fortunes primarily in the urban-based commercial trades and enterprises.[18]

From the earliest part of the twentieth century a sizeable proportion of the African population has been attracted to the mining industries. This is the case of bauxite in Guyana and Jamaica, and petroleum in Trinidad. Africans have also predominated in some aspects of the service and administrative sector, particularly the government bureaucracy and the military. This diversion into the service sector was mainly confined to second and third generation Africans who were relatively better educated than their forebears. A smaller proportion of the more educated Africans entered the professions such as law, medicine and teaching. However, much later in the century, East Indians and other ethnic groups have been increasingly attracted to these service and professional positions in Caribbean society. The post-colonial Caribbean experience saw a shift in positions of control. During colonial days white expatriates controlled the mining sector and occupied the higher positions of authority within the bureaucracy and military, while the people of colour were confined to the lower ranks of these occupations, thereby demonstrating a closer coincidence between race and class in the occupational and economic structures of colonial societies in these parts. During the post-colonial period, the British encouragement of Africans to fill the ranks of government services and the military, has been the basis of serious political conflicts. This has been the case specifically in Guyana where these services have more than disproportionately favoured the Afro-Guyanese ethnic groups as evidenced in the civil service, government agencies and police force, and as revealed in the report of a British appointed commission of enquiry into this problem during the 1960s.[19]

In general, the division of labour along ethnic lines which is more prevalent in the larger Caribbean territories tends to be reducible to basically two distinctive but not unrelated fields: (1) occupations related to political structures such as security and state bureaucratic activities in which the African elements of the population predominate, and (2) occupations related to economic production and exchange particularly private entrepreneurship, which tend to be dominated by East Indians, Chinese, Portuguese and other people of colour throughout the English-speaking Caribbean. At least implicit in the ethnic division of labour is the establishment of varying degrees of hierarchical relationships between the races in particular Caribbean societies. This division of labour makes for a kind of social stratification at some levels, and, at another level, opposing class forces coinciding closely with the degree of ethnic or racial polarization.

The post-World War II era, however, saw somewhat more significant loosening of the close ties between ethnicity and class. Several significant factors would seem to have been responsible for this trend. First, there were constitutional changes which allowed for universal suffrage and secret ballots at periodic elections, a factor which facilitated upward political mobility for people of colour. Secondly, the entrance of political parties into the political scene allowed for the organization and mobilization of a wider spectrum of political and economic interests which by and large aimed at cutting across racial and ethnic divisions. Thirdly, the expectation of political independence from British colonial rule led to the emigration of the bulk of the already small white population, leading to a realignment of the political and economic power structures, and allowing for greater access for the people of colour to the more pivotal, political and economic resources. The inevitable consequence of this trend was the fact that class divisions began to cut across rather than coincide with racial divisions in Caribbean society. It was, in fact, a situation in which for the first time race began to compete with class for playing the more significant role in the process of struggle and change in Caribbean politics.

It is usually reasonable to assume: (a) that class forces and their categories are generally weak in the context of the relatively low level of industrialization of the Caribbean political economy, and (b) that the obviously more visible factor of race becomes, at least by default, the crucial determining element in the political process. However, on closer examination of the historical experience of the Caribbean, precisely because class forces perceive themselves as relatively weak, they tend to utilize or manipulate other crucial factors or resources including both ethnicity and the state as necessary to further or consolidate their particular class interests in the society. Thus, C. Y. Thomas' hypothesis that the state apparatus in post-colonial Caribbean societies is invariably used as an instrument of class creation[20] must be supplemented by the further conception of weak class forces utilizing racial populations when necessary, and the state apparatus whenever possible, as crucial resources in the struggle for the attainment and consolidation of political power. This manipulative tendency is the typical approach of the Caribbean middle classes to attain and maintain political power.

THE MIDDLE CLASSES

 It has already been observed that the plantocracy which in partnership with the British crown controlled the colonial state in the English-speaking Caribbean, continually declined up to the eve of political independence, and gave way to the dominance of the more commercially and professionally based classes. The post-colonial period therefore saw a shift toward middle class rule. However, since the middle classes are sharply differentiated, the dominance of these classes is in effect a reflection of alliances between different strata within the middle classes. Hence, the gradual opening up of the political process toward increasing democratization saw the increasing control of state power by the professional and intellectual strata within the middle classes.

Table 2.4 gives some indication of both the middle class nature of Caribbean rule and the predominance of the professional and intellectual strata of these classes in the control of the Caribbean political process. As measured in terms of occupational characteristics, what could be termed working class elements are seriously underrepresented and in most cases significantly absent among the Caribbean ruling elite. This is observed in the relative absence of working class membership within Caribbean governing cabinets over the years (see Table 2.4). Similarly, we also find a preponderance of professional and intellectual elements at the level of heads of state of all Caricom territories. Of the thirteen Caricom heads in 1987, for example, six were professionals, four were intellectuals, while none could have been considered as being drawn from authentic working classes.[21] The post-colonial Caribbean state, then, is in effect a concatenation of different fractions of the middle classes, with the professional and intellectual strata in a somewhat hegemonic position, although these are largely dependent on both the commercial and bureaucratic strata for the consolidation of their overall ruling power.

Middle class rule and leadership in the Caribbean, and indeed the Third World as a whole, have often been berated by prominent Third World theorists such as C. L. R. James and Frantz Fanon, who maintain that these classes are, among other things, ineffective and intellectually bankrupt.[22] However, there is one quality of the middle classes that would seem to have been overlooked, that is, their capability to gain control and maintain political power which, in short, is rooted in their organizational capability. What therefore are the sources of the political capability of these classes? To say that the middle classes are essentially non-productive, is not, however, to say that they operate completely in isolation from the productive bases of Caribbean or other Third World societies. First, it should be recalled that the real power of the Caribbean middle classes inheres in their connections with international capital. Not only does the commercial section of

Table 2.4   Occupational background of Cabinet Ministers in the English-speaking
Caribbean

State	Occupational background of Cabinet Ministers						
Governing party	Business	Professional/ Technical	Intelle- ctual	Burea- ucracy/ Admini- stration	Working/ Peasant classes	Unknown	Total
Grenada							
NNP (1987)	–	4	2	–	–	2	8
NJM (1979)	2	7	6	2	1	–	18
Guyana							
PNC (1987)	1	9	6	5	–	2	23
PPP (1964)	–	4	3	–	3	–	10
Jamaica							
JLP (1987)	3	13	3	7	–	–	26
PNP (1980)	2	10	6	1	–	2	21
Trinidad and Tobago							
NAR (1987)	–	11	7	3	–	2	23
PNM (1986)	1	7	8	5	–	1	22
Total %	9	65	41	23	4	9	151
	5.1	43.0	27.2	15.2	2.6	5.9	100

Operational Definitions:

1. Business – positions in private enterprises, insurance, commerce, etc.
2. Professional/Technical – medical practitioners, attorneys-at-law, qualified engineers, professional politicians, trade unionists, etc.
3. Intellectual – educators (teachers, lecturers), journalists, etc.
4. Bureaucracy/Administration – positions in civil service, other service sectors in administrative capacity.
5. Working/Peasant classes – factory workers, peasant or semi-peasant farmers, labourers, etc.

Sources: *Caribbean Personalities*, various issues (1976-1980); Caribbean Community Secretariat, "Profile" (of Caribbean Heads of State), mimeo, May 1987; High Commissioner of the Republic of Trinidad and Tobago in Guyana, (a) "Ministers of Government, Members of Cabinet," mimeo (undated); and (b) "Profiles of Parliamentary Representatives, National Alliance for Reconstruction", mimeo (undated); Interviews with select Caribbean political and public personalities; *Elections Report*, 1964, Georgetown, 1964.

the middle classes live by this international capitalist connection, but it is through the existence of the middle classes that capitalist domination of Caribbean economies is facilitated and advanced.[23] It is, therefore, in the interest of foreign capital to foster the dominance of these dependent classes. The interests of both capital and middle class rule are consequently mutually reinforcing.

Secondly, it should also be recalled that much of the dominance of the Caribbean middle classes is based on a colonial heritage of selective political recruitment and privileged access to restricted economic resources. C. L. R. James' contention that the middle classes in the English-speaking Caribbean were deliberately cultivated by the British colonial authorities to govern, is indeed a very apt explanation of their claims to rule and whatever semblance of legitimacy is derived from such an inheritance.[24] The other inherited advantage of the middle classes' access to resources was evidenced by the colonial preference for granting loans and other forms of credit to these chosen elements for the development of private businesses, or for education abroad.[25] This access to colonial controlled resources allowed this section of the middle classes to become a new propertied class. The ownership of property, therefore, became one of the major inherited bases of the dominant power position of the Caribbean middle classes. The coincidence between the propertied middle classes and specific racial or ethnic categories such as Portuguese and Chinese represents a most significant feature of the Caribbean social system.

The combination of privileged access to basic resources and advanced education enabled this group to develop scarce skills which were quickly reflected in their prolific organizing abilities. Such skills soon became obvious in the variety of successful, although controversial, methods they adopted to further augment their power position – methods which borrow much from colonialism, including the exploitation of existing divisive tendencies within the society. More specifically, these tactics take the form of 'divide and rule', manipulative electoral and alignment practices, various forms of political repression by the state apparatus, and not least, propaganda, particularly control of the press and other media of mass communications.

There is also a self-justifying dimension of middle class rule, that is, that some of the problematic and disturbing consequences of that rule – political crises, instability and violence – are themselves used as justification for the ascendancy of the more politically conscious, skilled, capable and authoritative middle classes over the relatively more disadvantaged subordinate classes. Among the more negative, self-justifying consequences of middle class rule are:

- crises in governmental and political leadership resulting from the inherent fractious and conflictive nature of the middle classes themselves;

- fragmentation and polarization of racial, ethnic and other sections of the community as a result of the manipulative tactics of party politics controlled by middle class leadership;
- political violence and instability consequent upon middle class competitiveness in the pursuit of political power; and
- foreign intervention and destabilizing tactics usually facilitated by middle class divisiveness, competitiveness and general vulnerability within an ideologically sensitive geo-political environment.

Characteristic of the responses of the particular Caribbean states to these self-generated outcomes is the tendency to impose the more authoritarian and repressive approaches which are viewed as necessary to strengthen the states' capacity to govern effectively.[26] A fall back on the 'law and order' routine is invariably interpreted as an application of the principle of 'the rule of law' which is supposed to be a fundamental dimension of the liberal democratic constitutionalism. For example, the National Security Act which existed in Guyana for almost twenty-five years (1965-1989) during its independent existence is a classic case in point. In the more extreme cases, the party often substitutes for the state apparatus in repressing political opposition through its use of armed gangs, and strong armed thugs, as in the case of Gairy's 'Mongoose Squad' in Grenada during the 1970s[27], or Burnham's use of religious cults such as the 'House of Israel' to help terrorize and intimidate opposition political groups during the 1970s and early 1980s.[28]

But perhaps the most negative consequence of such officially sanctioned political extremities is the suppression of genuine democratic political practice. Inegalitarian developments affecting class relations are also reflected in differential access to political participation and decision-making; electoral advantages are premised on privileged access to material and state resources, while the benefits of political office are in many respects obtained through patronage, clientelism and partisan political loyalties rather than democratic choices or mobility based on merit.[29]

CARIBBEAN DEMOCRACY

There is a gap between the theory of liberal democracy championed by English-speaking Caribbean states, and Caribbean political practice. In theory, liberal democratic principles are enshrined in the constitutions of the various Caribbean countries which are patterned very closely on the British parliamentary or 'Westminster democracy'. Because of its derivation from the British parliamentary tradition Caribbean democracy is, theoretically, identified with the concepts of the rule of law, the independence of the judiciary, political representation in a centralized parliament on the basis of popular choice, a notion of political equality exemplified through the 'one man, one vote' principle, regular periodic elections, the principle of majority rule, political pluralism in the sense of encouraging competition among a multiplicity of political interests in the struggle for political power, and not least the assumptions of freedom of the press, speech, association, worship and the like.

However, in practice Caribbean democracy represents a fundamental distortion of democratic standards. Its close affiliation with colonial capitalist expansion in the region is largely reflected in the steep class and racial inequalities that underlie Caribbean political systems. For example, ownership of private property has always played a central role in constitutional development and the evolution of democratic practices in the English-speaking Caribbean. It is not for nothing, therefore, that the Moyne Commission noted that "vested interests" played a key role in influencing the Caribbean governmental processes during the colonial era. This was quite manifest in the rather gradual evolution and expansion of the popular franchise.

Colonialism in the Caribbean, far from representing the type of democracy exemplified in Britain at the time, was in fact a highly restrictive and circumscribed political universe with a virtually impassable divide between rulers and ruled. A combination of property (including slave) ownership, high income and literacy criteria ruled out any semblance of democratic political participation at different periods up to the time of World War II.[30] Additionally, the fact that during earlier colonial periods, the criteria for running for political office were even more restrictive than those for voting, put further distances between the official parliamentary representatives and political representation for the Caribbean masses.[31]

The coming of universal suffrage to the Caribbean after World War II constituted far-reaching constitutional changes which numerically transformed the electorate and the extent of popular political participation. Yet inherent contradictions in the colonial political structures at the time led frequently to the postponement or denial of the consequences of universal suffrage by the colonial authorities, particularly in the context of ideological conflicts. The dismissal of the popularly elected, pro-Marxist, People's Progressive Party (PPP) government by the Colonial powers in 1953 was a case in point.[32] The deliberate rigging of elections during the Burnham era in Guyana to offset what might have been a possible victory for opposing political forces, for the reason that the latter's support might have been racially based, was another typically Guyanese example of a ruling party unwilling to come to terms with the real consequences of electoral democracy.[33]

Post-colonial Caribbean states have to a large extent inherited a political culture based on the very inegalitarian and contradictory standards of colonialist democracy. Colonialist biases against radical and left wing politics, for instance, were later echoed in the destabilizing efforts of international capitalism, and the United States in particular, to undermine or eliminate radical political developments in these parts. The invasion of Grenada in 1983, as well as the unseating of the PNP in Jamaica in 1980 were prominent examples.[34] Such anti-radical or anti-Left biases were further reflected in policies such as *The Enquiry into Subversive Activities* in Trinidad and Tobago,[35] or *The Industrial Stabilization Act* directed against strikes in the same island during the 1970s,[36] an echo no doubt of the 'law and order' approach of colonial policies which were in earlier times instrumental in outlawing picketing and other forms of labour-related protests and mobilization. That these repressive tendencies were rooted in British colonial policies was suggested by the Moyne Commission itself which observed that the colonial system not only appeared to be autocratic but was, in fact, based on the essentially negative premises of the need for the preservation of law and order over and above ministering to social needs.[37]

The question of the representative character of parliament and other related democratic institutions is also very crucial, since it relates to both the class character and orientation of representatives *vis-à-vis* those of the 'represented' bulk of the population, and the strategy for the selection or election of representatives. The class gap between rulers and ruled, or between the political leadership and the masses in the Caribbean is, for example, reflected at the levels of both party and trade union structures. But what is most important here is that this kind of inequality gap often results in distortions of the principle of majority rule. This is not simply the general problem of the minority middle classes ruling over the majority labouring classes. In electoral terms, also, numerical minorities have often entrenched themselves in leadership positions over opposition political forces which together controlled the greater majority of votes in particular Caribbean countries. Apart from governments, this example is also notable in the hierarchy of trade union movements.[38]

This problem of minority rule is closely related to the second problem of electoral strategies. Not surprisingly, both wealth and privilege are still crucial in determining who controls the government as well as the leadership of contending political parties in the Caribbean electoral process. But even beyond the advantage which disproportionate control of material resources gives to political groups in electoral contests is the issue of electoral malpractices which take advantage of the mobilizational weaknesses of opposition political forces. The most remarkable example of this problem is the case of Guyana where elections between 1968 and 1992 were known to be massively rigged by the governing PNC using a combination of political tactics, including thuggery, threats, intimidation of voters, military commandeering of ballot boxes, deliberate efforts to exclude both independent and opposition scrutineers from the vote counting centers, and totally controlling the means of communication, such as the press and radio, to the disadvantage of other political contenders.[39] Similar electoral malpractices and democratic distortions were blamed on the Gairy regime in Grenada during the 1960s and 1970s.[40]

Related to the problem of electoral manipulation and resource control is the tactical mobilization of ethnic groups for partisan political support. Ethnic populations, therefore, constitute an important resource in the arsenal of particular political parties in the contention for power. This ethnic mobilization strategy was clearly seen in past elections in both Guyana and Trinidad where a variety of sizable ethnic-based constituencies exist, and provide easy opportunity for political manipulation in electoral contests. The obvious result of this skilfully manipulated process is the further fragmentation of the subordinate classes – a factor which undoubtedly contributes to the consolidation of middle class dominance, or the rule over the many by the few.

An even more significant outcome of selective and biased mobilization practices is the incidence of political violence so frequently associated with Caribbean democracy. Factional and fratricidal violence is continually witnessed at election time in such ethnically and socially polarized countries as Guyana, Trinidad and Jamaica where hundreds of people were killed in the inter-party electoral rivalries over the years. The violent take-over of the Grenada government by the NJM in 1979 was itself a response to equally violent repressive tactics on the part of the Gairy regime. Also, the bloody coup attempt by a dissident Muslim group in Trinidad and Tobago in 1990 was a similar response to what was perceived to be the unrepresentative character and the corrupt and oppressive practices of the fledgling National Alliance for Reconstruction (NAR) regime.[41]

Caribbean democracy, then, reflects a basic contradiction between the theory and the practice of liberal (or Westminster) political tradition. The relatively dependent nature of Caribbean economies renders the typically middle class Caribbean state weak and vulnerable to external pressures and control. Such weaknesses manifest themselves in terms of extremes of political behaviour, involving either the emergence of authoritarian-charismatic personalities and domination by the most manipulative types of political parties, or deliberate degeneration and deformation of the principles and procedures of popular political participation. Additionally, the dependent subordination of the Caribbean state to the ideological hegemony of the regionally or internationally dominant capitalist powers tends to determine and restrict the range of political choices. Within this limiting context, therefore, the choice of options challenging to the *status quo* tends to be sanctioned, thereby leading to a marginalization of left-wing and other groups interested in bringing about fundamental change.

A political culture develops in which political and social change is conceived essentially in piecemeal, incremental terms. Change in political personnel usually leaves intact the same inegalitarian class hierarchy dominated by the relatively privileged and more materially endowed classes. Meanwhile, the subordinate classes comprising the popular majority are usually fractionalized along racial, political and other sectional lines. The problem here is that class conflict, on which much of Leftist politics is based, tends to give way to sectional and partisan conflicts within the Caribbean political process. In this way, the prospects of class polarization and revolutionary change in the Marxist sense at least becomes relatively remote. At the same time, the option of violent class struggle becomes perilous since it soon degenerates into what Michael Manley terms the 'tribalistic'[42] or anarchistic type of violence which is often self-defeating to Leftist revolutionary or radical projects in the region.

The extent to which this particular political culture is influenced by external, international factors must also be addressed since it has implications for the development and scope of Leftist politics at both the national and regional levels.

FOREIGN INFLUENCES

The location, both historically and geographically, of Caribbean states within the periphery of the international capitalist system has rendered Caribbean democracy extremely vulnerable to foreign penetration, influence and control. Such vulnerability is often manifested in the frequency of external interventions and covert operations against domestic regimes and political organizations which tend to challenge, or threaten, the entrenchment of the powerful hegemon within the international capitalist system. Both overt military operations and the more subtle forms of destablization have been used quite effectively with extremely negative implications for the development of Leftist politics in the region. The pattern of foreign interventions, both overt and covert, which have at one time or another been used in this sense could be differentiated along the following lines:

- Military intervention, involving the use of regular troops to invade, occupy or conquer the particular target country. This approach is mainly historical, but applicable to target countries such as Guyana (1953), Dominican Republic (1965), Panama (1989) and Grenada (1983).

- Military destabilization, involving the use of mercenary troops to invade a target country, selective military aid to territorial neighbours of the particular target country, and military maneuvers by the dominant power within geographical proximity of the specific target country. Target countries included Dominican Republic and Grenada during the 1980s.

- Political destabilization, involving the conspiratorial use of systematic violence against leftist states or political movements, divide and rule tactics which inflame ethnic hostilities in order to discredit or undermine the authority position of a particular regime or movement, infiltration of the leadership of particular trade unions or political parties so as to influence the ideological orientation of the national movement, and certain subtle insultive or hostile diplomatic styles or responses. The main targets here were Guyana (1964) and Grenada and Jamaica during the 1970s.
- Economic destabilization, involving the deliberate efforts by the developed powers to sabotage the process of economic viability of the particular target country. This includes the blocking of loans and grants from international lending institutions, the deliberate flight of local capital, the fomentation of strikes, including lockouts by employers, restrictive control of markets by multi-national corporations, and the use of the debt trap to foster continuing and increasing dependence by the target country on the more economically developed countries, as well as to influence the ideological direction of particular target states. Targets included Grenada and Guyana (1980s) and Jamaica (1970s).
- Psychological-cultural destabilization, including the use of damaging propaganda by a hostile press or mass media and also, the use of religion and the churches to sermonize or campaign against a particular disliked ideology, regime or movement falls within this category. Guyana (1960s), Jamaica (1970s) and Grenada (1980s) were prominent cases of this type of destabilization.

The process of military intervention in the English-speaking Caribbean gradually shifted from overt operations in the early post-war years, to the more subtle use of military threat and maneuvers, including the movement of hardware and financial resources within more recent times. Overt military intervention to topple leftist-oriented governments in the Caribbean region were exemplified by the use of British troops to put down the Marxist Jagan government in Guyana in 1953.[43] In 1965 in the Dominican Republic, American military forces ousted the leftist Juan Bosch's government and installed in its place a government more favourable to US interests.[44] The most recent examples of such foreign military operations in the Caribbean were the US invasion of Grenada in 1983 to crush the ostensibly 'Marxist-Leninist' Revolutionary Military Council (RMC), which had earlier usurped power from the Maurice Bishop government,[45] the ousting of the Noriega government in Panama in 1989, which was accused of various crimes against the United States,[46] and the 1994 efforts to facilitate the return of the deposed democratically elected Jean Bertrand Aristide government in Haiti.

The use of mercenary troops to pressure or oust particular Caribbean governments from power was discovered, for example, in a plot orchestrated by Eric Gairy himself soon after his ouster, to use paid mercenaries to attack the People's

Revolutionary Government of Grenada.[47] Similar mercenary plots aimed at the destabilization of the Dominican government in 1981, and the Burnham regime in Guyana around the same time were also uncovered.[48] These events were only a few of the instances of mercenary plots against Caribbean regimes as wide-ranging as those of Haiti under the Duvalier dictatorship, Suriname under the Bouterse military rule and the smaller English-speaking Caribbean islands including Anguilla, although some of these operations were less politically motivated than related to drug smuggling or other criminal activities.[49]

The specific sources of foreign pressures on Caribbean political movements and activities involve not only the foreign policy concerns of hegemonic capitalist states, but also relationships to international donor institutions such as the International Monetary Fund (IMF) and World Bank. These latter institutions usually add to the large debt burden incurred by most Caribbean states stringent conditionalities which tend to perpetuate a vicious circle of dependence and indebtedness on the part of these states.[50] Foreign influence is further facilitated by the establishment of a variety of institutionalized facilities such as foreign-owned banks, military bases, and the recent establishment of Export Processing Zones (EPZs) within particular Caribbean countries.[51]

Underlying the rationale for US penetration into the region is the aggressive desire for ideological hegemony *vis-à-vis* the rise and development of any anti-systemic struggles, such as socialism and the more active types of nationalism, and not least to preserve the region as an avenue for economic exploitation by international capitalist interests.[52] The particular methodology for maintaining this kind of ideological and economic hegemony is the utilization of various forms of political and economic destabilization to stem, if not totally eradicate, the development of Leftist politics in the region as a whole. Tactics toward this end involve typically the use of proxy domestic groups and institutions such as Rightist political and labour organizations. The existing divisiveness within the Caribbean middle classes gives ample scope for the success of these disruptive tactics instigated by foreign sources.

Foreign intervention and destabilization are, therefore, critical factors contributing toward the isolation and ultimate marginalization of Leftist groups. In terms of the structure of dominance and subordination in the international political system, it is possible to discern the origins of destabilization in the aggressive hegemonic pursuits of dominant capitalist powers. The target countries are invariably those Caribbean and Third World states in which Leftist movements or parties significantly influence the domestic political process, and which seek to pursue both a relatively independent political line, and the implementation of alternative developmental projects. Thus, destabilization signifies the efforts of foreign powers to provoke domestic political instability in the relatively vulnerable countries with a view to re-orient specific groups and interests toward the ideo-logical direction of the hegemonic *status quo*.

The destruction wrought by destablization of Caribbean states and political movements is far-reaching in its consequences not only for the target countries, but for the initiating states as well. Democratic politics is often the first casualty in both political spheres. In the ostensibly democratic metropolitan countries, for example, mounting protests and quite often majority polling against these inter-ventionist strategies are often ignored or repressed. In the target countries, particularly the more Left-leaning Caribbean countries, democracy is further set back because intervention often preempts or frustrates public choice of political leadership and ideological direction. Within Leftist-controlled states in the region (e.g., Grenada, Nicaragua and Suriname during the 1980s), hostile foreign pres-sures and interventions led to a heightened repressive reaction, increasing bu-reaucratization and militarization, primarily because of their inevitable anxiety about their own security within a hostile geo-political universe.

CONCLUSIONS

By both their common historical experience and geographical location within a highly ideologized international framework, Caribbean states and political move-ments tend to encounter definite limits to their operational space for political maneuver and action. Geographic proximity to the United States as a dominant international power combines with increasing economic dependency on the part of peripheral and debt-ridden Caribbean states and the prospects of destabiliza-tion of deviant regimes and political movements, to form a formidable barrier to Leftist politics and attendant quests for fundamental political and social change. For this reason, the security issue becomes a disproportional consideration not only for the declining hegemonic power anxious to prevent alien forms of intrusion (such as Soviet or perhaps Japanese influence) into the hemisphere, but equally for Leftist Caribbean states which seek to protect their sovereignty against the usual threats of foreign penetration and destabilization.

The hierarchically-structured relationships at the international level tend to be duplicated or paralled at the domestic level. By this is meant that the dominant capitalist centers at the international level are closely interconnected with signifi-cant elements of the leading classes in the domestic political arena. In the Caribbean, this type of relationship is reflected in terms of middle class controlling influence over the subordinate classes. While the Caribbean middle classes are readily exposed to manipulation by external forces, they in turn readily manipulate the subordinate classes in the domestic political arena. In the loose democratic framework within which Caribbean states operate, working class support or acquiescence is essential for the maintenance of middle class rule, hence a strategy of manipulation and co-optation is crucial to the maintenance of this objective. What the middle classes lose to the external capitalist classes in terms of economic control is thus counterbalanced by significant gains in methods of domestic political control.

The consolidation of middle class power in the Caribbean is also facilitated by inherent divisiveness within the ranks of the subordinate classes. Working class disunity, for example, is reflected at several levels at once, including: (a) division within economic production mainly between a rural-based peasant sector and an urban-based industrial and service sector; (b) the usually high levels of unemployment which create opportunities for effective strike-breaking activities and the maintenance of low wages by employers or the state;[53] (c) a multiplicity of labour organizations which claim to represent parcelized constituencies of workers giving rise to a variety of jurisdictional conflicts;[54] and (d) ethnic and racial divisions, particularly in the larger multi-ethnic Caribbean societies such as Guyana, Trinidad and Tobago and Jamaica, which cut across class divisions while coinciding with political and ideological divisions within Caribbean societies.

The furtherance of Leftist objectives such as fundamental political change, economic transformation or even the far-flung perspective of introducing a socialist political and economic system requires a much higher degree of organized unity and cooperation than is allowed by the heightened state of divisiveness within both the working and middle classes themselves in Caribbean countries. What this means further is that the advancement of Leftist political pursuits is dependent on bridging much of these divisive gaps in Caribbean society. The approach needed here is usually a strategy of cross-class, cross-racial, and cross-organizational alliances and coalition building. How successful Leftist groups and political organizations were in utilizing these strategies will be dealt with more closely in subsequent chapters.

3

Rise of the Organized Left

In general, the rise of Leftist politics in the English-speaking Caribbean is rooted in the nature and impact of class politics as introduced by colonial capitalism. Thus, the development of Caribbean Leftist politics is essentially a response to the problems intrinsic in the character of a dependent capitalist Caribbean economy. At the same time, however, Caribbean Leftist forces have manifested such a wide variability in their orientation and practice as to reflect significant degrees of autonomy relative to the constraints and limitations imposed by existing economic conditions.

This chapter is an attempt to examine the historical origins and structure of Leftist political movements and organizations in the region. Our particular interest here is to understand how anti-systemic or counter-hegemonic movements emerge within a highly oppressive and dominant ideological-political system such as characterized British colonialism during the first half of the twentieth century. Further, we seek to examine the class character of these movements and the different ideological and political lines along which they diverge. It is the crucial Gramscian issue of why, in other words, political movements and organizations differentiate and fracture along the particular lines they do, and with what impact on the political struggle for change and development.[1]

Two relevant theoretical issues which follow from the foregoing considerations are whether the behaviour of organized Left political groupings is necessarily the expression of the interests of any particular class, and secondly, whether ideological and political divisiveness is inevitable in peripheral capitalist societies such as those in the Caribbean, and to what extent this inevitable ideological divisiveness contradicts the search for class and organizational unity in the Leftist struggle for political and social transformations. Against the background of the Caribbean experience these crucial issues will be investigated with specific references to: (a) the social origins of Left political forces and the conditions facilitating their development, and (b) the nature and basis of the differentiation and/or fragmentation of Left political movements and organizations.

HISTORICAL ORIGINS

Central to the definition of Leftist politics is the idea of movements, groups and individuals seeking to challenge or change the dominant ideological and political system by a variety of either conventional or non-conventional means. The Left, therefore, involves individuals, movements and organizations in continual resistance against pressures emanating from institutionalized formations within the controlling centers of political power, while at the same time exerting their own pressures for significant changes in or of the institutionalized arrangements. Conceptualizations of the Left, however, might differ depending on the particular historical and social context. The Left in the Caribbean context, although comparable with other Left movements outside the region in terms of their middle class, intellectual-type leadership, and an ideological orientation anchored in a critique of capitalism and imperialism, and advocacy of some form of socialism, tend, nevertheless, to be rather peculiar in their consistent embrace of Black consciousness philosophies and an *a priori* commitment to non-violent democratic struggles. Defined in terms of resistance to the *status quo*, the earliest pre-modern, political deviation in the Caribbean must be sought in the history of protest and resistance against plantation and colonial domination, going as far back as the period of slave revolts and other varieties of resistance including strikes, sabotage, avoidance strategies and marronage (runaways).

The post-slavery, or emancipation period, witnessed a shift from the earlier types of resistance against the dominant plantation system to the employment of a kind of economic guerilla warfare on the part of the newly freed labour forces, for, following emancipation, ex-slaves developed the peculiar embryonic form of labour organization called the 'task gang' which became their main bargaining units for wages on the sugar estates.[2] The skilful use of threats to withhold crucial labour when the sugar canes were ripe for cutting was a tactic which caused much consternation among members of the post-emancipation planter class. The East Indian labour force imported from India to replace the more flexible African plantation labour force also had its crucial moments of resistance activities manifested particularly in strikes and absenteeism.[3] The post-emancipation period also saw the birth of embryonic political organizations in the form of 'Reform Associations' founded by typically middle class men wishing to protest the inequities of a foreign and colonial-dominated plantation system.[4] Through the reformist ideology of these early political associations, the middle classes were able to co-opt and thereby contain the largely spontaneous protest and resistance of the Caribbean masses.

Perhaps the earliest efforts toward leftist advocacy were produced within the rudimentary beginnings of the labour movements in the Caribbean. The revival in 1919 of the Trinidad Working Men's Association under the legendary Captain Cipriani, for instance, took the form of a political party or protest movement which made extremely radical demands on the existing colonial system, including self-government, universal suffrage and equal job opportunities regardless of race.[5] About the same time, Hubert Nathaniel Critchlow created his British Guiana Labour Union (BGLU) in the neighbouring mainland territory which, apart from maintaining a militant trade unionist posture, agitated for political demands not unlike those of the Cipriani movement in Trinidad.[6] Both Cipriani and Critchlow were avowed 'socialists', and the latter travelled to the newly revolutionized Soviet Union as if to prove the point.[7] Cipriani's movement collapsed in 1933 essentially because it lost much needed popular support.[8]

It was from the BGLU that the first Caribbean-wide trade union movement was spawned. At a BGLU convention in 1926, several trade union and political personalities met and formed the British Guiana and West Indian Trade Union Conference (BG&WITUC) which in 1945 culminated in the formation of the Caribbean Labour Congress.[9] The significance of this regional labour movement for Caribbean Leftist development is that from its inception it militantly combined labour concerns with conscious political struggle and attracted to its ranks some of the most prominent leftist labour and political organizers in the region. The aims of the BG&WITUC included: (a) West Indian federation with self-government or dominion status for each territory; (b) the establishment of formal channels of communication among labour organizations throughout the region; (c) the institutionalization of compulsory education, workmen's compensation, an eight-hour day, and a national health insurance scheme; and (d) universal adult suffrage.[10] Also, in one of its annual conferences held in 1944, the BG&WITUC was very vigorous in its protest and condemnation of the British colonial policy of banning prominent Leftist individuals from travelling throughout the English-speaking Caribbean. Chase concluded that by 1955 the list of banned Leftist labour leaders included Quintin O'Connor and John LaRose of Trinidad and Tobago, and Ferdinand Smith, Billy Strachan and Richard Hart of Jamaica.[11] The Caribbean Labour

Congress, founded in 1945 in culmination of the efforts of the BG&WITUC, suddenly collapsed in 1947 as a result of cold war pressures which brought about an ideological split in the movement, with the more moderate elements withdrawing from the body during its 1947 convention in Guyana.[12]

Much earlier in the 1920s a variety of Leftist individuals from the English-speaking Caribbean became very prominent not only in the local and regional milieu but on an international scale as well. Perhaps the most notable of these individual Leftists were George Padmore and C. L. R. James, both of Trinidad and Tobago, and Hugh Buchanan of Jamaica. Both Padmore and James combined involvement in internationalist Marxist politics with a strong commitment to Pan- Africanist causes. While Padmore became a member of the British Communist Party in 1927 (a cause he later rejected) and took up the cause of Pan-Africanism, James became a staunch Trotskyist and was an ardent champion of the Negro cause particularly during his sojourn in the United States in the 1930s. According to James, Blacks are destined to play the vanguard role in any future class revolution in capitalist society, since Blacks are doubly exploited and oppressed, first because of their general working class status, and second, because of their race.[13] Hugh Buchanan became an independent Marxist early in the 1920s while living in New York and was later to return to Jamaica to initiate an organized Marxist movement in the island during the 1940s and 1950s.[14] Caribbean Leftist individuals outside of their home region were also active, both theoretically and practically during this period. In the United States, for example, a group of West Indian intellectuals, including Richard B. Moore, W. A. Domingo, Cyril Biggs, Otto Huiswood and Grace Campbell, were involved in the formation of the African Blood Brotherhood which briefly became immersed in American Communist politics.[15]

The interest of these Caribbean Leftists in the cause of the Black struggle for liberation in the United States, Africa, the Caribbean and around the world inevitably brought them into varying levels of contact with the Garveyist Movement during the 1920s. Garvey's struggle to organize the people of African descent against the conditions of oppression and dispossession throughout the world was immediately attractive to Caribbean Leftists including prominent Marxists such as Buchanan, McBean and others.[16] However, Garvey's apparently enthusiastic acceptance and adoption of capitalism for Blacks soon became anathema to most Caribbean Leftists, particularly Marxists like C. L. R. James who strongly advocated a class committed approach to fundamental social change. For James, as for most Caribbean Marxist intellectuals at the time, and very much unlike Garvey's perspectives, the strategy for successful Black struggle was ultimately bound up with the need for some form of alliance with the wider white American working classes.

What was indeed peculiar about the earliest beginnings of Caribbean Leftist political movements was the overwhelming impact of foreign influence on the genesis of the movement. This was natural for three main reasons. Firstly, access to Leftist ideological literature was obtainable only from foreign quarters, particularly among the British, European and American Left and labour movements, at the time. Secondly, serious Leftist thought and agitation within the colonized periphery were, during the heyday of colonialism in the 1920s and 1930s, almost tantamount to treason and destined for certain repression at the hands of the colonial authorities, and thirdly, West Indian students abroad provided resources and leadership for the creation of the early Left movements such as the Jamaica Progressive League (JPL), the precursor of the PNP in Jamaica.

The People's National Party of Jamaica, therefore, the first organized nationalist and pro-Leftist movement in the Caribbean, had its origins outside the region, in the formation in 1936 of the JPL in Harlem, New York. The JPL was founded on 1 September 1936 mainly "for the purpose of securing self-government for the island of Jamaica".[17] Beyond this initial nationalistic demand, however, was a demand for greater democracy in the form of universal adult suffrage which was then operable only in the metropole, but denied to British colonial possessions at the time.[18] While these demands were fairly radical for the times, the JPL was a natural precursor to Leftist politics, not only as the founding organization for the national, Leftist PNP in Jamaica, but more significantly in its frequent adoption of a class analytic perspective in its advocacy of liberation from colonialist oppression in Jamaica and throughout the world. But even beyond this generalized advocacy of the rights of the world's oppressed, members of this founding group often adhered to more specific class analytic perspectives on the Jamaican colonialist conditions. The Reverend Ethelred Brown, the original secretary of the JPL, reflected this class consciousness perspective in describing his experience when he returned to Jamaica in 1952 on the invitation of the PNP. He observed in Jamaica that:

There is the persistent and unashamed indifference bordering on cruel inhuman callousness of a section of the better-off people of Jamaica in regard to the suffering of their less favored brethren. This callousness was painfully brought to my attention as I was driven over a road bounded by either side by acres and acres of land owned by one man. I asked my friend if the owner of these acres could not be persuaded to cut up a portion of his vast property in lots to be sold or leased to the land-hungry peasants of the island. He replied that the owner in question when he was faced with such a suggestion asked, 'What would become of his cows?' [19]

Equally significant was the fact that this pioneering political organization was created at a time when the English-speaking Caribbean was experiencing momentous labour disturbances ranging from massive street demonstrations and protests to strikes, riots and other extremes of political violence activities, and involving most of the islands and Guyana between 1935 and 1938.[20]

It was, however, not until about this time that what could be termed modern political organizations were founded in the English-speaking Caribbean. The Moyne Commission report which was established by the British government to inquire into the disturbances of the 1930s left little doubt that the causes lay fundamentally in the extremely unequal and exploitative relationship between employers and labourers. The commission defined these relationships as "quasi-feudal"; it further complained of a "lack of proper labour legislation", and attributed the disturbances to "long years of repressed grievances" with regard to labour conditions.[21]

International factors also played a large role in these events. Among these were: (a) the post-World War I crisis in international capitalism which witnessed a slump in the late 1920s, the effect of which was to create severe economic hardships (e.g., low wages and unemployment) particularly among the labouring classes throughout the Caribbean; (b) the demonstration effect of better conditions in both metropolitan countries and the foreign military bases in the Caribbean, coupled with the influence of the returned war veterans, on the relatively underpaid local workers; and (c) the local consumption of foreign news about events such as the militancy of European workers against capitalist exploitation, and the Italian attempt to colonize Abyssinia (now Ethiopia) in 1936 which served to raise the level of consciousness of the average Caribbean worker and hence to stimulate his interest in continued agitation, strikes and other political protest activities.[22] (See Table 3.1 for a political geography of the 1935-39 labour disturbances.)

How significant was this period of labour disturbances for the rise of the modern Left wing political movements in the English-speaking Caribbean? Above all, the events introduced a peculiar anti-colonialist brand of Caribbean radicalism. In addition, the period laid the foundations for the later development of Left political forces in several important respects. Firstly, it represented the beginnings of a simultaneous process of conscious collective agitation of the working peoples throughout the region in the determined pursuit of their particular class interests. It reflected a surprisingly high degree of Caribbean working class consciousness, given the fact that the level of class formation in Caribbean society was still relatively embryonic and amorphous. Such levels of consciousness were manifested not only in the spontaneous strikes and riots for wage increases and better working conditions, but in relatively organized hunger marches and ultimately the establishment of working men's associations in most of the Caribbean territories, despite the then existence of a variety of anti-labour laws including laws against trespass and picketing.[23]

Table 3.1 Geographic spread of labour unrest in the English-speaking Caribbean, 1935-1939

Country/Year	Causes	Significant Events	Results
St Kitts 1935	Worsening economic conditions; demand for increased wages.	General strike: march round island, violence on plantations, 3 killed, 8 wounded, many arrested.	Strike lost: Worker's League and Universal Benevolent Association formed.
St Vincent 1935	Protest against increased customs duties.	Looting, press censured, police intervention, 3 killed, 26 injured.	Working men's Association formed, backed by middle classes, contested elections and won seats.
St Lucia 1935	Demand for higher wages.	Plantation workers strike, warship on demonstration exercise.	Strike lost; First St Lucia Trade Union, General Union of Agricultural and Urban workers, formed 1939.
Barbados 1937	Clement Payne's oratory, problems of unemployment and poverty.	Spontaneous mass violence; middle class sympathy for movement.	Barbados Progressive League formed 1938: objectives: (a) to organize trade unions, (b) run candidates for elections, and (c) promote land settlement.

Table continues

Table 3.1 (cont'd) Geographic spread of labour unrest in the English-speaking Caribbean, 1935-1939

Country/Year	Causes	Significant Events	Results
British Guiana 1935-1937	Protest against deteriorating economic and working conditions; labour union (BGLU formed 1919) involved.	Widespread spontaneous strikes, disturbances.	Man Power Citizens Association formed 1936, registered 1937.
Trinidad 1934, 1937	Protest against rise of cost of living, and possible victimization of workers.	Disturbances on sugar estates (1934), strike on oilfields and throughout island, arrest of labour leader, Uriah Butler; 14 killed, 59 wounded; hundreds arrested (1937).	Oil Workers Trade Union formed 1937, followed by All Trinidad Sugar Estates and Factory Workers Union, Seamen and Waterfront Workers Union, and Public Workers Union.
Jamaica 1937-1938	Demand for higher wages, more work and land.	Disturbances in Kingston (1937), Riot at Frome Estate, several killed.	Bustamante Trade Union formed July, 1938.

Sources: W. Arthur Lewis. *Labour in the West Indies, The Birth of a Workers' Movement*, Port-of-Spain, 1977; pp. 19-21; William H. Knowles, *Trade Union Development and Industrial Relations in the British West Indies*, Berkeley, 1959, pp. 40-45; Zin Henry, *Labour Relations and Industrial Conflict in Commonwealth Caribbean Countries*, Port-of-Spain, 1972, p. 25; *West India Royal Commission Report*, (The Moyne Report), Cmnd. 6607, London HMSO, 1945, p. 196.

The second facilitating factor for the development of Leftist politics was the manifestation of the organized inter-relationship between working class and political struggles. Indeed, the first modern political party in the English-speaking Caribbean, the PNP in Jamaica, grew out of activities directly related to the labour disturbances of the period.[24] Similarly, the Barbados Progressive League, which was vociferous in its advocacy of land reform among other progressive objectives, was born (in 1938) of this very spate of worker's resistance to the oppressive politics of expatriate planter domination and colonial rule.[25] Another example of the political activities of the labour movement at the time was the fact that the St Vincent Working Men's Association actually contested and won seats at national elections in 1935.[26] More specifically, the movement developed a typically anti-colonialist ideology combined with black consciousness as evidenced in the vigorous opposition to the Italian colonialist conquest of Abyssinia, and in some of the advocacy of prominent labour leaders of the time, such as Butler in Trinidad, H. N. Critchlow in Guyana and Clement Payne in Barbados.[27] It was also during these formative years that the Jamaican, Marcus Garvey, founded his People's Political Party (PPP) to struggle against colonial control and for the improvement of the conditions of the black working classes throughout the Caribbean and indeed the entire Western hemisphere.[28] The third important factor which enhanced Left political development during this period was the instance of a high degree of unity among the masses or working classes, when town and country, worker and peasant were united in a single determined effort toward the attainment of better material conditions. This was evidenced in the fact that the disturbances rapidly spread from the relatively overpopulated cities to the countryside throughout the region. Such a unity was also facilitated or forged by the charismatic type of leadership as displayed by Butler and Cipriani, in Trinidad, and Bustamante in Jamaica among others in the labour movement.

However, notwithstanding these significant advances in Caribbean working class struggles, the ensuing movement was limited in many respects. Not only was it dominated by essentially economic and therefore ideologically reformist aspirations which stopped short of the more far-reaching political struggles such as demand for political independence and transformations of the dominant capitalist economic order; not only, also, did it develop a penchant for messianic leadership and hero worship as witnessed in the cases of the Butler and Bustamante following in Trinidad and Jamaica respectively, but more crucially it became controlled by elements within the more politically assertive, but nevertheless contentious middle classes. Ken Post's analysis of the 1938 Frome riots in Jamaica, for example, is clear on the limitations of the movement primarily because of its ultimate middle class bias: "politics of protest", he asserted of the Frome events, was met with "politics of control".[29]

The necessity to transcend the contradiction of middle class control of working class political life in the Caribbean gave rise to political and ideological splinters within the middle classes themselves. There was need for alternative approaches to the more fundamental resolutions of working class problems, and hence the rise of an alternative political movement which found in Marxism the key, not only to the explanation of the crisis of the period, but to the eventual liberation and emancipation of the masses and subordinate classes of the Caribbean population. Perhaps the earliest movement within this Marxist trend was one created and led by Hugh Buchanan in Jamaica in 1937. Its newspaper, the *Jamaica Labour Weekly*, became the singular most ardent voice for the articulation of labour grievances, and a champion of democracy for the labour movement as a whole. Beyond this the Buchanan movement strongly advocated the need for political independence, anti-imperialism, and the study of Marxism.[30] Two years after its founding, the early Jamaican Marxist movement gained affiliation to the PNP. Within the PNP, this group of Marxists, best known as 'the inner circle', was destined for a very interesting but not altogether unexpected short-lived fate.[31]

The Marxist 'inner circle', comprising such early Marxist stalwarts as Ken Hill, Frank Hill, Arthur Henry and Richard Hart (otherwise known as the 4-H's), represented a significant step beyond the scattering of Caribbean individuals such as the Trinidadian's C. L. R. James, Rienzi, Cirpriani and others, who were persuaded by Marxism or socialism since the 1920s. Not only did the inner circle represent perhaps the first attempt to organize a Marxist core movement in the English-speaking Caribbean, but it was extremely militant in its efforts to address and resolve the economic and political problems facing both the working classes and the nation as a whole. It was within this very organized and militant tradition, also, that the Political Affairs Committee (PAC) was founded in Guyana in 1946 by Cheddi Jagan, Jocelyn Hubbard, Ashton Chase and others. The objectives of the PAC in Guyana were identical with those of the 'inner circle' in Jamaica, in as much as it strongly championed the cause of the labouring classes, the struggle toward political independence, and the study of Marxism.[32] However, the Guyana PAC went beyond the Jamaican 'inner circle' to found a mass political organization of its own, that is, the creation in 1950 of the People's Progressive Party (PPP), which was destined to play a very dynamic role in the political life not only of Guyana but of the Caribbean region as a whole. The PPP was fortunate in that no significant rival mass party existed at the time in Guyana. The significance of this observation is borne out by the later experience of a similarly Marxist-oriented party in Trinidad, the West Indian Independence Party (WIIP), founded in 1955, which would seem to have been crushed in the virtual stampede of popular support for the more nationalist-oriented rival party, the People's Nationalist Movement (PNM), led by the popularly acclaimed national personality, Dr Eric Williams.[33]

A crucial distinction between the present (post-colonial) phase of Left political developments in the Caribbean and that of the earlier (colonial) period is the fact that Leftist politics during the colonial phase tended to be more orthodox, and characterized by more external (or foreign) inputs into the struggle for change. In particular, European ideological influences and contact of Caribbean nationals with Left political developments in metropolitan countries, particularly the influence of British Labour and Communist parties on returned students and war veterans, loomed large in the creation and development of Left forces during this period.[34] At this time also, a relatively orthodox adherence to Soviet Marxism tended to characterize a particular variety of Left movements such as the PPP and WIIP at the time. It was both the external metropolitan influence and the ideological orthodoxy which served to distinguish the Left movement of the colonialist period from such developments following independence in the English-speaking Caribbean. By contrast, Left developments in the post-colonial Caribbean tend to be more rooted in localized conditions, more ideologically diversified and also more fragmented in organizational patterns.

INTELLECTUAL CONTROL

During the post-colonial period, the middle class character of Caribbean Left movements and trends is epitomized in their essentially intellectual leadership and control. The individuals who initiated the organization of radical and Leftist politics during this period were mainly writers, lecturers and those directly involved in other forms of intellectual activities. Most of these post-colonial Left organizations in the English-speaking Caribbean came, directly or indirectly, out of intellectual institutions such as the University of the West Indies, and the University of Guyana, as well as the educational arms of trade union movements. As an organized movement, therefore, the intellectualized Left in the Caribbean is essentially a post-colonial phenomenon. In general, it could be distinguished from earlier Left movements in the region by: (a) its quest for a more independent ideological orientation; (b) a focus on indigenous values which are perceived as a counterweight to colonial domination and dependance; (c) a focus on Third World issues above the more global internationalist considerations; (d) attempts to interrelate an essentially class reductionist, economistic perspective with cultural level analysis such as the race issue; and (e) interrelating anti-imperialist considerations with an anti-dictatorial critique of Caribbean democracy.

Perhaps the most impressive intellectual Leftist venture to come out of the English-speaking Caribbean was the establishment of the New World group in Jamaica, Guyana and Trinidad during the 1960s. *New World* was formed by a group

of intellectuals from the University of the West Indies, and independent professionals from Guyana and elsewhere in the Caribbean. The New World group was
basically concerned with extending the political and cultural awareness of the
Caribbean people, and for this reason employed a strategy of educating various
interested publics through a series of lectures and a variety of publications, the
most important of which were the New World Quarterly periodical located in Jamaica
and New World Fortnightly in Guyana. The main concerns of New World were, in
keeping with the trends of the times in the region, the contradictions apparent in
the process of constitutional development which promised political independence while leaving untouched the problems of economic dependency and
the prospects of increasing poverty in the region.[35] Further concerns of the group
were the growing state violence and tendencies toward dictatorial politics, and
what was conceived to be increasing cultural disorganization throughout the
region.[36] Their ultimate objective was the transformation of thought and lifestyles
of the Caribbean masses.[37] The New World group and operations, however, did
not survive the 1970s as a result of declining popular support and lack of adequate
financial resources.

Following the demise of New World, two other similar, essentially intellectual
enterprises with Caribbean-wide scope were to emerge during the 1970s. These
were the Moko fortnightly review which appeared in Trinidad in 1969, growing out
of the Scope bulletin of the University of the West Indies (UWI), and the Abeng
newspaper which appeared in Jamaica the following year, similarly inspired by
UWI campus activities. The specific campus-based activity which more than any
other directly influenced the emergence of these two radical periodicals was what
has now come to be known as the Rodney Affair of 1968.[38]

The Rodney Affair was the incidence of widespread riots and anti-government
demonstrations in Kingston, Jamaica as a result of the banning of Dr Walter
Rodney, a Leftist Guyanese-born UWI lecturer, by the Jamaican government which
was no doubt responding to pressures of the cold war experience, particularly with
the heightening of tensions and conflict between the US and Cuba in the region.
The events in Kingston had repercussions throughout the Caribbean with similar
incidents of violent public protest emerging in other campus territories, notably
Trinidad and Guyana. Both Moko and Abeng were able to use the Rodney incident
as an appropriate launching pad for their newspaper. For example, the very first
issue of Moko, in October 1968, was entirely dedicated to this Rodney Affair,[39] while
Abeng dedicated itself to issues which were at the very heart of Rodney's quest for
relevant and committed scholarship, in particular the issues of Black and Caribbean awareness and revolutionary consciousness.[40] Not unlike New World, both
Moko and Abeng sought to be independent and objective media of intercommunication among the local peoples. Their orientation combined both cultural and

political interests as applied to localized or regional issues, as well as a focus on fundamental change.

Following a similar Leftist intellectual derivation of the former movements, the Ratoon group was created in 1969 mainly among academics at the University of Guyana. Ratoon emerged at the same time when the Rodney issue in the islands, and Black Power in the United States, propelled the need to debate the problems and contradictions of race and class exploitation in the region. It came at a time also when the issues of dictatorship as against mass democratic politics became foremost in the Guyana context, in particular with the emergence of the Burn-hamite regime which had by 1968 shed all pretense to government through democratic coalition strategies and proceeded to rule almost through fiat.[41] The 1968 elections were rigged by the Burnhamite regime in order to facilitate its singular and exclusive domination over Guyana's political life.[42]

These issues formed the basis of the critical attacks on the existing Guyanese political system (dominated as it was by the Burnham-Jagan political nexus) by Ratoon through its periodical pamphlet under the same name. This group even-tually became part of four such interest groups in Guyana which formed the nucleus of the now-existing Working People's Alliance (WPA), a Leftist pressure group created in 1975 which became a political party in 1979. This transition to practical politics parallels the experience of many of the later Leftist groups which were originally inspired by intellectual movements and trends, the most notice-able example being the New Jewel Movement in Grenada which originated from a coalition of discussion groups such as JEWEL, MAP and OREL, and eventually ended up as the government of Grenada following the coup in 1979.[43]

Other similar movements which had surfaced but attained far less prominence than the aforementioned groups during this period in the region include the New Beginning Movement, which was based in both Port of Spain, Trinidad, and Toronto, Canada, the Antigua-Caribbean Liberation Movement (ACLM) led by Tim Hector in Antigua, and the Marxist-oriented Movement for National Liberation (MONALI) in Barbados. These relatively more obscure movements also managed to produce periodicals which richly contributed to the ongoing Leftist debates in the Caribbean.[44] Also notable as a moderate Leftist, although religious, organiza-tion is the Caribbean Council of Churches (CCC), which would seem to be at least sympathetic to the Marxist oriented liberation theology and frequently takes an anti-imperialist position. Further, the CCC supported many of the goals of socialist ruling parties in the region and defended such beleaguered Caribbean states as Cuba, Grenada under the PRG, and Nicaragua under the Sandinistas which were all threatened with destabilization by the United States government.[45]

In general, the contribution of the intellectuals to the formation and develop-ment of Leftist movements and trends in the English-speaking Caribbean has been significant in several respects. Essentially, the intellectual involvement not only lent additional respectability to Leftist politics, but their creative inputs, particularly in the form of organizational capability, levels of knowledge and skills, and newspaper and periodical developments, facilitated the dissemination of left-wing ideas across classes and throughout the region, and the attraction to the movement of much needed international support. At the same time, however, their monopolizing stranglehold on the movement almost cemented the exclusion of the working and subordinate classes from key leadership positions within these movements, thereby facilitating the divide and rule strategies of foreign interventionist forces in the region.

CLASSIFICATION OF THE CARIBBEAN LEFT

There are basically two closely interconnected trends at work in the diversification of Caribbean Left forces in the post-colonial phase. The first is the fact that diversification followed lines similar to what obtained among the Left in continental and metropolitan countries. The second is a somewhat creative attempt to merge foreign ideologies and political theories with localized conditions, to forge a more indigenous ideology which could inform and guide more relevant political and social practice. Thus, the various European Leftist influences, ranging from Fabianism and Labourism to various forms of Marxism including Leninism, Trotskyism, Maoism and Castroism, have all played their individual parts in influencing the creation and development of different Left political tendencies, movements and organizations in the region.

These different types of ideological commitments, therefore, play a key although not exclusive role in the classification of Left political movements in the Caribbean region. A second and perhaps more fundamental element in our classification is the observed political practices of the movement or organization. This approach discerns the nature and behaviour of the political movements/organizations in terms of the relationships between theory and practice or between rhetoric and performance. However, practice alone is inadequate as a basis of classification with respect to the Caribbean Left since only a few of the Left parties in the region (particularly those which have at one time or another commanded political power) have had the opportunity to demonstrate any sustained and regularized patterns of political performance. Thus, much of the analysis about party commitment is based on ideological or political platform statements gleaned from party manifestos and theoretical organs, their class alliance tendencies, and their international political affiliations.

Within these rather broad criteria, the wide spectrum of political forces identified as the Caribbean Left could be classified into three main groups: namely,

Table 3.2 Classification of left-wing political organizations in the English-speaking Caribbean

Country	Left-wing political organizations: ideological orientation		
	Reformist	**Radical**	**Revolutionary**
Guyana	People's National Congress (PNC)	Working People's Alliance (WPA)	People's Progressive Party (PPP)
			Working People's Vanguard Party (WPVP)
Jamaica	People's National Party (PNP)		Workers' Party of Jamaica (WPJ)
Grenada		New Jewel Movement (NJM) (1978-83)	OREL (faction within NJM)
		Maurice Bishop Patriotic Movement (MBPM)	
Trinidad and Tobago		National Joint Action Committee (NJAC)	People's Popular Movement (PPM)
		New Beginning Movement (NBM)	February 18th Movement
Barbados	Barbados Labour Party (BLP)		Workers' Party of Barbados (WPB)
Antigua		Antigua-Caribbean Liberation Movement (ACLM)	
St Vincent		Movement for National Unity (MNU)	Youth Liberation Movement (YULIMO)
		United People's Movement (UPM)	
Dominica	United Dominica Labour Party (UDLM)	Dominica Liberation Movement (DLM)	Socialist Workers Party (SWP)
St Lucia		Progressive Labour Party (PLP)	
Bahamas		Vanguard Nationalist and Socialist Party (VNSP)	

the reformist, the radical and the revolutionary (see Table 3.2). There are, of course, several elements in common among the Caribbean Left forces. First, each of the groups identified within this political-ideological spectrum is interested in the pursuit of some form of change within or of the political system. Secondly, each proposes to pursue some variety of socialism. Thirdly, they tend to resent the relatively subordinate status of the particular states they represent (in fact, Third World states as a whole) relative to the dominance and dictates of the more powerful states in the international political system. Each, for example, supported the call made popular during the 1980s for a New International Economic Order.[46] Fourth, each in its own way bases its strategy for change on assumptions of support from the masses or subordinate classes of the population. But beyond these relatively superficial factors, the resemblances between the various types of Left movements and political organizations in the Caribbean Left cease. What, then, in more specific terms are the significant differences between these Left forces? These differences will be characterized in terms of: (a) reformist responses, (b) radical challenges, and (c) revolutionary alternatives.

Reformist Responses

As was intimated before, reformist movements perceived of change in incremental and gradualist terms, i.e., change *within*, rather than *of*, the political and ideological *status quo*. In Caribbean terms, reformist movements represent those political organizations or parties which espouse the more liberalist tradition of rule and profess at best only modifications of the institutions which grow out of the Westminster parliamentary tradition. The two principal Left parties which follow this general reformist patterns are the PNP of Jamaica, and the PNC of Guyana. However, the PNC for the sake of the perpetuation of its exclusive rule, introduced some alterations in the Westminster system, such as the attempt to permanently institutionalize the dominance (called 'paramountcy') of the party, while at the same time claiming to support the multi-party pluralistic features of the system. On the other hand, both the PNP of Jamaica and the Barbados Labour Party (BLP), which once claimed to be socialist, have accepted without question the parameters of the Westminster colonial legacy.

Another dimension of the Reformist Left is their anti-colonialist, and often anti-imperialist, stances and rhetoric. Michael Manley claimed, for instance, that "we are broadly the anti-imperialist democratic Left."[47] However, this anti-imperialism might not necessarily be followed through in concrete political practices. The Caribbean reformist Left embrace the principle of state autonomy or the right to sovereignty *vis-à-vis* external (foreign) interference, while at the same time attempting to maintain sufficient ties with metropolitan imperialist states in the interest of obtaining economic assistance. In essence, they preach self-help but not international isolation or autarchy. This approach is reflected, for instance, in the PNCs nationalization of the Canadian and American owned bauxite industry in the 1970s while attempting to maintain the traditional international market controlled by the said foreign-owned companies, ALCAN and ALCOA.[48] This same kind of contradiction applies to Michael Manley's approach to the nationalization of the Jamaican bauxite industry during the same period.[49] There appeared to have been a great deal of reluctance on the part of these two governments to seek alternative markets, and only when this option was completely unavoidable were barter arrangements with the Soviet Union negotiated and established.[50]

A third aspect of Left reformism in the Caribbean is the tendency toward an all-class alliance so as to ensure the basis for the ultimate attainment of political power. In this alliance, the middle classes play the dominant role, although the rhetoric often addresses working class or mass support. Ideologically, these reformist movements tend to be populist, or strongly nationalist, while at the same time entertaining clearly modified versions of socialism. In this sense, socialism is usually qualified by some limiting adjective such as, for example, 'co-operative socialism' as in the PNC Guyana case, or 'democratic socialism' as in the case of PNP under Michael Manley in Jamaica. It was for this reason that Errol Barrow's BLP's advocacy of a 'Barbadian socialism' has been criticized by a rival party as a cover for imperialism and the politics of the traditional ruling class.[51] What is perhaps most curious about the Reformist Left in the Caribbean is its usually ambiguous relationship with Marxist movements. The attitude of the PNP toward the Marxist WPJ in Jamaica, for instance, was indicative of this dilemma of the reformist movement wishing on the one hand to identify with working class issues, as in the 1976 cooperation between the two parties, and at other times to distance itself from Marxism and radicalism in the interest of retaining its middle class electoral dominance and maintaining its foreign economic links.[52] Thus, the PNP's break with WPJ support in the 1980s was predictable, since its association with Marxism is consistent with the case of the PNC and its rather ambiguous, contradictory and at times hostile relationship with Marxism and Left organizations in Guyana.

The Radical Challenge

What are termed Radical Leftist movements are of relatively recent origin in the Commonwealth Caribbean, having developed out of local conditions and events during the post-colonial period. In particular, these radical movements are typically 'Third World' oriented in contrast to either the reformist parties which always sought close links with the developed metropolitan countries, or the more extreme Marxist-Leninist revolutionary parties which pursued strong ties with Moscow or China. In short, they seek greater political and economic independence as a result of being more conscious of the causal relationships between economic dependency on metropolitan powers and underdevelopment in Caribbean and other Third World countries. As such, they pursue fundamental change in the nature of the political-institutional patterns and relationships, particularly those responsible for maintaining the external economic linkages which increase economic dependency. Yet the language of the Radical Left is usually more cautious than that of the Revolutionary Marxist parties, and more often stops short of the demand for total transformation of the political and social system.

The focus of the radical movements has been on democratic institutions which reflect the relationship between rulers and ruled. Their objective is to change the structure of these institutions such that they reflect more faithfully and meaningfully the will of the masses and subordinate classes in Caribbean society. Thus, the now-defunct United Labour Front (ULF) in Trinidad, the similarly emasculated NJM of Grenada, and the currently active WPA of Guyana, have all in the early stages of their development challenged the Westminster parliamentary system, and advocated what they regarded as a more meaningful representative institution, called 'People's Assemblies' which give scope for more direct popular participation.[53] Moreover, this more direct democratic approach is thought to have a greater potential to encourage more local initiative as well as to limit the extent of external economic and political penetration. This particular type of institutional change is suggested in the claims of the ACLM that it is interested in building "a new social economy" with "direct and continuous mass participation in political and economic planning", and for which the masses must possess "assemblies of their own creation."[54]

In general, the ideological orientation of the Radical Left tends to be rather eclectic, reflecting a curious blend of Marxist tenets with more indigenous ideological perspectives such as Black Power and other conceptualizations relating to the development of Third World consciousness. Perhaps the most outstanding theorist of this Marxist-oriented Black Consciousness movement was the late Walter Rodney, one of the key leaders of the WPA in Guyana before his brutal assassination in 1980. As early as 1969 when the Black Power movement was in its ascendancy in the United States, Rodney developed the perspective of linking the Black struggle with the problems of imperialism and international capitalism. He contended, for example, that imperialism in its manifestations within Caribbean and other peripheral societies is basically White-racist in character, hence, the struggle against it is necessarily reduced to a struggle of the generally Black Caribbean masses against an essentially White controlled establishment, both domestically and internationally.[55] The Black masses should therefore seize political power, then institute a cultural revolution oriented toward the development of Black consciousness. However, Rodney was at the same time conscious of the significance of class distinctions which overlap racial categories in such a struggle. 'Black', therefore, represented for Rodney the toiling masses of African and East Indian ethnic populations in the Caribbean, while Whites on the other hand included the lighter-skinned races such as Europeans, Portuguese and Chinese who were considered part of the dominant exploiting capitalist classes.[56] To offset charges of racism against his philosophical orientation, Rodney concluded:

Black Power is not racially intolerant. It is the hope of the Black man that he should have power over his own destiny. This is not incompatible with a multi-racial society where each individual counts equally.[57]

The WPA itself attempted to evade any charge of racism in its very specific electoral program based on what it conceived as "multi-racial power" which is indicative of the Party's sensitivity to the racial question in multi-racial countries like Guyana.[58] Similarly, the ULF in Trinidad boasted about involving both African and East Indian working classes in its struggle against the existing regime,[59] particularly since this party combined both the African-dominated Oilfields Workers Trade Union (OWTU), and the East Indian-dominated sugar unions as its popular support base.

The more practical manifestations of the Black/White ideological and class struggle were seen in the events in Trinidad and Tobago in the 1970s, led by the National Joint Action Committee (NJAC), which was founded in 1969. It was a period when Black Power consciousness in the Caribbean was fuelled by several events including: (a) Black students protests in Canada against what was discerned to be racial discrimination involving Sir George Williams (now Concordia) University in Montreal and Caribbean students, (b) the banning of the charismatic Trinidad-born Black Power leader, Stokeley Carmichael, by the Trinidad and Tobago government, and (c) the coercive and military tactics of the PNM government to repress the movement.[60] These events engulfed the working classes of the small island and led ultimately to extremes of political violence and the near collapse of the PNM governing regime, particularly after a serious mutiny in the Trinidad army inspired by the Black Power protest movement which they were initially ordered to suppress. The realization that extremes of repression can also come from Black governments like the PNM must have been somewhat of a rude awakening to the Black Power protesters, and should serve to suggest, unlike the strict black/white dichotomy theses of Rodney and NJAC, that blackness is itself not necessarily a guarantee of revolutionary or progressive consciousness and behaviour.

The Marxism of the Radical Left in the Caribbean represents a relatively independent position *vis-à-vis* the more internationalist Marxists who traced their ideological lineage to either the Soviet October Revolution of 1917 or the Chinese Revolution of 1949. The infatuation with Black Power and other Third World ideology on the part of the Radical Left in the region, as well as the ambiguity they display as regards their commitment to private enterprise capitalism, serve to distance this grouping from the more orthodox Marxist-Leninist parties which claim to pursue 'scientific socialism'. But what is perhaps the most peculiar element of the Radical Left in the Caribbean is their consistent critique of Caribbean democracy and hostility to all dictatorship and authoritarian governments in the region.

Thus, the NJM was extremely hostile to the dictatorial style of Eric Gairy, the leader of the ruling Grenada United Labour Party (GULP) before its overthrow in 1979, while in Guyana, a very consistent and determined struggle against the Burnhamite PNC dictatorship was waged by the WPA under the slogan "People's Power No Dictator."[61]

Leadership of the Radical Left comes mainly from the intellectual section of the middle classes, which is usually more politically conscious and articulate compared to the other classes in the Caribbean. However, the middle class basis of the Caribbean Radical Left did not inhibit these groups from aiming at the full mobilization of the working class and labouring elements of the population, and to seek as the basis of their popular support an alliance between the industrial workers and the rural agrarian classes. However, their interest in the development of the working classes did not consistently go as far as seeking the total revolutionary transformation of Caribbean society, a position advocated by the more orthodox Marxist-Leninist Left in the region.

The Revolutionary Alternative

Revolutionary Left movements in the English-speaking Caribbean have invariably identified themselves as Marxist-Leninist organizations, although a few have tended to extend their ideological commitment to embrace Mao Zedong thought, Castroism and, in some instance, Trotskyism. They seek fundamental transformations of the socio-political and economic structures, that go far beyond the radical quest for extensions of democratic institutions. They advocate 'scientific socialism', and are as such strongly critical of capitalism, particularly in its Caribbean manifestations. The main Caribbean political parties which followed this line, as indicated in Table 3.2, are, in order of their organizational strength and popular appeals: the PPP of Guyana, founded since 1950; the WPJ, which developed out of an earlier Workers Liberation League (WLL); and the Workers Party of Barbados

(WPB), which grew out of MONALI, an earlier Marxist movement based on the Cave Hill, Barbados, campus of the University of the West Indies. Another similarly extreme Marxist-Leninist party, but of relatively less political significance, was the Working People's Vanguard Party (WPVP), which had a very checkered and inconsistent historical development in the Guyana political process.[62] While however, the PPP, WPJ and WPB were pro-Moscow in international orientation and linkage, the WPVP originally claimed to be Maoist in orientation. In addition, there were some smaller splinter groups in Trinidad and Tobago which professed similar scientific socialist principles based on Marxist-Leninist ideology. The People's Popular Movement (PPM) and the February 18th Movement in Trinidad and Tobago during the 1970s fell within this category.

What, however, is most notable about these Revolutionary Left movements is not only that most were splintered and minuscule in terms of popular following, but that most tended to be either short-lived, or displayed very inconsistent and even contradictory historical developments. Among those which have mushroomed into an extremely short-lived existence were the following Marxist-Leninist movements in Trinidad and Tobago: West Indian Independence Party (WIIP), which surfaced in 1955 and faded shortly thereafter; the Workers and Farmers Party led by C. L. R. James which unsuccessfully contested the Trinidad general elections of 1976; the United Revolutionary Organization (URO), 1971; and some Maoist organizations, notably the NUFF, which emerged as a guerilla organization in 1972 but was soon eliminated by the Trinidad state apparatus, and the National Liberation Movement (NLM), which surfaced temporarily in 1974. In St Vincent, the Youth Liberation Movement (YULIMO) surfaced in the 1970s as a Marxist-Leninist political organization, but soon suffered the fate of a leadership split characteristic of most of the revolutionary Left, and was later absorbed within the larger and relatively more moderate national movement, the Movement for National Unity (MNU).[63]

The logical consequence of their relatively orthodox Leninist ideological position was their internationalist commitments which served to further distance the Revolutionary from the Radical Left in the Caribbean. This internationalism, however, was not simply the question of developing fraternal relations with other Left parties in other countries, nor an approach to the analysis of local problems based on factors and circumstances at the international level of operations. For this type of internationalist outlook was equally applicable to Radical Left movements. What distinguished Revolutionary Left internationalism from that of the Radical Left parties was that the Revolutionary Left saw their own local struggle as part of a wider historical plan which transcended local or national boundaries and was inevitably bound up with the success and struggle of similar movements throughout the world. In addition, essential to the internationalism in the struggle of the Caribbean Marxist-Leninist parties was their unanimous claim of historical lineage from the Soviet October Revolution of 1917. The WPJ, for example, put it this way: "history records that 20 years after the Great October Socialist Revolution led by Lenin, and 90 years after Marx and Engels made socialism a science, the Movement of Jamaican working people made closer contact with communism."[64]

Another significant difference between Revolutionary and Radical Left movements is that the former usually claim to represent exclusively working class interests, although the sources of their leadership might be largely middle class, and tactical alliances entertained with the dominant classes if the ultimate realization of their socialist objectives is to be better assured. The working class is, however, recognized by the Revolutionary Left as the only revolutionary class, but becomes conscious of itself as such only under the organization and leadership of a Marxist-Leninist vanguard party.

IN RETROSPECT

The development of Leftist politics in the English-speaking Caribbean has moved from relatively sporadic, individual commitments to anti-colonialist and Marxist socialist positions following World War I and the 1917 October Revolution in Russia, to the more organized radical and revolutionary movements following the Great Depression and labour revolts of the 1930s, but particularly after World War II. At the same time, it was a move from a more internationalist perspective and outlook among individual socialists such as C. L. R. James and George Padmore, most of whom operated outside of the Caribbean area, to a relatively more inward-looking movement of the more localized intellectual, professional and political groupings engaged in the practical political struggles against emerging dictatorships and authoritarian rule in the region. Leadership of Caribbean Leftist politics was, from the earliest stages, drawn essentially, although not exclusively, from middle class individuals, particularly the intellectual and professional strata, including lawyers, writers, journalists and university academics.

Although the Caribbean Leftist movements would seem to represent something like a microcosm of Leftist developments on a world scale; although, that is, the Caribbean Left reflect all ranges of Leftist perspectives – reformist, radical and revolutionary – there was, nevertheless, a peculiar element which sets these Caribbean movements apart from the rest of the world. This peculiarity involves their consistent interest in the cause of Black liberation which is indeed a specific response to the particular conditions of their historical location and experience. The earlier phase of the movement in the 1920s and 1930s embraced Pan-Africanism, while the post-independence radical Leftists in the region were themselves ardent champions of the Black Power philosophy which originated among Blacks in the United States. Thus, the question of the relationship between race and class became the peculiar hallmark of Caribbean Leftism among issues which are still debated and formed the central focus of the Left agenda in the Caribbean during the 1980s and 1990s. It is to this question of the Caribbean Left's agenda, programs and practices that we turn in the next chapter.

4

The Left
Agenda

The ultimate test of the significance of the Caribbean Left lies in their contribution to both theory and practice in the struggle for change. This contribution is reflected in what could be generally conceived as the Left's political agenda which summarizes their programs, policies and practices. What, however, is perceived here to be the Caribbean Left agenda represents a summation of the separate agendas of the different Left groupings and movements spread throughout the region, each projecting different emphases depending on the particular theoretical perspectives and practical experiences of struggle of the particular Leftist groups within the existing social order, both domestic and international.

How the aggregated Left agenda is determined is largely dependent on what these groups perceive to be the demands of their particular time and socio-political conditions. For this reason, the Left agenda reflects the limitations imposed by those times and conditions, and bears out our main argument that the demands of the international and domestic political environment set limits on the maneuverability of Leftist movements, and tend to pressure and orient their practice away from their preferred ideological and political objectives. Hence, the Caribbean Left agenda is usually Leftist only tentatively, while constantly shifting toward the Right in practice.

Such shifts were represented in tendencies to move away from rigidity and dogmatism in the early years of Caribbean Leftist development, toward a relatively more flexible and pragmatic position in later years, particularly during the 1980s. However, these shifts were far from being uniform or monolithic among Left movements throughout the region. In fact, different kinds of Left orientation responded to international and national events differently. Further, the historical and social events differed in their relative impact on different types of Left movements in the Caribbean. In general, however, ideological shifts became most dramatic in response to issues such as imperialism, class and race, dictatorship and democracy, the transition to socialism, and the forging of Left unity. During the 1980s in particular, these issues constituted the most important items on the Caribbean Left agenda.

The priority status given to these particular issues was determined by several considerations, most notably their common appeal, their relative degree of influence on political policy and practice, and their capacity for mobilizing popular support. The priority issues – anti-imperialism, democracy, race and class, socialism, and Left Unity – and the variations in the levels of commitment given them over time, will therefore be examined more closely.

Anti-Imperialism

Foremost on the Left agenda, particularly during the post-colonial period, was the question of the response to imperialism. This issue occupied the attention of the Caribbean Left in general, although a much stronger commitment to anti-imperialism was held by the more radical and revolutionary Marxist groups. The main considerations surrounding this issue involved the question of (a) the role of imperialism in defining the existing socio-economic conditions in the Caribbean, (b) its impact on the political movements in general, but particularly the Left in the region, and (c) the necessary strategies to be employed in response to the negative effects of imperialism.

As regards the general background role of imperialism, the Caribbean Left generally focused on the relationship between foreign capital penetration and domestic capital formation, the role of the Caribbean state in both combating imperialism and helping the process of developing domestic capital, and the capacity of imperialism for intervention and destabilization. The general position of the Left was that imperialism represented a system of foreign capitalist relations which stifled the formation and growth of national capital and undermined authentic democratic political life in the region as elsewhere in the Third World. It was in relation to the negative impression of imperialism that domestic capital was sometimes seen in a highly positive light. Rodney, for example, suggested that national capital usually played what he regarded as "a patriotic role", since it "does not automatically represent imperialist exploitation".[1]

In general, Caribbean leftists tended to be unanimous in their rejection of imperialism. Such a rejection was often encapsuled in the rhetoric of the radical or revolutionary Left as in the case of Tim Hector's recommendation of a "swift surgical effort to dismantle the colonial capitalist state" as a necessary culmination of the decolonization process in the Caribbean.[2] Further, imperialist states, particularly the United States, were thought to be basically aggressive since they actively sought to destroy the Left movement in the region and elsewhere in the Third World. The invasion of the Dominican Republic in 1965, and Grenada in 1983, as well as the covert destabilization of Leftist regimes in Guyana (1963 and 1964) and Jamaica (1976 and 1980) were naturally viewed in this light.

Because of its basically aggressive nature, all struggle toward socialism, the WPA suggested, must be situated within the anti-imperialist struggle.[3] Imperialist aggression has also been perceived in covert, subversive activities as in the case of CIA destabilization of Guyana in 1964 and Jamaica in 1980 through a combined tactic of 'divide and rule' and inter-party and inter-ethnic political violence. Further, Cheddi Jagan of the PPP in Guyana suggested that the CIA and related governmental agencies in the US successfully infiltrated the Caribbean Left during the 1960s through the use of other leftist groups or leaders such as Norman Thomas in the US, with the hope of dividing and ultimately destroying the movement.[4] The Caribbean labour movement, political parties, social organizations and even regional organizations such as CARIFTA (now Caribbean Community (Caricom) were seen by the Revolutionary Left as major instruments of imperialist destabilization in the region.[5] The PPP, for instance, had regarded Caribbean regionalization efforts such as CARIFTA and its successor Caricom as a "vehicle for US monopolies", formed during the 1980s "to contain national liberation".[6] The perception was also formed that some Left political parties became very crafty agents of imperialism as they were pitted against other leftist parties in the struggle for political power.[7]

In general, the anti-imperialist strategy of the Caribbean Left involved continual struggle and the implementation of alternative approaches to economic development. Rejection of imperialism ranged from conceptual shifts in international alignment patterns to the advocacy of revolutionary transformation. While, for example, the Reformist Left such as the PNP of Jamaica, and the PNC in Guyana argued for closer relations with Cuba and the non-aligned movement as the crucial element of their anti-imperialist strategy, the more radical parties such as the ACLM of Antigua argued that there should be one continuous revolutionary process leading directly from decolonization to socialist transformation, and involving, if necessary, the use of force. For this reason Tim Hector, leader of the ACLM, enthusiastically applauded Castro's military intervention in Angola in support of the Marxist MPLA government against imperialist-sponsored guerillas like the rival UNITA forces.[8]

Specific and more practical targets were identified within the general and continuous anti-imperialist struggle. Among the most prominent targets were usually what were regarded as neo-colonialist elements and institutions, which included sections of the middle classes and multi-national corporations. The ACLM, for instance, viewed the Caribbean middle classes as being basically small and weak, yet because of their "alliance with imperialist capital", they foster the entrenchment of a political elite and the consequent "bankruptcy of the political parties and political system in general".[9] Similarly, multi-national corporations in Trinidad and Tobago were the primary targets during the anti-imperialist 'Black Power' struggle led by NJAC in 1970.[10]

Also, Left unity was fostered as a bulwark against imperialist aggression, an issue to be more fully discussed later. But it could be mentioned at this stage that Left unity tactics included: (a) the seeking of alliances between Leftist opposition forces and ruling parties, as in the case of the PPP in Guyana offering what it called "critical support" to the PNC regime,[11] and a similar tactical alliance between the WPJ and the ruling PNP in Jamaica during the 1970s;[12] (b) Caribbean-wide consultative meetings among regional Leftist groups, leading to the setting up in both Guyana and Nicaragua of a semi-institutionalized arrangement to facilitate mutual cooperation and intercommunication between Left groups, particularly at times of imperialist aggression;[13] and (c) the seeking of closer unity with the Eastern Bloc countries, Cuba and socialist-oriented states in the region while strengthening their ties with the non-aligned movement.

Obstacles to the anti-imperialist struggle were perceived to be varied, and included most prominently right-wing political parties, elements within the dominant middle classes, trade unions and religious organizations. The rightist JLP, for instance, was viewed by the Jamaican and Caribbean Left as an instrument of foreign, particularly US, penetration into Jamaica, and indeed the region as a whole. Also, the roles played by the Barbadian Labour Party, the Freedom Party in Dominica and, of course, the JLP in Jamaica in aiding the US invasion of Grenada in 1983 were perceived as classic examples of what could be termed the "Trojan Horse" effect. In Guyana, the PNC and the right wing United Force (UF) played a similar role in 1964 in supporting British and US intervention to put down the Marxist Jagan (PPP) government. Certain regional institutions such as Caricom and the OAS were also regarded as avenues for foreign manipulation and the frustration of leftist developments in the region.[14] This position was consistently held by the Radical and Revolutionary Left which for a long time wavered on issues of support for regional and political integration.

During the 1970s, though, the Caribbean Left displayed a general optimism about the impact of the anti-imperialist movement in the region and, indeed, worldwide. Because of periodic recessions witnessed in the world capitalist economy during this period, the Caribbean Left regarded imperialism as in crisis and therefore in the process of some form of transformation. In addition, particularly since the socialist successes in Third World countries like Vietnam and Nicaragua, and more specifically because of successes of socialist parties like the PNP, NJM, and so on in the English-speaking Caribbean, the Caribbean Left contended that the 'balance of forces' was in favour of world-wide socialist advances.[15] However, these predictions soon proved to be premature and failed to anticipate the Grenada fiasco of 1983 which revealed serious internal weaknesses in the Leftist movement, not only in Grenada, but in the Caribbean region and the world as a whole. It was during the 1980s also that a combination of international and internal pressures led to drastic modifications of anti-imperialist perspectives and protests among the Caribbean Left.

Dictatorship and Democracy

Another important issue that dominated the Caribbean Left agenda was the problematic nature of Caribbean democracy and the rapid rise of dictatorial leaders and governments throughout the region. This phenomenon of rising dictatorship surfaced during the 1960s with the creation of newly independent states in the region. Leftist discussion on this issue revolved around three main, interrelated considerations, namely, the history and structure of the Caribbean State, strategies to combat dictatorship and authoritarian rule, and perceptions of a new and more complete democracy relevant to socialist transformation in the region.

The essentially colonialist nature of Caribbean democracy was the prime target of Caribbean leftist attacks. The Caribbean application of Westminster democracy reflects the familiar contradiction of power controlled by a minute propertied and privileged class, despite its claims to the egalitarian principle of one man, one vote and majority rule. Essentially, the working and less privileged classes are disadvantaged and virtually left out of the decision-making processes while being entrapped within an exploitative capitalist system which accompanied the imposition of this form of democracy during colonial times. One of the major arguments of the Caribbean Left was that the Westminster system imposed an inflated concentration on parliamentary politics which is not necessarily representative of the interest of the masses. According to this argument, parliamentarism tended to undermine the power of the party to undertake its necessary vanguard or leadership role, by concentrating political power in the parliamentary wing of the party which does not necessarily include the party's most experienced and capable leaders.[16] But even more significantly, Caribbean parliaments are thought to foster what Miles Fitzpatrick, a prominent Guyanese Leftist politician, termed "boss" rule.[17] The character of leadership portrayed by political leaders and heads of states such as Eric Williams of Trinidad and Tobago, Edward Seaga of Jamaica,

Eric Gairy of Grenada, Eugenia Charles of Dominica and Forbes Burnham of Guyana were seen as classic examples of parliamentary 'boss' rule.

Much of the discussion on political strategy and tactics among the Caribbean Left, particularly the Radical Left, centered on exposing the methods and means whereby authoritarian leadership might be defeated. The methods used to sustain dictatorial powers in the English-speaking Caribbean included: (a) the development and use of private armies by ruling parties to intimidate and silence political opposition; (b) the use of the state apparatus, including the armed forces, administrative machinery, the courts and state financial and other resources to augment popular mobilization in support of party projects; (c) control of the mass media to contain independent or mass criticism of the regime; (d) imposing legal restrictions on opposition protest activities; and (e) simple political fiat or arbitrariness on the part of the ruling group or political leadership.

Intimidatory and illegitimate methods were utilized by the Gairy regime in Grenada prior to the 1979 NJM coup. Gairy frequently utilized a private thug army, called the 'mongoose gang', against NJM and other opposition forces on the island.[18] In Guyana, too, the Forbes Burnham PNC regime unilaterally invoked what it termed "the paramountcy of the party" principle to merge state resources with party resources and the rigging of general elections as a bulwark against opposition pretensions to power. Forbes Burnham carried intimidatory tactics to the extreme. At a party congress, he defined the political situation in Guyana as "a war" between his ruling party and the opposition forces who were regarded as "enemies of the people."[19] He further contended that the PNC "will not rest" until its enemies "are crushed and utterly destroyed".[20] He defined legitimate strikes in state-controlled enterprises such as the sugar industry as *ipso facto* "political strikes" which must necessarily be met by the severest forms of "political sanctions"; "match steel with more highly tempered steel" as he put it.[21] Burnham's rhetoric was equally matched by the actions of his government and ruling party. Opposition political meetings were often violently broken up by organized and officially condoned thuggery while the armed forces were occasionally used to break strikes.

The WPA in Guyana would seem to have had the most traumatic experience with dictatorial pressures and repression, and therefore represents a classic case for the study of organized responses to dictatorial rule. Some of the WPA responses to dictatorship involved what appeared to be a calculated attempt at shunning or avoiding the regime. In a public announcement, the WPA boasted that it had never taken sides with the Burnhamite dictatorship, nor has it ever made "the mistake of agreeing to discuss or wishing to discuss with the ruling party of the dictatorship, the social system, or any matter other than arrangement for 'free and fair' elections . . . "[22] After Burnham's death in 1985, however, the WPA advocated dialogue with rival parties, including the ruling PNC, as a means toward mitigating some of the harsher measures of dictatorial rule.[23] The principle of dialogue, advocated by the WPA in 1989, was accepted and adopted by the PNC regime, but the efforts toward this end proved to be short-lived.

Another form of response by opposition forces to dictatorship was the use of the typically Caribbean art of ridicule. For instance, Burnham was nicknamed 'King Kong' by Walter Rodney to describe a man who wanted to be king but became a brute instead. Rodney further characterized Burnham's rule in terms of what he called "the Burnham touch" which was defined to be the opposite of the mythical 'Midas touch'.[24] While the Midas touch was supposed to turn everything into gold, the Burnham touch turned everything into filth in Rodney's mocking imagery.

Perhaps the most forceful weapon of the Left against dictatorship in the region was the mobilization of collective action including boycotts, civil disobedience or passive resistance, strikes and mass demonstrations, and ultimately, but rarely, armed responses. Discussion of these responses formed a very prominent part of the Left agenda. The PPP in Guyana had initiated the boycott tactic since 1964 when it boycotted parliament in protest against electoral manipulation by British colonial authorities. This form of protest continued during the 1970s in opposition to the Burnhamite tactic of electoral rigging. The tactic of civil disobedience was introduced in 1973 by the PPP opposition forces after massive rigging of the elections of that year by the Burnham regime. The civil disobedience tactic involved PPP appeal to supporters to boycott the government-controlled radio and mass media, and to withdraw their produce from national and city markets.[25] Strikes also formed part of the strategy as in the case of the 1977 GAWU strike which paralyzed the sugar industry for 135 days and brought the national economy to the brink of collapse. Rodney, himself, had regarded "mass withdrawal of labour" as "the ultimate weapon against dictatorship".[26]

Another approach to the problem of dictatorship was the creation of anti-dictatorial alliances. Since the 1960s, for instance, the PPP initiated what was then referred to as the Civil Liberties Action Committee (CLAC) comprising a variety of citizens' religious and grass roots political groupings, to combat the early development of PNC dictatorship.[27] Also, in 1985, the WPA initiated the Patriotic Coalition for Democracy (PCD) comprising all opposition political parties that were cheated in the 1985 elections, the objective being to fight for free and fair elections and a more open democratic system in Guyana. Similar alliances initiated by Leftist groups in the Caribbean were reflected in the Grenada experience in 1979 when the NJM formed the Committee of Twenty-two to oppose the Gairy dictatorship, and the creation of the ULF in Trinidad out of a combination of several Left leaning labour organizations in the 1980s in opposition to the PNM monopoly of political power. More on the issue of alliance politics will be discussed in a subsequent section of this chapter.

Beyond the critique of Westminster democracy and attacks on dictatorship, the Caribbean Left had some definite proposals as regards what constituted a more meaningful democratic system. According to this conception, socialism demanded a more extensive and inclusive form of democracy which was not as class restrictive as the current form of Westminster democracy practiced in the English-speaking Caribbean. Genuine democracy, it was thought, required a more decentralized distribution of power centres to replace the centralized parliamentary system that existed in the region since colonial times. The establishment of 'People's Assemblies' to embrace every conceivable regional or special interest was thought to be better equipped to give the hitherto neglected populations a more direct say in the political decision-making process. The ULF at its inception considered the necessity to build what it termed "independent organs of power" in every factory, estate, community or bloc throughout Trinidad and Tobago.[28] In similar vein, the ACLM in Antigua talked about the creation of Workers and Farmers Democracy on the island and indeed elsewhere in the Caribbean.[29] The Dominican Liberation Movement (DLM) during the 1970s supported the idea of the "spontaneous generation" of organs of power among the different constituencies within the island.[30] And the WPA of Guyana spoke of establishing "Workers' Assemblies" to guarantee what it termed "people participation" in economic-based institutions such as sugar, bauxite, transport, etc., which are in effect "storehouses of worker's power".[31]

It was the Radical Left more than any other which favoured a much more decentralized grassroots democratic system, at least until the Grenada fiasco of 1983. After that date the Radical Left was seen to return to the advocacy of Westminster electoral politics.[32] Compared to the Radical Leftist groups, both the Reformist and Revolutionary Left, seemed to have been more content with the established centralized parliamentary system under Westminster democracy. However, the Revolutionary Left more than the Reformist, advocated a greater emphasis on working class control of both parliament and industries. But all agreed that the 'democracy' issue was closely intertwined with the issue of the transition to socialism.

Transition to Socialism

The transition to socialism became a very prominent issue on the Caribbean Left agenda during the 1970s and early 1980s. Although this issue was of general concern to all Caribbean Leftist political organizations, it was pivotal to those parties which had occupied positions of power in Caribbean political systems. This meant that governing parties such as the PPP (1960s), PNC (1968-1985) in Guyana, PNP (1970s) in Jamaica, and NJM (1979-1983) in Grenada equated this issue with the practical considerations of economic and political development. At the theoretical level, also, the transition issue became a major preoccupation of Leftist intellectuals in the region, in particular, the New World group and the leadership of such intellectually-led political organizations as the WPJ of Jamaica and the WPA in Guyana.

Socialism itself has been variously conceptualized depending on the different positions on the ideological spectrum occupied by the various Left political organizations in the region. These differences were reflected in three distinct forms of socialist experiments in the English-speaking Caribbean: (a) cooperative socialism as practiced by the PNC government in Guyana between 1970 and 1985; (b) Democratic Socialism as interpreted and applied by the PNP government in Jamaica between 1972 and 1980; and (c) Scientific or revolutionary socialism as adapted to Caribbean conditions by the New Jewel Movement's PRG government in Grenada between 1980 and 1983.

The major distinction between these three varieties of Caribbean socialism revolved around: (a) the extent of their commitment to the Westminster brand of democracy; (b) the relative significance of the state in directing economic development; and (c) the level of their association with foreign, socialist and communist states.[33] As regards commitment to Westminster democracy, the PNP's 'democratic socialism' totally accommodated itself to the parliamentary and electoral processes as a necessary vehicle toward socialist transformation. On the other hand, the PNC's 'cooperative socialism' attempted to drastically modify Westminster parliamentary democracy to suit its own private agenda which included "paramountcy of the Party over the government and state". At the further extremes, the NJM's People's Revolutionary Government rejected the Westminster system as being too limited to effect a genuine economic-democratic transformation of Caribbean society.

Although all regarded the state as pivotal in economic development, they differed as regards the modes of intervention of the state in the economy. While the PRG in Grenada saw the state as basically hegemonic in the sense of giving leadership and guidance to an increasingly supportive population – a situation in which mass mobilization substitutes for free market economic processes – the PNP in Jamaica seemed to have been more inclined toward giving equal weight to the three sectors – private, state, and cooperative – in a mixed economy approach. The PNC's position was much more complex. Its commitment to the 'party paramountcy' principle meant that the party was the supreme authority in the nation, and the state represented merely its 'executive arm'. At the same time, however, the PNC defined its socialist experiment as 'the Cooperative Republic', suggesting that eventually the cooperative sector will become dominant, although the party never intimated the mechanisms by which cooperatives will eventually supersede either the state or the party or the private sector in dominance over the economic system.

Yet a third area of difference between the three transitional approaches resides in their relative degree of association with socialist bloc countries in the international environment. While the Grenadian PRG linked its own developmental strategy with closer association with the Soviet Union, Cuba and Eastern bloc socialist countries and sought membership in the communist economic union (COMECON), the other ruling Left parties in the English-speaking Caribbean chose to maintain a relatively more equidistant position between the Soviet Union and the US and other Western capitalist countries. But the subtle difference between the Jamaican PNP approach and that of the PNC in Guyana was that while the PNC's relations with these foreign socialist countries tended to be relatively more formal and official, those of the PNP seemed to have been rather more fraternal and friendly.[34]

Notwithstanding these differences, there were several areas of agreement among these various socialist experiments in the region. Perhaps the most obvious was their insistence on a mixed economy approach which combined state, private and cooperative sectors as critical to their developmental thrusts. The mixed economy approach also had its adherents among the non-ruling Left such as the WPA, the ULF as well as the more orthodox Marxists, the WPJ and PPP. The parties also agreed on the necessity for state intervention in economic development, nationalization of selective foreign-owned economic enterprises, particularly those such as sugar, bauxite and tourism, which are pivotal to the economies of these countries, and the involvement of the labour movement in political and economic mobilization, although some like the PNC tended to subordinate labour to the dictates of the party while others like the PPP advocated workers' control or something akin to a partnership between the workers and the state.[35] In general, also, the Caribbean Left advocated a progressive foreign policy which included support for national liberation movements abroad and membership in the non-aligned movement.

Debate was intense over the issue of whether the cooperativist approach had the capacity to facilitate either economic development or socialism. Only the moderate reformist parties, particularly the PNC, placed any significant emphasis on cooperatives as an instrument of social transformation. The radical and revolutionary parties recognized that cooperatives had a role, albeit a subordinate role, to play in the transition process. Some groups, however, like the New Beginning Movement, referred to the cooperativist approach as wholly idealistic and utopian.[36] A similar view was shared by the PPP and other revolutionary parties such as the WPJ which contrasted cooperative socialism and other similar Third World varieties of classless Communitarian socialism, with a scientific socialism which focuses on class struggle as the basic motor of development.[37]

Class struggle was the principal lever of change advocated by the Radical and Revolutionary Left in the region. In Antigua, class struggle was viewed essentially as an internationalist struggle against foreign capital and the ultimate 'dismantling of the capitalist state'.[38] A more nationalist interpretation was given by the WPA which talked about the need for a "veto of the working class" in the event of conflicts between capital and labour in the process of socialist transformation.[39] Class conflict was viewed in terms of its historical significance, as in the case of the PPP which called for an "intensification of the class struggle" in what was discerned as "the epoc of transition" to socialism.[40] What, however, distinguished the perception of the Radical Left from that of the more Revolutionary Left on this class struggle issue was their different explanations of the social origins of class behavior: the radicals tending to view working class activism as stemming from naturally spontaneous origins, while the revolutionaries such as the PPP and WPJ believed in the need for a more organized vanguardist development of class struggle.

In general, however, approaches to socialism in the Caribbean differed along lines closely parallel to the distinction we have made between reformist, radical and revolutionary politics of the Left. The reformists (e.g., PNC in Guyana and PNP in Jamaica) preferred a transition that embraced a much greater pro-capitalist ingredient. This entailed dealings with both East and West on equal terms, a mixed economy approach that retains much of capitalist production and exchange processes, and reliance on middle class leadership. The radical groups such as the NJM in Grenada and the WPA in Guyana tended to lean toward the 'non-capitalist path' which stressed greater worker participation in industry, breaking with dependence on Western capitalist systems, greater state involvement in economic processes, and rotating leadership patterns. The more revolutionary Caribbean Left, including the PPP and the WPJ, preferred the 'socialist orientation' approach which embraced a much greater pro-Moscow line in international relations, workers control of both industry and the state, and political leadership that is at least interested in the fulfillment specifically of working class demand, if not commanded by the working classes themselves.

In the final analysis, though, the issue of class leadership will have to confront the critical issue of race, colour and ethnicity which in the Caribbean context has been in fierce competition with class as the main controlling force in Caribbean political life.

CLASS AND RACE

While the element of class has usually been taken for granted in the Left analysis of Caribbean politics, the issue of race and ethnicity has been generally neglected, often to the peril of Leftist prospects for political mobilization and change. Even in multi-ethnic Caribbean societies such as Trinidad, Guyana and Jamaica, where the ethnicity issue is pivotal to the understanding of the political process, this issue has invariably been subordinated to class considerations among the prominent Leftist groups. This subordination of race to class is a classical Marxist response to the problem, and therefore was more prevalent among the more orthodox Marxist Left in the region.

The relative neglect of the racial issue by the Caribbean Left has been observed by Trevor Munroe, leader of the WPJ, who contended that in Jamaica, the Marxist Left "has clearly failed to deal adequately with race, to take up and consistently carry forward the positives of Garveyism".[41] That the class issue was consistently made to supersede the racial issue is reflected, for example, in the contention of Janet Jagan of the PPP in Guyana that while race cannot be ignored in Guyanese politics, the "decisive factor" as she put it, was "not race but economics".[42] It was also this typical Marxist "base-superstructure" argument that led Cheddi Jagan to conclude during the early part of his political career, that "race is only skin deep."

This 'base-superstructure' subordination of the race issue was equally reflected in the ultimate argument of the Marxist Left that the racial problem would eventually disappear with the advent of socialism and classless society. *Caribbean Dialogue*, for example, argued that "the solution to racism" lies ultimately in the "abolition of the social system" which oppresses the working classes when socialism is eventually realized.[43]

The realities of the Caribbean struggle for change have nevertheless brought home to political analysts the central importance of race and ethnicity in the determination of certain critical outcomes, such as voting patterns and group violence, in the Caribbean political process.[44] Because of these realities the Left could not have totally ignored the race issue although it was usually made subordinate to the class issue. Over the years, however, discussion of the race issue shifted from its very subdued position to a more prominent focus among the Caribbean Left.[45]

The earliest considerations about the special place of race in the Leftist political spectrum were expressed outside the Caribbean region by a group of Caribbean intellectuals residing in the United States who constituted themselves into the African Blood Brotherhood (ABB) during the 1920s. Many of these were initially Garveyists who championed the glories of their African origins and the development of African consciousness among the black masses in the United States and beyond. The ABB also recognized the special place of Blacks in the Marxist revolutionary schema, since Blacks were doubly exploited, first as Blacks under White domination and additionally as occupants of the lowest rungs in the capitalist class structure.[46] C. L. R. James, during the 1930s, extended the ABB argument to embrace Trotskyist perspectives. James held that blacks have a historical mission to make common cause with the entire Third World proletariat in their struggle against white-dominated imperialism.[47] During the 1940s, Richard Hart, one of the founders of the socialist movement in Jamaica was equally concerned about the race issue within the Marxist framework of analysis. Munroe noted that Hart recognized the revolutionary significance of both black resistance, particularly during slavery and the cultivation of racial self-respect – two factors which were necessary to break the historical dominance of whites over blacks.[48]

It was natural that most of the progressive forces in the Caribbean would support the Garvey Movement, since it was the earliest movement to champion anti-colonial nationalism and the democratic inclusion of blacks in the Caribbean political process. While the progressive forces agreed with the identification of colonialism with white racism, not all, however, agreed with the 'Back to Africa' content of the Garveyist programme. The 1950s, however, saw an upsurge of inter-ethnic conflict and violence in several Caribbean territories including Trinidad and Guyana, which brought the racial issue once again into prominence on the Left political agenda in the region. The split in the Marxist PPP of Guyana in 1955, for example, was attributable to race, first in the perception that the cause of the split related to the personal ambition and racist objectives of Forbes Burnham, the author of the split,[49] or to the entrenched racism within the PPP itself;[50] and secondly to the racial 'divide and rule' manipulative policies of the colonial authorities who used race to stem the potential tide of Marxist political development in Guyana and indeed the Caribbean region as a whole.[51]

It was not until the 1960s, following a series of intensively violent racial events in Trinidad, Jamaica and Guyana that the issue of race became firmly placed on the Left political agenda. Focus on the race issue took three distinct forms: first, it was conceived and utilized particularly by the older Leftist groups as basically a tactical instrument in electoral competition for political power; secondly, it became, mainly with the more recently added radical third parties within the Caribbean Left, a predominantly moral issue, usually in the form of blaming the older parties for the escalation of the problem, or in appeals for unification of the subordinate classes and ethnic elements of the population; thirdly, the racial issue became elevated on the Left agenda into the more academic issue of seeking appropriate means toward conflict resolution.

The classic case of using race as a tool of political mobilization is that of the electoral competition between the PNC and PPP in Guyana. This sinister development followed the split in the PPP-led nationalist movement in 1955. Much of the analysis of race by these two parties centered around the need to mobilize ethnic constitutuences for electoral victories, and casting blame on each other for causing the racial conflict in the first place. At the same time, however, both parties neglected consideration of the wider roles that racial consciousness can play in a revolutionary situation, whether against colonialism or in the construction of socialism. A similar programmatic neglect of the racial question has been observed in the case of the PNP in Jamaica where, as Trevor Munroe argued, race consciousness played a crucial role in the electoral campaign which brought Michael Manley to power in 1972.[52]

The Left parties which emphasized the more positive politicization of race were mainly drawn from the new radical parties which emerged during the 1970s. These parties included NJAC and the ULF in Trinidad and Tobago, the NJM in Grenada and the WPA in Guyana. For these parties, race mobilization was positive to the extent it aimed at imperialism, but negative when used as a necessary means in the competition for power in the domestic political arena. Their argument on the positive side of race politics was that the development of race consciousness was as of much significance as class in countering the foreign, white-dominated, capitalist (or imperialist) system in the Caribbean. The concept of 'Black Power' was introduced by these parties to foster the solidarity of the non-white races, particularly the working class blacks and East Indians, against white-dominated imperialism.[53] Secondly, these parties attacked the conventional Left and ruling parties in the region for introducing a localized variety of racial domination which favored the advancement of foreign capital. For this reason, the Eric Williams' PNM regime in Trinidad, the Eric Gairy regime in Grenada and the Burnham PNC regime in Guyana were seen to represent a special brand of African middle class domination of localized politics to the detriment of the other non-white races, particularly East Indians and Amerindians, who constitute two of the main elements of the subordinate classes in the region.[54] Finally, these parties attacked the racial mobilization strategies of conventional parties in the electoral contest for power, as essentially divisive and inimical to the realization of socialist objectives.

It was mainly from these very radical quarters that a perception of conflict resolution with regard to the racial divisive issue was introduced in the Left agenda during the 1970s. The main manifestation of this conflict resolution approach was the necessity for multi-racial solidarity as against either white-dominated imperialism, or internal dictatorship which was seen to oppress the subordinate working classes comprising the major ethnic groups, such as blacks and East

Indians. The WPA in Guyana talked about "multi-racial power" as necessary for both effective opposition to the Burnhamite dictatorship and the institutionalization of a more inclusive democratic process.[55] Similarly, NJAC in Trinidad advocated the need for "unity of the oppressed" classes and races comprising both Blacks and East Indians.[56] It was within this context also, of opposition to imperialism and promotion of working class (East Indian/black) solidarity, that the PPPs offer of "critical support" for the PNC against imperialism and its proposal for a "National Front government" must be understood.[57] Ultimately, these unification efforts went far beyond the simple racial issue and became a concerted movement toward economic development and socialist transformation. In this case, ethnic conflict resolution became only one dimension in the movement toward resolving class contradictions and divisiveness within the Left movement itself.

The PPP itself had been perceived by other Leftist groups, particularly the intellectuals of the New World Movement, as embodying both race and class contradictions in its own leadership structure.[58] The fact that the PPP had neglected the emergence, during the 1960s, of attempts to promote East Indian leaders to the exclusion of black contenders for positions within the party hierarchy, had lent much credence to this charge. Much earlier, the party was challenged by some of its most prominent Black leadership for attempting to cultivate and recruit the rich East Indian business class at the expense of both the Blacks and the working class elements of all race groups.[59]

Eusi Kwayana's contribution to this race issue within the leftist movement was most noteworthy. Kwayana, a co-founder of the WPA in Guyana, had taken up this race issue since 1956 with his attack on Jagan's apparent pro-Indian stance. However, Kwayana became even more controversial during the early 1960s, when, following the most bloody period of ethnic political violence in the country (1962-64), he recommended as a solution to the problem the geographic separation of the races, or 'zoning' as it was popularly called. Kwayana's 'zoning' concept met with widespread criticism from both within and outside the Left, since it was seen in terms of narrow racial chauvinism, and anti-nationalist divisiveness which could further the fragmentation of so small a country (territorially and demographically) as Guyana. However, Kwayana contended that the suggestion was recommended mainly for discussion and to be implemented only as a last resort if other more meaningful considerations failed.[60] Within this period, also, Kwayana founded the African Society for Cultural Relations with Independent Africa (ASCRIA) which, much like the Garvey Movement before it, advocated the promotion of African self-pride and cultural development in order to strengthen the race *vis-à-vis* the other more advantaged ethnic groups in the system. After a sojourn which included close association with the PNC regime, ASCRIA finally became absorbed within the WPA pressure group which it helped form in 1975.

As one of the co-leaders of the WPA, Kwayana appeared to have shelved the African-centred racial issue in preference for a more multi-ethnic and class-based approach. However, Kwayana's race-centred preoccupation seemed to have resurfaced in 1990 when he renewed his charges, this time more subtle, against the PPP for racism over the issue of 'choice' of a compromise presidential candidate to challenge the Burnhamite PNC monopoly at elections. The PPP had insisted that Cheddi Jagan be that presidential candidate, whereupon Kwayana and the WPA spearheaded a challenge to this choice first by supporting a counter-choice of a prominent Afro-Guyanese candidate, Ashton Chase, and second by claiming that all politicians who played principal political roles during the 1960s, the period of the bloody racial-political violence, should voluntarily disqualify themselves from competing for power positions during the 1990s.[61] Kwayana was obviously pointing to the PPP since he saw Jagan as the main contender from the notorious period of racial confrontation of the 1960s, although both himself and Chase were also prominent among the national political leadership of the 1960s in Guyana.

The PNC's perspective on the racial problem was as simplistic as it was contradictory. For the PNC there was only one source of the problem of racial divisiveness in Guyana: Jagan. The solution, which the PNC claimed to have brought to Guyana, revolved around equally simplistic factors: effective law enforcement, the co-optation of PPP leaders, mainly of East Indian descent, and the introduction of 'cooperative socialism' which was supposed to transform race consciousness into national or socialist consciousness. Naturally, the PNC's 'cooperative socialist' programmes met with forceful criticism from other Left parties and groupings in Guyana and the Caribbean, particularly since the proposals led to a series of both economic and political crises in the country. PPP supporters condemned the PNC projects as essentially anti-East Indian, since in the process the East Indian-dominated rice industry was virtually destroyed.

Also, both the PPP and WPA saw the excessive growth of the military and security forces in Guyana as a domain for ethnic, class and political repression. Further, cooperative socialism was criticized by most Left forces within Guyana and the Caribbean region as a ploy to entrench the domination of an essentially Black, petty bourgeois clique under the personal control of Forbes Burnham.[62] However, mainly because of its rather simplistic approach to the race issue, and its conviction that the problem was finally solved under the manipulative proclivities of the party, the PNC was the only so-called Left party in Guyana that persistently rejected calls from other Left groupings for compromise solutions toward Left unification and solidarity.

LEFT UNITY

Beyond the issue of race and class was the concern for the unity of the Left movement, particularly in the face of hostile external and internal forces. This issue emerged in the Left agenda in the form of specific attempts to challenge or escape the wrath of repressive regimes and imperialism in the region. Approaches to Left unity also surfaced in the form of collaborative efforts toward the realization of ideological objectives such as socialism, or organizing solidarity platforms on international concerns such as national liberation struggles. In short, Left unity in the Caribbean ranged from desperate survival strategies to the development of the more far-reaching capabilities for political triumphs or successful social transformation.

This unification or solidarity issue became a most urgent agenda item after the Grenada debacle in 1983 which saw perhaps the most successful Caribbean Leftist experiment disintegrate before the very eyes of the entire Leftist movement in the region. From its inception, the Caribbean Left represented small splintered groupings, each operating in relative isolation from the other and often becoming a hot bed for some of the most hostile sectarian political squabbles the region had ever witnessed. For example, small Leftist groupings like the WPJ, the Communist Party of Jamaica, and the Jamaica Trotskyist group hardly mentioned each other in their statements, programmes or projects, let alone united on any single issue. Before 1983, also, Left parties such as the PPP and WPVP in Guyana were more at war with each other than collaborating in challenging a common oppressive regime. In Trinidad, extreme parties such as NUFF suffered the fate of self-imposed isolation from other potentially-friendly political forces in the country, by experiencing a lonely defeat at the hands of an increasingly unpopular Trinidad state apparatus.[63]

Some small steps in the direction of Left solidarity alliances were, however, taken as early as the 1950s when Jamaican Marxists contrived a class collaborationist effort in the early formative stages of the PNP. The attempt soon failed mainly because of cold war fears internalized within the PNP. Similarly, efforts made in the 1960s to bridge the gap between the Jagan-Burnham rift within the Guyanese Left, including Jagan's offer of parity in his government to the opposition PNC party, and the efforts of an independent intellectual grouping from *New World* sources, called the Committee for National Reconstruction, met with the staunchest of rebuffs from Burnham, undoubtedly influenced by similar cold war considerations.

One case that led to region-wide Leftist solidarity during the 1970s was what came to be popularly known as the 'Rodney Affair'. The Rodney Affair had three major dimensions, each drawing sizeable support from various politically conscious and progressive quarters in the Caribbean and beyond. The first event happened in Jamaica in 1968 when this prominent young Guyanese and Caribbean intellectual was denied a reentry visa into Jamaica to resume his position as lecturer in history at the University of the West Indies in Mona. Students and academic staff at the UWI in Jamaica went on a vigorous protest march which spilled over into riots in Kingston, the capital city, leaving several persons killed or injured.[64] Solidarity with the Rodney cause was immediate throughout the other campuses of the UWI, notably Trinidad and Barbados which also saw widespread protest demonstrations led by students and academics. The events also spawned the creation of a variety of intellectual centres and productions throughout the English-speaking Caribbean, the most prominent of which were the already mentioned periodicals *Abeng* in Jamaica and *Moko* in Trinidad, dedicated to the discussion of Leftist and radical issues affecting the Caribbean as a whole.

The second solidarity event around this Rodney Affair was in 1974 when Rodney was denied a job at the University of Guyana by the Burnham government which considered the native scholar a threatening political rival. The University of Guyana Workers Union (UGWU) and the entire Guyanese Trade Union Movement, under the TUC, were quickly drawn into the affair in protest against the job denial. Solidarity from other progressive trade union bodies from throughout the West Indies, particularly the UWI workers union in Jamaica and Trinidad, was ever forthcoming in support of Rodney, the UGWU and the Guyana TUC. The Burnham government, however, remained unyielding.

Yet a third Rodney event with more far reaching Caribbean-wide significance was Rodney's tragic and controversial death in June 1980. Rodney was killed when a bomb exploded in his car. This event was a shocker not only for the Caribbean Left, but for the entire academic and intellectual community far beyond the Caribbean itself. The government of Guyana was almost unanimously accused by all groups of being responsible for Rodney's death either directly through assassination, or indirectly through facilitating his death. Many point to Burnham's angry speech shortly before Rodney's death exhorting the leaders of the WPA, of which Rodney was a most prominent leader, to "make their wills", and threatening to "meet steel with even sharper steel", as directly preparing the ground for Rodney's assassination.[65] The possibility of CIA involvement was also discerned in this deadly scheme by many within the Left and academic communities in the region.[66]

Apart from issues and events which give rise to relatively spontaneous and reactive types of responses by the Caribbean Left, unity efforts were also conceived or forged in relation to particular common objectives. These unity projects took various forms including electoral, nationalistic or survival alliances. Electoral alliances were usually the most short-lived. Some examples were the strategic support given the PNP by the WPJ during the 1970s in the electoral contest against the right wing, US-sponsored JLP. This fragile alliance lasted until 1980 when the PNP lost the elections of that year to the JLP. Other temporary electorial alliances included the ULF coalition with the National Alliance for Reconstruction (NAR) which defeated the dominant PNM at the polls in 1986 in Trinidad and Tobago. Shortly after the NAR assumed political office, internal dissent led to a split involving ULF elements within the party.

In Guyana, the PCD represented an outstanding example of an attempted electorial alliance among political opposition groups including the major Leftist parties in the country. The PCD originated from the initiative of the Working People's Alliance which was among several opposition parties strongly opposed to the rigging of the national elections in Guyana by the Burnhamist PNC government. The PCD in essence represented a multi-party, multi-class alliance which also aimed at jointly contesting the 1992 elections under a single opposi- tion presidential candidate in the hope of defeating the Burnhamist monopoly on Guyanese electoral politics. The PCD further aimed at setting up a coalition government after the 1992 elections (which they hoped to win on the assumption that together they controlled majority popular support in the country). However, the Leftist coalition partners, particularly the PPP and WPA, soon quarrelled among themselves on four major issues: (a) whether and to what extent the PNC should be involved in future coalition governments, (b) the extent to which socialist or anti-imperialist objectives should form part of the platform of either the electoral alliance or a future coalition government, (c) the formula for the sharing of parliamentary seats and cabinet posts by the various parties in any possible future coalition government, and (d) who should be the common presi- dential candidate in 1992.[67] The coalition broke down shortly before the 1992 elections on account of failure to agree on all of the issues. The PPP eventually won the 1992 elections by forming its own separate alliance with sympathetic citizens, called the 'Civic Slate'.

Beyond strictly electoral alliances, Left parties in the region also attempted to forge more far reaching kinds of alliances such as those embracing national considerations whether of the anti-imperialist or pro-socialist variety. The PPP's offer of 'critical support' to the PNC government, subsequent cooperation talks between these two parties, and proposals for a National Front government, were all initiated, according to the PPP, in the interest of "anti-imperialist unity".[68] WPA's response proposal for a National Patriotic Front government reflected similar nationalist and anti-imperialist consideration.[69] But, perhaps, the most ambitious effort toward anti-imperialist unity was the Caribbean-wide attempt, following the Grenada NJM fiasco of 1983, to develop a permanent structure for 'Regional Consultative Meetings', involving Left groups not only in the English- speaking Caribbean, but in the wider region including Nicaragua, El Salvador and

Suriname. These region-wide meetings, initiated by the PPP in 1984, met first in Guyana in that year, and in the following year, Nicaragua. The main objectives of these meetings, according to the PPP, were "the exchange of experiences and ensuring the cohesion of the movement".[70] The one unification effort with definite socialist interest was that of the Guyana TUC in 1985 to bring the three Leftist Guyanese parties together, the PPP, PNC and WPA, under the banner of what it termed "revolutionary democracy", as a means toward "a political solution to the economic crisis" facing Guyana since the mid-1970s.[71] However, these varying attempts at nationalist, anti-imperialist or socialist unity failed for several reasons, including: (a) disinterest on the part of major elements in the arrangements; (b) personal and political rivalries due to electioneering; (c) lack of time for organizational efforts outside of election campaigns; and (d) lack of popular support.

Then there were mere survival alliances, involving mainly those minuscule or splinter groups which were weak because of lack of resources or sizeable support. Thus, in the 1970s the WPVP in Guyana merged with the small rightist Liberator Party (LP), to form the Vanguard for Liberation and Democracy (VLD) which soon faded from the political scene. Survival strategies were also implicit in other attempts in Trinidad and Tobago at inter-organizational recombination following organizational splits, as in the cases of the Raffiq Shah group which had split from the ULF, reemerging under the banner of the Committee for Labour Solidarity; and the Panday faction of the same ULF split, becoming eventually absorbed within the NAR. Another similar recombination was that of the small Marxist YULIMO grouping in St Vincent which, after several unsuccessful attempts at uniting with other small Left parties in the island, became finally absorbed within the relatively more moderate Movement for National Unity (MNU), which is now more committed to electoral than to extra-parliamentary struggle.[72]

Despite its importance, the unity issue occupied a relatively marginal place on the Caribbean Left agenda. Not only was it rather late in coming as a serious political issue (i.e., during the 1980s), but it hardly went beyond tactical and relatively transient considerations such as winning elections and countering dictatorial governmental policies or foreign interventionism. Only in exceptionally few cases, if at all, did collaboration efforts aim at resolving entrenched racial and class divisions in the interest of working class unity for the realization of socialist objectives.

In sum, there seemed to have been a kind of division of labour as regards the different unity objectives as emphasized by the different types of Left movements and organizations in the region. While, for example, the Revolutionary Left stressed unity against imperialism, the radical Left emphasized solidarity against dictatorship and racism. The Reformist Left, on the other hand, tended to view alliances essentially in instrumentalist terms, mainly as a convenient means toward electoral successes or securing political power. The PNP's quarrel with both its own Left wing and the WPJ, particularly after its electoral defeat in 1980, must be seen in this light. Also, the PNC's coalition with the United Forces in 1964 to defeat the PPP at the polls represented such an instrumentalist and transient arrangement.

REFLECTIONS ON THE LEFT AGENDA

The Caribbean Left agenda was not necessarily a single or common agenda reflecting an underlying unity or consensus among the various leftist groups in the region. If anything could be said about the Caribbean Left it is that they represented a complex and polyglot set of individuals and groups, reflecting more ideological pluralism than political uniformity. At the same time, however, one could detect the emergence and projection of some common themes which represented the priority items on the Caribbean Left agenda. The Revolutionary Left stressed anti-imperialism, the Radical Left stressed anti-dictatorship and anti-racism, and the Reformist Left stressed issues of the transition and power struggle.

However, the Caribbean Left agenda was as important for what it left out of focal consideration as for what it prioritized. Among the most critical issues slighted or ignored by the Caribbean Left – issues which became focal points in the very definition of the newer Left in the more developed countries – were: (a) the women and gender issue; (b) the politics of choice, particularly sexual preference and abortion rights; (c) the environment; (d) the relative merits of violent versus non-violent strategies of change; and (e) certain Left theoretical issues such as some aspects of post-modernist or post-structuralist debates.

Although many Left parties in the region boasted of strong women's chapters, these were usually more conscious of women's roles in political mobilization than of the fundamental issue of women's rights or assertiveness vis-à-vis male or capitalist exploitation. Women's equality in these bodies was usually taken for granted rather than viewed as a special problem for debate. The closest one gets to the women's issue being discussed as a problem in its own right is usually at the academic level where, particularly at UWI and the University of Guyana, a clear agenda is increasingly emerging on this long-neglected issue.[73] It is also within this slowly emerging women's issue perspective that the politics of choice regarding pregnancy or abortion rights is also being discussed. However, the only closely related issue that has never made it on the Caribbean Left agenda, and is very unlikely to make it soon given the typically male chauvinistic culture of the Caribbean, is the gay rights issue which has for the last several years become prominent as a modern Leftist issue in North America and Europe.

The problem of the environment is, at best, only marginally discussed within the Caribbean Left. To the extent that this issue has ever been raised, it represented a concern about immediate practical problems that surfaced in piecemeal and specialized settings, rather than a concern of more lasting consideration. The WPA in Guyana, for example, raised the environmental issue in connection with the wildlife and biological damage to the environment caused by large scale gold mining operations in particular sections of the Guyana interior.[74] What, however, needs to be elevated more prominently on the Caribbean Left agenda is the threat of industrialized pollution (particularly bauxite and gold mining) to the health of surrounding, vulnerable populations (particularly populations representing endangered species and tribes such as some Amerindians in the Guyana interior), and the ill environmental effects of widespread deforestation which comes in the wake of willy-nilly free market industrialization in vulnerable Third World countries such as Guyana.[75]

On the issues of violence there appears to be a general consensus on the part of the Caribbean Left to publicly disassociate themselves from all uses of or adherence to violent techniques. This public position, however, says nothing about either the private use of violence between competing groups as in election times, or the use of state violence to repress possible political threats to regime stability. Even the violent seizure of power by the NJM against the Gairy government in 1979 was publicly asserted as an example of relatively peaceful resistance.[76] Burnham and the PNC's obvious use of the most extreme violence in the 1960s against the PPP government, and again in the 1970s against the political opposition, were all publicly denied in the strongest terms by that party. Yet the issue has so far failed to make a serious place on the Caribbean Left agenda. The marginal way in which this issue surfaced on the Left agenda was in the circumstances where a beleaguered Leftist party, the WPA, was itself at the mercy of PNC-initiated violence, in which case members of the WPA became seriously concerned about how to counteract state violence. Rodney's death itself might have resulted from an activation of this concern for an appropriate response to Burnhamite violent repression. The issue of violence was also raised by the PNC after sensing popular disenchantment with its policies when it raised the spectre of future opposition political violence in the hope of gaining public sympathies.[77]

But there are strong reasons why this issue might have been beneficial to the Left if given a more prominent place for discussion and debate on the agenda. First, the violent and suicidal extremism of the splintered Left such as the NUFF in Trinidad (1970s) and the Coardist NJM faction in Grenada (1983) might have been avoided and the corresponding movements thereby saved. Secondly, the dissemination of serious research findings on political violence in the Caribbean might have influenced a reversal of the usual public association of Leftism *ipso facto* with violence, when in fact the Caribbean Left tend in general to be much less violent compared to the more right wing political forces in the region.[78]

While some subjects tended to be underemphasized on the Caribbean Left agenda, commitment to the very priority subjects tended to shift in intensity over time, depending on the particular circumstances. Usually the stimulus for such shifts in priority is based on particularly dramatic historical events at either the domestic or international levels. At the domestic level, significant changes such as electoral defeats, internal party splits, economic crises, or extreme violent acts usually impact most strongly on the Left agenda with far-reaching consequences for either the particular Leftist organization or the movement as a whole. At the international level, the events which tend to have similar effects include foreign military intervention, political and economic destabilization, and fundamental structural changes in international political and economic arrangements.

For these reasons, the strong and almost fanatic anti-imperialist emphases on the agenda sharply shifted during the 1980s to a more pragmatic approach by the major Left parties to the issue of international capitalism and imperialism. For example, the PNP in Jamaica took this route following its defeat at the polls in 1980, at the hands of US instigated destabilization. The almost complete turn-around from democratic socialism of the Manley PNP government after its 1990 recent electoral success is undoubtedly a strong indication of pro-imperialist modifications in the interest of maintaining political power. Similarly, the PPP in Guyana noticeably modified its strong anti-imperialist stance when it recognized that its own chances of reversing a series of artificial electoral defeats at the manipulative hands of its PNC rival, depended ultimately on the assistance of outside forces close to the imperialist powers. The PPP's lobby of the US, particularly the Carter Center and Democratic Party congressmen, for support for its campaign for free and fair elections in Guyana, was a case in point.

Sudden economic crises, such as the OPEC oil crisis of 1973 which negatively impacted on most non-oil producing Third World countries, or the debt problem which forced Caribbean states to urgently seek IMF loans, as in the cases of Jamaica (1977) and Guyana (1978 and again in 1989), have also contributed to a softening of the traditional animosity to US imperialism on the part of these respective governments. The PNC, which started out as pro-imperialist in the early 1960s, took a sudden anti-imperialist turn in the early 1970s, only to turn again toward imperialism during the 1980s in the wake of both foreign debt and the prospects of economic destabilization. By the early 1990s, the Hoyte administration of the PNC regime had embarked on a frantic policy of what it termed 'divestment' or privatization of government-owned enterprises and restrictions on labour demands as a result of its contractual commitments to IMF conditionalities.

The WPA in Guyana also represented an example of a strong anti-imperialist, anti-dictatorship and pro-socialist party that turned around to a more moderate stance by the end of the 1980s. This reversal became obvious following the assassination of its prominent leader, Walter Rodney, in 1980. That the WPA started out as staunchly anti-imperialist, anti-PNC dictatorship, and Marxist-Leninist socialist in orientation, is clearly indicated in its launching Manifesto in 1979.[79] But by the mid-1980s, the WPA had taken a more neutral position *vis-à-vis* US imperialism, sought "dialogue" with the ruling PNC, eliminated all references to socialism in its manifestos and platforms, moved from "People's Assemblies and economic democracy" to the concept of "due process and Westminster Democracy", and as some argued, would appear to have actively considered the prospects of forming an alliance with the PNC in opposition to what it perceived as the resurrected racist politics of the PPP during the 1992 elections campaign.[80]

Two major international events which, one would have thought, might have had serious negative implications for the Caribbean Left, seemed in fact to have had the reverse effect. These were the foreign military intervention in Grenada in 1983 and the ideological and political debacle among Communist powers in the East, following experiments with Glasnost and Perestroika in the Soviet Union. Both events seemed to have stiffened the resolve of the Caribbean Left, the first because it brought an instant heroic solidarity in the face of hostile outside forces, and confirmed earlier Left predictions about US intervention in Grenada; the second because the Caribbean Left claimed to have already experienced similar experimentations with liberal democracy and free market capitalism which the Soviet Union was only now advocating.[81] US military intervention in Grenada had the immediate effect of drawing together Left forces from all dimensions, ranging from moderate PNC and PNP, to the more radicalized WPJ and PPP elements, and extending solidarity beyond the English-speaking Caribbean to embrace such countries as Suriname, Nicaragua and the Left guerilla forces in El Salvador. Glasnost and Perestroika also served to reinforce earlier Caribbean Leftist resolve to seek the electoral route to power, to embrace western democracy and to involve private capital as an indispensable aspect of their economic development strategies.

5

The Quest
for Power

The adaptability of the Left within the Caribbean political process has always been problematic. Much of the problem resides in the limitations inherent in Westminster-styled democracy as applied to a relatively unstable Caribbean political milieu. This chapter focuses on the methods used by the Caribbean Left for gaining political power within the parameters of the Westminster democratic framework. In this regard, the Caribbean Left's predisposition toward both the electoral or violent road to power will be examined. The rudiments of Westminster democracy introduced in the English-speaking Caribbean via colonialism, with its typically middle class characteristics, have already been discussed in chapter 2. In this chapter we focus on the problematic implications of this largely 'de-contextualized' democracy[1] for progressive political practices in the region. Apart from the inequalities which derive from capitalist and middle-class control, it is necessary to stress here: (a) the continuing tendencies toward demagogic and authoritarian styles of political leadership in these parts; (b) the occasional degeneration of this process into arbitrary and personalized usurpations of power;[2] and (c) the inherent potential for political violence and instability. These factors inevitably lead to a rather exaggerated emphasis on security questions on the part of both the state apparatus and metropolitan political and economic concerns.[3]

To fully understand the particular predicament of Leftist political movements within the colonialist legacy of Westminster democracy, it is necessary to briefly re-examine Leftist perspectives on particular types of democracy in the region.

The more radical and revolutionary Left, for instance, take a Marxist position on the issue. This means that these groups accept some aspects while rejecting most of what is implied in Westminster democratic forms. The classical Marxist notion, for example, suggests that liberalist or 'bourgeois' democracy tends to mask essential inequalities inherent in the class divisions of capitalist society. As a result, Marxism is intrinsically skeptical of the extent to which parliamentary democracy, as exemplified in the Westminster form is really representative of the masses of the population. However, both Marx and Engels regarded the attainment of universal suffrage as a significant stage in democratic political development, and a benefit particularly to the hitherto oppressed and unpoliticalized masses of the population.[4]

While accepting the majoritarian principle, the 'one man, one vote' egalitarian assumption and the libertarian perspectives of Westminster democracy, the Caribbean Left nevertheless emphasizes its minority class nature, and its essentially unrepresentative character as applied to the Caribbean context. For this reason, Caribbean democracy is regarded as inadequate as a means toward revolutionary transformation of Caribbean society, or at best a necessary but not a sufficient condition for mass emancipation.

There are, of course, varying levels of commitment to Westminster democracy depending on the type and orientation of the particular Left movement. The older Left, for example, the PNP and PPP, tend to be most conformist within the Westminster electoral and parliamentary tradition, while the newer Radical Left, on the other hand, tend to be most critical of this tradition, and work actively towards its transformation, as the advocacy of 'people's democracy' or 'workers' assembly' suggests. The central question in this chapter is how the methods used in the acquisition and maintenance of political power are themselves dictated by the limiting conditions of Westminster democracy, and contribute to both the rightward shift and the eventual marginalization or emasculation of the Left movement in general. These issues will further shed light on the extent of the responsiveness of the Caribbean masses to leftist politics, selective or general mobilization strategies, Left/Right confrontations and Caribbean democracy, and ultimately the increasing militarization of the Caribbean state and the region as a whole.

ELECTORAL PARTICIPATION

The significance of electoral strategies is best conceived through a prior understanding of Caribbean political culture and the mass receptivity of left-wing politics in the region. Public opinion surveys and election statistics represent major dimensions of understanding this political culture. Both these data sources suggest that the Caribbean population at large is far from enthusiastic about Left wing politics, except in peculiar circumstances, such as where Leftist politics coincides with either nationalism as in the decolonization struggles in the 1940s and 1950s, mainstream liberalism as in the case of the PNP in Jamaica, or racial self-defensive strategies as in the case of the PPP (and PNC) in Guyana. Beyond this, however, several other factors contribute toward the marginalization of Leftist influence in Caribbean electoral politics. These include the extremely complex, sophisticated, and sometimes confusing message of the Left campaigns, and the lack of material support for Left parties and political movements.

As regards public opinion polls, Carl Stone's analysis of the level of acceptability of different political ideologies by the Jamaican masses is very suggestive of the relatively low, although not insignificant, level of popularity of Leftist politics in the island. One poll in 1977, for instance, suggested a 23 percent positive response in favor of communism in Jamaica. Stone concluded that while "anti-communism" represented the "main public opinion tendency", support for communism is nevertheless represented by a "not insubstantial minority".[5] It must be noted also that this survey was done in the 1970s, a time when Michael Manley's radicalization policies were highly popular and the international political atmosphere tended to favour "ideological pluralism".[6] Stone, in explaining this phenomenon, contended that the radicalization of Manley's PNP served to legitimize "far Left Marxist tendencies" in the island".[7] Whether such a "substantial minority" still holds for communism today in Jamaica when the pressures for conformity to an increasingly conservative and anti-communist domestic and international political environment are greater than ever, is rather doubtful.[8]

It must be noted, however, that the 1977 Jamaican example of a substantial pro-communist minority is not necessarily representative of the Caribbean outlook in general. Elections statistics in the other Caribbean territories are not nearly as flattering to the Left as in the case of Stone's observation of Jamaican public opinion in the 1970s. Electoral support for Left wing parties in the smaller islands has usually been significantly low. In the 1984 elections in St Vincent and the Grenadines, for example, both the Movement for National Unity (MNU) and the United People's Movement (UPM), the two main Left parties, failed to make any significant impact on the voters.[9] Similarly, the 1984 election in Grenada, following the US invasion in 1983, reflected only about five percent popular support for the Maurice Bishop Patriotic Movement (MBPM), the successor to the New Jewel Movement.[10] Of course, MBPM support varied from constituency to constituency, with its most significant support coming from St John's and St Mark constituencies which were characterized by very high unemployment rates. In Dominica in 1985, the Leftist Dominica Labour Party (DLP) which had dominated Dominican electoral politics since the 1960s, lost the elections to a right-wing party, the Dominica

Freedom Party headed by Eugenia Charles. The DLP lost much of its support because of a variety of splits in the party and the dictatorial tendencies of one of its leaders, Patrick John. In the 1986 Trinidad and Tobago elections, the single radical contender (NJAC) earned less than one percent of the total votes, while the other radical party, the ULF contested within the ambit of the moderate coalition, the NAR, which won the elections.[11]

In the larger Caribbean territories such as Guyana, Jamaica, Trinidad and Tobago, the left-wing parties do much better at the polls. Michael Manley's PNP in Jamaica has been the most successful in terms of winning elections over the years, since its inception in 1942. The PPP in Guyana is extremely popular at the polls, its electoral strength based mainly on rural, particularly East Indian ethnic support. Both PNP and PPP electoral support range from about 40 to 60 percent of the polls as gauged from the results of a series of elections held between 1953 and 1992. The ULF always boasted of a substantial minority support at the polls in Trinidad and Tobago. In 1981, for example, this party gained eight out of 36 seats in the Trinidad Parliament in the elections of that year, and became the official parliamentary opposition party at the time.[12]

Although the general level of popular reception of the Left seemed to be low, there were cases where the Left obtained appreciable mass support, which undoubtedly buttressed their commitment to the electoral and parliamentary road to political power. In addition, the conduct of electoral practices in the region encouraged the feeling on the part of the Left that their electoral performance was not a true reflection of their popular strength. Justification for this view was found in the electoral rigging and malpractices in cases like Guyana under Burnham (1964-85) where the major Left parties were artificially left out of power since 1968. In other cases, as for example the 1984 Grenada elections, the Left complained of unfair advantages enjoyed by the more conservative parties such as the New National Party (NNP) which obtained a disproportionate amount of financial backing from the US government in their electoral campaign.[13] The fact also that the post-invasion elections in Grenada were conducted under foreign military occupation created the kind of political atmosphere in which a Left party like the MBPM might be shunned even by Bishop's traditional supporters.

A major problem affecting the smaller Left parties in the English-speaking Caribbean was the rather entrenched two-party (government versus opposition) system intrinsic to the Westminster democratic process. This two-party dominant system made it difficult for third parties to thrive in electoral politics.[14] When, in addition, this two-party dominant system is reinforced by the tendencies toward clientalism, tribalization and racial divisiveness in the partisan electoral mobilization process, then the prospect of any new third parties significantly challenging this system becomes exceedingly remote.

MOBILIZATION STRATEGIES

In general, electoral strategies under the Westminster democratic tradition in-volve the mobilization of particular constituencies or voting blocs by each party or candidate in the contest for parliamentary seats. In this ostensibly multi-party, pluralistic context, such an approach amounts to a highly competitive zero-sum or 'winner take all' power struggle. It is necessary, therefore, for parties to recruit to their side as many constituencies as possible to ensure victory at the polls. At the same time, it is important for each to prevent other parties from making successful inroads within whatever constituency it has its strongest appeals. Thus the notion of maintaining 'strongholds' while at the same time encroaching on strongholds of the opposing party becomes typical of this potentially conflictual mobilization strategy in Caribbean parliamentary elections.

The particular constituencies relate not only to geographic locations within particular political systems, but also to social groups, associations, institutions and the like, which themselves might cut across geographic boundaries. The most fundamental of these social groupings or institutions are trade unions, and what theorists refer to as ideological institutions, namely the church, the state and the press.[15] Recruitment within these institutions, therefore, usually involves the most intensive efforts on the part of political parties interested in winning parliamentary elections. These institutions constitute probably the most highly contested terrain in the pursuit of political power. The extent, therefore, to which the Left could successfully mobilize within these major institution-alized constituencies, is the extent to which their growth, development and eventual success are assured.

Trade unions in particular represent the most natural terrain for left-wing political mobilization. Thus, the Caribbean Left either develop strong links with the trade union movement or foster their own labour organizations. As earlier observed, the ULF in Trinidad was an example of the organic linkage between trade unions and Left political organizations, having itself been created out of a coalition of four main trade unions in the country. Also, the creation of GAWU within the ambit of the PPP in Guyana, as well as the growth of the WPJ out of the struggles particularly of the university workers union in Jamaica, are further examples of these strong linkages. For elections purposes, the trade union arms of the party are often used as a focal point, a virtual campaign machine, for electoral mobilization purposes. A classic example of electoral mobilization along these labour-centered lines is the perennial competition between the PNC and PPP for the support of the TUC in Guyana elections. In the past, the TUC invariably supported the PNC, but this did not prevent the PPP trying each time for TUC endorsement. At critical moments, this extremely close linkage between parties

Table 5.1   Position and Opinions on Communism

	Anti-Communism	Non-Communism	Pro-Communism
Mass Media	*Daily Gleaner* *Star*	*Daily News* JBC (TV) JBC (Radio) RJR (Radio)	
Political Parties	JLP	PNP	
Mass Public	67%	10%	23%

Source: Carl Stone, "Ideology, Public Opinion and the Media in Jamaica", *Caribbean Issues*, Vol. 14, No. 2, August, 1978, p.65

and trade unions in the Caribbean foster extremely volatile conflict and political violence.

Most of the fundamental social institutions which provide supports for electoral struggles, however, reflect a conservative and anti-Left political orientation. The clearly anti-Left orientation of the press in Jamaica, as is reflected in Carl Stone's survey (Table 5.1), for example, tends to closely parallel the responses of the established press in the rest of English-speaking Caribbean. Jagan's reference to the extremely counter-revolutionary role of the mainstream Guyana press during the 1960s is a case in point.[16] The compensatory attempt by the Left to counter this trend by creating their own press often runs into the same conservative reaction or state repression from established presses and political institutions. The frustrating experience of the *Mirror* and *Dayclean* newspapers, of the PPP and WPA, respectively, at the hands of the PNC-controlled press and state apparatus in Guyana was a clear example of this type of anti-Left repression.[17]

The established churches, however, seemed to have moved from a very orthodox anti-Left position during the colonial period, to a much more ambiguous one today. Within recent times the CCC took an increasingly anti-imperialist position, and emphatically opposed the US invasion of Grenada in 1983.[18] On domestic policies, the CCC often supports radical programs. For example, during the 1979 workers' strike in Guyana against PNC-IMF policies, the CCC gave financial support to the strikers.[19] Historically, however, the established churches supported the colonial authorities and the conservative, pro-colonialist parties in the country. For example, during the 1957 electoral campaign, these churches actively opposed and mobilized popular opposition against the ruling PPP, mainly because of the latter's educational policies which sought to relinquish church control of schools.[20] Similar conservatism and anti-Left policies of the established churches

were reflected in the 1964 elections when these churches supported pro-colonialist parties against the struggle for independence mounted by the PPP in Guyana.

Other religions also played prominent and sometimes deadly roles in Guyana's
elections over the years. A prominent Muslim group, for instance, formed its own
party, the Guyana United Muslim Party (GUMP) to fight the 1961 elections. It lost badly
at the polls. The Hindus in Guyana split over support for one or another of the major
parties, the PPP and PNC, with the Maha Sabha going over to the PNC and the Dharmic
Sabha remaining with the PPP. But perhaps the more notorious of religious support
for political and partisan power struggles was that of two deadly religious cults
for the ruling PNC during the 1970s and 1980s, i.e., Jonestown or 'The People's
Temple' movement, and the House of Israel headed by Rabbi Washington.

The Jonestown cult was totally disposed to Burnham and the PNC as a possible
thug recruiting base in the event of the need to rig elections or break up opposition
political forces. According to Joseph Holsinger, administrative assistant to Rep.
Leo Ryan (D-California) who was fatally shot at Jonestown, Jim Jones' security force
"acted as a terrorist organization to intimidate the opponents of Burnham's
regime".[21] Tim Wheeler, in an article on Jonestown, quoted from John Nugent's
book, White Night, to support his claims that Jones had made a commitment to
Burnham to help in the rigging of elections. Wheeler put it this way:

John Peer Nugent in his book, White Night, confirms charges that Jones served as a tool of
Burnham's political machine. He described Jones' first meeting with Burnham, well known
for his CIA connections. In Dec. 1976, Jones informed Burnham that his dedicated cadre of
supporters would assist him if he needed an election or referendum battle organized . . . the
'People's Temple' 2,000 would be his . . . [22]

In fact, as Wheeler contended, the Jonestown forces turned out in full support
a year later when Burnham decided to unilaterally postpone the elections due that
year. Wheeler quoted Nugent as follows: "People's Temple squads turned out with
all the alacrity they had demonstrated for politicians in San Francisco to support
the referendum delaying the poll."[23]

Rabbi Washington's 'House of Israel' was equally notorious as a source of thug
pressure on political opposition to Burnham's regime. This cult was willing to
break up opposition political meetings, to organize and participate in multiple
votings for the PNC in elections during the 1970s and early 1980s, even to become
assassins of Burnham's opponents, including priests of what was conceived to be
the White establishment churches. In 1978, for instance, a prominent member of
the House of Israel was charged and convicted for the assassination of a Roman
Catholic priest who was a participant in anti-government demonstrations.[24]

Electoral alliances as a means toward bolstering electoral chances were also
prevalent among the Left in the Caribbean. The PNC, for example, between 1958
and 1961, entered marriages of convenience with other reformist or conservative

parties in the interest of a collaborative strategy to defeat the PPP at the polls.[25] Mention has already been made in a previous chapter of the attempts by the PCD in Guyana and the NAR in Trinidad to use similar coalition strategies for electoral campaigns, with varying levels of success. Also, the short-lived WPJ-PNP electoral collaboration in the 1980 Jamaican elections had its moments of electoral successes despite the overall defeat of the PNP which Manley blamed on his association with the "communist" WPJ.[26]

Trevor Munroe, leader of the WPJ, contended that his supportive tactic brought the PNP many more votes than the latter would have otherwise obtained. Munroe asserted as follows:

The fact is that instead of our Communist Workers' Party of Jamaica causing the PNP to lose votes, we brought them a number of votes which they would not otherwise have got. In some divisions and constituencies in which WPJ was most active – like in Greenwich, South West St Andrew, in Maxfield, South Central St Andrew – the PNP not only did not lose, but won a great majority. In other divisions in which our comrades played the leading role – such as in Siloah in North East St Elizabeth, or in Gray's Inn in South East St Mary – these divisions were amongst the few won in the constituency by the PNP.[27]

Other forms of inter-organizational alliance strategies were also created. The success of the NAR against the PNM in Trinidad was an indication of the possibilities of the United Front approach as was the Seraphin coalition government in Dominica in 1974. Then there were the particular elections tactics of linking the coalition strategies with a compromise package in anticipation of better electoral support. The PPP's proposed National Front Government suggested, for example, that regardless of which party won the single party majority in the 1992 elections, the winner should share power with other significant parties, in contrast to the traditional winner-take-all zero-sum situation implicit in the Westminster electoral model.[28] The PPP, however, did not clarify its criteria for sharing parliamentary seats in such an arrangement, and the post-1992 PPP government composition indicates that its earlier compromise proposals were not to be implemented. Except for the WPA, this National Front proposal was met with less than enthusiastic support by the other parties targeted as part of the governmental coalition.

INSTITUTIONALIZED REPRESSION

The use of the state apparatus as a major instrument in party competition for political power is also very prevalent in Caribbean politics. Much of this repression is directed against Left political movements in the region. The variety of repressive techniques used by ruling parties and the state apparatus include censorship of opposition press and propaganda media and the use of political violence to break up opposition political campaigns. These approaches have already been effectively employed in the cases of Grenada under Eric Gairy during the 1960s, and Guyana under Forbes Burnham during the 1970s. Examples of anti-Left emergency regulations included the National Security Act in Guyana (1964) and the declaration of emergency in Dominica in the 1980s to contain opposition challenges to the ruling regime.[29] State harassment, which was also used against the Left, took the form of political discrimination in employment and promotions, or dismissal of workers from government jobs. On several occasions, government employees in Guyana were dismissed for allegedly being associated with opposition political groupings and activities.[30]

A most effective use of the state apparatus for the maintenance of political power was the subtle manipulation of constitutional, legal and legislative forms to influence electoral outcomes. It was in this sense more than any other that the Westminster principle of 'the rule of law' was often used to subvert genuine democratic processes in the Caribbean. As an indication of how electoral manipulations were done under the guise of maintaining Westminster democratic forms, the PNC example in Guyana was definitely the most outstanding in the region. Between 1968 and 1985 the PNC managed to rig four elections using the following steps:

- by administratively shifting responsibility for registration of voters from the constitutionally-established Elections Commission to the party-controlled Ministry of Home Affairs, the PNC contrived to extensively pad the electoral list in 1968 mainly with its own supporters, while disenfranchising a great number of non-PNC supporters;
- by the introduction of overseas and proxy voting, the list became further padded with fictitious names and non-Guyanese persons who were ineligible to vote. By the use of proxies many of these fictitious, dead or non-Guyanese persons were made to vote in favour of the PNC in the 1968 and 1973 elections;
- blatant tampering with ballot boxes. Geniune ballot boxes were switched with fictitious boxes flooded with PNC votes. The process was made possible by: (a) removing the ballot boxes from the voting area to a central place of counting, and (b) preventing non-government supporters or opposition scrutineers from following the ballot boxes. In 1973 two PPP supporters were shot and killed by the military when they insisted in following ballot boxes in a PPP stronghold;
- military intervention in the elections, ostensibly in the interest of security, but actually to commandeer and transport ballot boxes, and prevent opposition forces seeing what happened to these boxes on the way to the central counting center;
- reducing the Elections Commission to a tool of the ruling party, by appointing a chairman who was more than sympathetic to the PNC rule.[31]

In addition to these institutionalized methods, the ruling PNC regime has often been associated with organizing multiple voting for its candidates by intimidating or pressuring electoral officials, and deliberately ejecting opposition scrutineers from polling places. These methods were particularly acute during the 1985 elections.

But beyond electoral rigging, other forms of institutionalized repression became most important as means toward the control of political power in the Caribbean. These included the regularized use of such state institutions as the courts, the legislature, government ministries and the security forces as instruments in the containment of the more radicalized or Left political forces in the region. Eric Gairy's regime in Grenada during the 1960s and 1970s, that of Edward Seaga in Jamaica in the 1970s and 1980s, not to mention the more extreme Burnhamite regime in Guyana between 1968 and 1985, were all notorious for their arbitrary manipulation of state institutions to contain or destroy the Left. The various methods used included witchhunting, proxy violence, anti-protest and anti-strike legislation, and the banning of Leftist individuals and books from particular Caribbean territories.

The uses of these repressive methods go back to colonial times. The colonial administration, for example, used constitutional manipulation, incarceration, banning of what they termed 'subversive' literature, and restriction of movement of individuals, quite liberally in their attempts to contain the Left. The 1953 suspension of the Guyana constitution to undermine and oust the first elected Leftist government in the British Empire; the jailing of the leaders of both the PPP in Guyana, and the Marxist 'inner circle' of the PNP in Jamaica in the early 1950s; colonial restrictions of the movements of the Jagans in Guyana and Richard Hart in Jamaica from travel to other British Caribbean islands; and the banning of Marxist literature throughout the English-speaking Caribbean during this period are cases in point.

The post-colonial Caribbean state followed closely in the wake of the repressive colonialist legacy. Eric Gairy's use of his private thug army, 'the mongoose gang' in Grenada, to liquidate the NJM paralleled Burnham's use of his 'plain clothes death squad' to silence political opposition. Burnham combined with his overtly coercive methods, the subtler approaches such as the denial of resources and government employment to opposition political groupings, and the co-optation of key leaders from these very opposition sources. However, the Left forces in Guyana seemed to have been specially singled out for repression, compared to the more Rightist forces like the United Force (UF). For instance, the WPA experienced the very worst of it. A WPA press release on Friday, 18 September 1981 headlined: "PNC Unleashes Savagery on Peaceful Picket and People's March: 28 Arrested, Some Hospitalized."[33] The tragic and violent death of Walter Rodney in

1980 and other leaders of the WPA during the 1970s followed in this similar pattern of Burnhamite state repression of political opposition. Similarly, in Grenada, Eric Gairy's 'mongoose gang' targeted Maurice Bishop and the NJM leaders for violent death which materialized when Bishop's father was killed and Maurice Bishop himself very narrowly escaped death at the hands of his 'mongoose' attackers.[34]

Repressive legislation also played a significant part in curbing the Left and democratic movements throughout the English-speaking Caribbean, particularly during the 1980s. Among these could be listed most prominently, the anti-protest legislation in Antigua and St Vincent which attempted to criminalize anti-government protest even at the level of verbal criticisms of government ministers and state policies.[35] Tim Hector's successful challenge of such a repressive anti-democratic piece of legislation in the Antigua courts, therefore, represents an important step in the level of Left struggle in the smaller Caribbean islands.[36]

Closely allied to this anti-democratic type of state control of the Caribbean Left is also the issue of banning of Leftist individuals from travel anywhere throughout the English-speaking Caribbean. Those affected by this form of travel restriction during the post-colonial period were C. L. R James and Stokely Carmichael (now Kwame Toure) who during the 1960s were prevented by the Eric Williams' government from entering the territory of their birth, Trinidad and Tobago; C. Y. Thomas and Walter Rodney, two Guyanese nationals banned during the 1970s by the JLP government from working in Jamaica; and Jamaican national Norman Girvan and Guyanese Steve De Castro denied work permits by the Eric Williams' regime in the 1960s, to continue their employment at the St Augustine (Trinidad) campus of the University of the West Indies.

Perhaps the most disturbing form of repressive control was the state's use of witchhunting techniques to harass, intimidate and contain the Left. The paramount example of the use of this technique was the establishment in 1965 by the Eric Williams' regime in Trinidad and Tobago of a 'Commission of Inquiry into Subversive Activities in Trinidad and Tobago' (CISAT). The primary objective of CISAT was to investigate the activities of radicals in the OWTU, and those 'Marxists' who were associated with the short-lived WIIP. Relying essentially on the unsubstantiated allegation of a renegade 'Marxist', John Rojas, the CISAT sought to identify individuals whom it thought were committed to "change of government through force or intimidation", or to the use of "legal and constitutional means with the objective of changing the democratic pattern of society".[37] C. L. R. James, for instance, was identified by Rojas as one who agitated for revolution in Trinidad and Tobago. The evidence Rojas used for his allegation was a purported "conversation" he had with James.[38] CISAT, therefore, concluded that both James and George Weekes, leader of the OWTU and a founding member of WIIP, were both "communists", and therefore had "to be watched".[39]

Thus, the overall pattern of state and institutionalized repression in the English-speaking Caribbean amounted to attempts to short-circuit effective communication and mobilization among the Left political groupings and individuals throughout the region. It succeeded to the extent that it prevented the forging of Left unity among the minuscule and splintered groups on the Left and had a discouraging effect on some of the most militant and dedicated leftists. C. L. R. James not only quietly went back to England, but was noticeably subdued in his unwillingness to frontally address the issue in Guyana where he was invited to speak. Rodney and Thomas returned to their native Guyana where the former was assassinated, and the latter continued to suffer harassment as he struggled to make his own political impact under the Burnhamite dictatorship.

POLITICAL VIOLENCE

Beyond electoral manipulations and state repression, the quest for control or maintenance of state power has often resulted in the higher extremes of political violence. The Caribbean state is also invariably involved, whether directly or indirectly, in those violent events that are usually associated with inter-party struggles for power. Left parties and movements were involved in a sizeable proportion of political violence events, whether as victims or as perpetrators. The types of political violence associated with the Left range from demonstrations and strikes at the lower extremes, to mass riots, guerilla warfare and armed rebellion on the higher levels. The occasions precipitating such violent activities were usually elections, inter-group (ethnic, racial or cultural) rivalries, the intransigence of the state or controlling authority, or foreign interventions.

The major proportion of inter-organizational political violence represented confrontations between leftist and rightist political forces, the most outstanding example of which were the 1963-64 riots in Guyana in which the collaboration of the UF and the PNC on the Right sought, with the aid of foreign financial and military support, to displace the ruling leftist PPP government, and the 1976 JLP-initiated violence against the newly installed democratic-socialist PNP government of Michael Manley in Jamaica. The similarities between the 1962-64 events in Guyana and the 1976 events in Jamaica were remarkable, as they indicated the power, resources and managerial coordination of rightist-inspired political violence in these parts. What was even more remarkable was their resemblance to the foreign-inspired rightist destabilization and destruction of the Marxist Allende government in Chile in 1964,[40] and the US establishment of Contra forces against the Sandinista regime in Nicaragua in the 1980s. Most prominent among the coincidences in these separate events were:

- evidence of foreign involvement, particularly the CIA and the US government, in the financing and arming of the rightist forces. Large caches of arms were to be found among rightist forces in both Guyana and Jamaica during these incidents.
- as a pretext for destabilization of the Left, efforts by the Right and foreign authorities to link the Left with Cuban and Soviet global designs.
- the overwhelmingly urban concentration of the violence, reflecting its essentially minority middle class character.
- the use of widespread arson or bombing of governmental property alongside the use of guerilla sniping activities by right-wing groups and parties as a major weapon in destabilization of the Left.
- the establishment of secret guerilla plans and organizations. In the Guyana case, it was the 'X-13' plan; in the Jamaica case, it was 'Operation Werewolf '. Economic sabotage and embargo against particular leftist regimes were also imposed by foreign (US) government and multinational corporations.

Michael Manley referred to the Jamaica destabilization events as a "deeper and wider conspiracy" and "planned terrorism".[41] On the other hand, political violence initiated by the Left against the Right tended to be more sporadic, loosely organized, even chaotic, less dependent on foreign resources or leadership, and fell far short of the provisions in armaments, compared to rightist-initiated violence. Among the most significant of Left-inspired violence were: (a) the student-inspired demonstrations leading to riots in Kingston, Jamaica, against the JLP regime in protest against the banning of Walter Rodney in 1968[42]; (b) the massive demonstrations of NJAC in Trinidad leading to arson, riots and military mutiny in 1970; (c) the disorganized and sporadic guerilla activities by NUFF against the police in Trinidad in the 1970s; (d) NJM coup against the Gairy regime in Grenada in 1979; and (e) Patrick John and the LP-attempted coup against the Eugenia Charles' Dominica Freedom Party (DFP) government in 1981. What the Left-initiated violence had in common with that of the Right was its minority, middle class character. However, the Left in particular have so far failed to mobilize significant mass or working class support in armed insurrectionary campaigns in their quest for power.

The one protracted incident in the region which more than any other involved significant working class action was the 1977 sugar workers strike against the Guyana Sugar Corporation (GUYSUCO) and the Burnham regime in Guyana. This event represented a virtual struggle of attrition between the two major rival political parties, PPP and PNC. Despite the extensive repressive force used by the PNC against the strikers, the union (GAWU), the supporting PPP party, and the people of Guyana, this protracted struggle was surprisingly non-violent. The sugar workers' strike called by GAWU, the trade union arm of the opposition PPP, started out as an industrial issue with the union demanding increased workers' wages through a promised profit sharing in the industry's earnings. Both GUYSUCO, the government-owned sugar company, and the PNC government under Burnham bluntly refused to talk to the workers unless they resumed work. In addition, the PNC dubbed the strike 'political' and concluded that the party was justified in using the extremist means to force the workers to return to work. To this end a series of extreme repressive measures were introduced by the regime, including: (1) invoking the National Security Act which extended the police powers of arrest and detention; (2) arrest and detention of many sugar workers; (3) using 'volunteers' including the military forces and civil servants to break the strike; (4) seizing of foodstuffs intended for strikers and their families; (5) attempting to displace GAWU by imposing a new union of PNC creation as bargaining agent for sugar workers, and establishing a 'cooperative' to recruit strike breakers on a permanent basis; (6) sowing conflict between affiliates of the TUC, particularly the Public Service Union and GAWU; (7) suspending the license for newsprint for the *Mirror* newspaper, the PPP propaganda organ; and (8) threat to ban imported foodstuffs such as garlic, onions and split peas, which were used as a main staple by the East Indian population who constituted the bulk of the striking sugar workers.[43]

The 1977 sugar workers strike escalated into a serious test of will between the two major Leftist parties. It appeared that this otherwise peaceful industrial strike was deliberately escalated and politicized by the PNC whose primary purpose was the ultimate destruction of both GAWU and the PPP. In turn, the PPP seemed to have used the occasion to resurrect its civil disobedience campaign started since the rigged elections of 1973, but subsequently postponed for tactical and ideological considerations. The PNC from the beginning dubbed the strike 'a political war'. PNC counter-pickets at the time read: "Start war PPP – PNC must win", and "This is the end of the PPP and GAWU".[44] The strike might have ended much sooner, through the constructive mediation by the TUC and a British Trade Union official, had it not been for the dogged refusal to negotiate by GUYSUCO, Burnham and the PNC regime.[45]

The conflict became inevitably widened to include attempted mediation by the TUC, the Ministry of Labour and the British TUC, international support for the strikers from the OWTU in Trinidad and a British Trade Union, and a local sympathy strike by a sister trade union, the National Association of Agricultural Commercial and Industrial Employees (NAACIE), and material assistance from some elements of the established church in Guyana. The PNC, too, was able to mobilize in its support some trade unions such as the Public Service Union (PSU), the Postal and Telegraph Workers Union (PTWU), the Guyana Labour Union and the General

Workers Union, most of which were involved in the mobilization of scab labour to break the strike.[46] In the process also the PNC moved to create its own rival church representative body, the 'Guyana Council of Religion', headed by the Rabbi Edward Washington of the notorious House of Israel, to displace the heavy Roman Catholic influence in the already established Guyana Council of Churches.[47]

Private cane farmers were also drawn into the contest, most probably by the machinations of the PNC. Much of the arson reported in the canefields was directed against the private farms in the hope that these farmers, who had initially declared their solidarity with the strikers, would be forced to harvest their cane soon enough. In the Guyana parliament, one PPP parliamentarian, Dalchand, accused the PNC, the security forces and government agents of setting fires to the cane.[48]

In the end the strike left both parties totally exhausted, financially and spiritually, and brought the entire country to the brink of economic ruin. The strike had cost the country about $1 million (US) per day.[49] After 135 days of mutually exhaustive struggle, GAWU unilaterally ended the strike. The PNC had refused to yield, and all sides lost; but the tragic outcome for the national economy as a whole and the working classes in particular had spelt the beginning of the end of the PNC's capability for popular mobilization, manipulation and control, and hence also its monopoly on power.

In its intransigent response to the sugar workers' strike, the PNC managed to alienate a large section of the working population, significant sections of the church and religious community, and much of its foreign support. In addition to this cost to the regime, the PNC failed in its bid to displace the legitimate sugar workers union (GAWU), though it had indeed set up a parallel, rival union called the Guyana Agricultural and Allied Workers Union. Comic irony was also involved in that the very strike breakers, mobilized by the PNC to undermine GAWU, themselves struck against GUYSUCO for higher pay, while prominent PNC officials successfully intervened on their behalf. Meanwhile, the authentic sugar workers' demands for the same thing were not recognized, let alone entertained, by GUYSUCO and the PNC regime.

The GAWU 1977 strike in Guyana undoubtedly represented the most protracted, organized and disciplined resistance by the Left anywhere in the English-speaking Caribbean. By and large, Leftist-inspired political violence in the region had always remained sporadic, spontaneous and ill-equipped compared to political violence initiated by Rightist forces. The River Antoine terroristic incident in Grenada in 1980,[50] the NUFF guerilla tactics in Trinidad during the 1970s, the 1985 anti-IMF gasoline riots in Kingston, Jamaica, were classic examples of the more sporadic, adventuristic political violence inspired by the Left.

By contrast, Rightist political and social forces in the English-speaking Caribbean received vast amounts of financial, material and military resources from foreign sources to enable a more deeply entrenched and sustained struggle for continued political domination in the region. The JLP-initiated violence in Jamaica was reinforced by similar disruptions by the newly-formed Jamaica Conservative Party led by Charles Johnson in 1980, both of which benefitted from millions of US dollars in funding from Jamaican expatriates abroad, living mainly in the United States.[51] Similarly, extensive arms caches were discovered by the Canadian police on militants of the Guyanese Conservative Party based in Canada,[52] intended to overthrow the PNC government in Guyana in 1985. In addition, the massive sums spent by the US government and the CIA to fund: (a) the racial-political disruptions against the Jagan government in Guyana during the 1960s,[53] or (b) the Eugenia Charles government in Dominica to provide initial justifications for the US invasion of Grenada in 1983,[54] are further evidence of massive foreign support for Caribbean right-wing political forces in conflict against the Caribbean Left.

On the other hand, the Caribbean Left received very little foreign support. 'Friendly', socialist sources, for instance, applied very rigid ideological tests as a yardstick to measure the extent of material support to be given[55] (the criteria of being 'socialist-oriented'). None of the Caribbean Leftist states or political organizations were recognized as such by the Communist bloc countries during the 1980s.[56] Cuba by this time had already backed off from its initial policy of supporting revolutionary forces abroad.[57] Thus, the Left in the English-speaking Caribbean by the 1980s had become virtually isolated from its material support base both at home (that is, regionally) and internationally as well; hence, the overall weakness of the Caribbean Left movement to sustain any successful strategy toward the attainment of lasting political power in the region.

THE IMPACT OF POWER STRUGGLE ON THE LEFT

Power struggle involving Left parties took the form mainly of electoral contests which gave rise to varying levels of political conflicts and violence. In electoral struggles, the moderate Left tended to be more victorious than the radical or revolutionary Left, the sole possible exception being the PPP in Guyana. On the other hand, only the NJM in Grenada could be said to have come to power exclusively by violent means. However, in the power struggle, the more radicalized Left tended to be marginalized within the Westminster political process. And even under circumstances where Left parties can have claims to widespread mass support, as in the case of the PPP in Guyana, and the more moderate PNP in Jamaica, a combination of internal and external forces often operated to undermine their possible victory at the polls. But regardless of whether these destabilizing developments were within these parties or outside them, the combination of negative experiences had a severe toll on the prospects for the advancement of these parties within the Caribbean political system. The power struggle tended to foster a situation somewhat like Darwin's universe of the survival of the fittest and the complete submergence of the unprepared and ill-equipped among organized political contenders.

The experience of the Marxist party with the longest record of electoral participation, the PPP of Guyana, should serve as a guide to understanding the problems of the more radicalized or revolutionary Left in the struggle for power through popular vote in the region. The PPP experience showed that a major impact of electoral participation was the pressure toward conformity to the liberal democratic norms. This conformity was manifested in the party's extremely flexible approaches ranging from major compromises with more moderate political forces, to the sometimes hard and inflexible pursuit of vanguardist politics. Political concessions to opposition forces by the PPP took place as was earlier mentioned during the 1960s period of political violence when, as the ruling party, it acquiesced to the demands of the Guyana Trade Union Movement and opposition forces on its very controversial Labour Relations Bill which sought to make labour representation more democratic.[58] This approach represented one example of a party trying to retain power and popular favour in the wake of both internal and external hostilities to its pro-socialist programs. An even more extreme example of such political compromises was the offer by the PPP to share political power equally with the opposing PNC in 1963 in the interest of the stabilization of the violent unrest which racially and politically divided the country at the time.[59] Echoes of this same position of compromise were seen much later in the PPP proposals of "critical support" for the PNC government and for a National Front government in the 1980s.[60]

But the more relevant example of compromise in electoral strategies was the attempt by Left parties to distance themselves from their usual advocacy of socialism when it was felt that the voting population became hostile to this particular ideological platform, and to champion instead a return to the familiar notion of pluralistic democracy. During the 1985 Guyana election, for example, the PPP downplayed the issue of its Left Front proposals, the WPA submerged its earlier advocacy of socialism in favour of the more moderate platform of a "Democratic Republic", while the ruling PNC skillfully avoided its earlier aggressive advocacy of "cooperative socialism", all under the perception that the electorate was tired of, or rejected, socialism.[61] This perception followed the long experience of economic hardships – unemployment, rising prices, shortages of essential consumer goods – not to mention increasing political repression which the population, rightly or wrongly, associated with the 'socialist' advocacy of the ruling PNC regime. Thus, by distancing themselves from the socialist thrust in their electoral campaign, the Left parties had hoped for greater support from the population. This expectation of increased popular support for the Left was entertained even though experience had shown that the ruling regime usually rigged the elections to its sole advantage. Another aspect of this tendency was the rather ironic struggle by the radical Left parties for a return to the already familiar Westminster democratic tradition, despite their earlier advocacy of its transformation into more direct or decentralized forms of popular democracy. This approach was more greatly enhanced by those Left parties which faced severe repression under authoritarian conditions, such as in Guyana.

The ultimate dilemma of power which Left political movements and organizations faced in the English-speaking Caribbean was how to correct the continual failure to attain power through the legitimate electoral process, without recourse to extralegal or violent means. How far, in other words, could the peaceful approach adopted by the Left be reconciled to the frequent use of repressive violence by the state apparatus against the Left? Given the persistent commitment of the Caribbean Left to non-violent and peaceful struggle, they would seem to have had very little choice but to continue to tinker and experiment with specific styles and strategies within the Westminster parliamentary electoral process. However, the failure of NUFF in Trinidad and the Coardite NJM elements in Grenada in their use of violence toward the realization of power objectives was a strong reminder of the unhappy fate that would seem to befall the extremist Left in the English-speaking Caribbean. Political violence strategies utilized by both Right and Left, moderate or extremist, led not only to failure on the part of the perpetrators to gain or consolidate political power, but eventually to undermine the basis of overall economic and national development.

Left political struggles have also had their impact on the Caribbean democratic process. Much of the tangible benefits that accrued to the Caribbean population in the name of political democracy resulted directly or indirectly from the struggles for political alternatives that have always characterized left-wing politics in general. At the same time, however, periodic successes of the Left have frequently led to both internal and external assaults on many of the democratic institutions and processes in the region. The characteristic reaction to the Left inclusion in the Caribbean democratic process is a kind of defensive propensity on the part of the state and international capital to the extent that struggle for democracy becomes almost synonymous with national and regional security issues.

This penchant for state and regional security is reflected, for instance, in the increasing tendencies toward militarization in the region. In this respect, Guyana and Jamaica, the two countries with the most successful history of Leftist politics, tended to be the most militarized, as evidenced by military expenditure, strength of armed forces, and quantum of armaments and military hardware.[62] Given, therefore, the combined emphases on increasing military strength and the purchase of anti-protest weaponry by the police, it is not surprising that, as Dion Phillips concluded, "Caribbean military organizations have become influential in their prophylactic role against democratic revolution."[63] Add to this the role of foreign financing to local right-wing parties, as in the cases of Seaga's JLP, Blaize's NNP in Grenada, and Charles' DFP in Dominica, in elections during the 1980s, and the toll on genuine electoral and political democracy becomes enormous.

The Left response to repression took the form largely of non-violent struggle – the use of the courts, demonstrations and strikes – in the hope of attracting the adherence of the Caribbean masses, and at least the sympathies of the international community. Non-violent approaches were, however, more prominently utilized during the 1980s compared to the relatively more violent periods of the 1960s and 1970s. The overall toll of the power struggle on the Caribbean Left had been tremendous, as reflected not only in the rightward shift of the Left movement as a whole during the 1980s, but more tragically in the loss of valuable leaders either through violent repression and assassination as in the cases of Walter Rodney and his colleagues in Guyana and Maurice Bishop and colleagues in Grenada, through purges as in the case of Sydney King, B. H. Benn and Moses Bhagwan of the PPP in Guyana during the 1960s,[64] and D. K. Duncan and others of the PNP in Jamaica during the 1980s or through retreat and resignation as in the cases of C. L. R. James in Trinidad during the 1960s[65] and the hierarchy of WPJ leadership in Jamaica during the 1980s.

Ultimately, the struggle for power led to a series of both externally induced and internal crises which contributed significantly to the further debilitation and marginalization of the Caribbean Left. External pressures included foreign, financial, military and material support for the Right against the Left, while internal crises were occasioned by the exclusionary tendencies inherent in Caribbean electoral-democratic practices, state and institutionalized repressiveness, contentious squabbles and strains within Left political leadership, and the attrition occasioned by continual involvement in intermittent political violence unleashed mainly by right-wing political forces in the region. That these stresses and strains precipitated the devastating disintegration of the Caribbean Left during the 1980s is the central topic of the following chapters.

6

Leadership-Mass Contradictions

This chapter is concerned with the problematic of middle class leadership of the Left and working class movements in dependent capitalist countries with specific reference to the Caribbean context. The major issue here resides in the extent to which middle class control becomes a negative factor in the efforts of the Left towards successful mobilization of the masses and working classes, and eventual realization of political power and social transformation. In short we are interested here in what in Gramscian terms could be referred to as the organic quality of the movement – whether, that is, it tends to be strongly rooted in the masses or grass roots of the particular population and therefore lasting and durable, or whether, as is the argument of this chapter, the precarious relationship of the Left leadership with the Caribbean masses condemns the former to a largely conjunctural existence destined to eventually disappear or atrophy.

One of the main theses of this study is that the dominant explanation for the decline of the Caribbean Left resides not in the peculiar characteristics of the particular ideological preferences or orientation of the movement, however flawed that particular ideology may be, but rather in the problematic relationship between the elitist leadership style of the Left and the increasingly alienated masses of the Caribbean population. By 'elitist leadership style' we refer to three closely interrelated considerations: (a) that the main leadership personnel of the left is drawn essentially from the relatively privileged professional and intellectual sections of the Caribbean middle classes, (b) that their invariable pursuit of centralized political power is usually done at the expense of their promised pursuit of mass empowerment, and (c) that the nerve centre of the Left leadership in the region tends to be sooner or later co-opted into the economic and political establishment, i.e., by forces compatible with the dominant capitalist and international hegemonic interests. This chapter aims to illustrate the foregoing arguments with evidence drawn from a close observation of the mass work of the Left throughout the English-speaking Caribbean.

Several other closely interrelated factors to be further examined in this chapter help to explain the limitations and shortcomings of middle class Left leadership in the region. These include: (a) simple failure to pay adequate attention to mass work and mass demand, (b) preoccupation with ideological conformity to a singular or vanguard party line, (c) racial, tribalistic, or what could be termed ethno political electoral and other mobilization patterns, (d) emphasis on an internationalist outlook at the expense of developing a more nationalist basis of mass political education, and (e) apathy or alienation of the Caribbean masses themselves. It is further asserted here that these factors directly or indirectly contribute to the eventual disintegration of the Left movement as a whole in the region. This in essence is the problematic of the elite-mass gap or Left elitism manifested in the Caribbean context.

THE ELITE-MASS GAP

Here we are concerned not simply with class divisions per se, but how such divisions degenerate into lethal or destructive (usually zero-sum) polarization of forces in peripheral capitalist, particularly Caribbean societies. We are not simply looking at the differences, for example, between the dominant middle classes and the working or subordinate classes in the Caribbean, but at the particular nature of the social distance between them. In effect, we are interested in the situation which distinguishes a dominant few from the subordinate masses of the population. For in the Caribbean context we are witnessing not simply inequality differences between separate entities, but more importantly, relatively autonomous and increasingly polarized forces which are often in conflict while simultaneously working in tandem with each other. Thus, the Caribbean working classes are not totally dependent on the middle classes, although in some crucial respects such as in gaining employment and other forms of economic involvement they often do; but in other critical respects such as ideological and political affiliations, the Caribbean masses usually demonstrate a remarkable capacity for independence and diversity in relation to various middle class positions in the political system.[1]

The Caribbean political elite is drawn directly from these middle classes. In fact the political elite represents the inner core of these classes from which the

Table 6.1   Class differentiatiated parliamentary representation of the PPP:
1953, 1964, and 1992

Election Year	Parliamentary representation by occupational class background: %				
	Professions	Business	Workers	Other	Total
1953	44	17	17	22	18
1964	42	25	4	29	24
1992	53	18	10	18	28

Sources: *Report of the General Election* 1953, pp. 26-32. *Report House of Assembly, Election* 1964, pp. 25-26. PPP/Civic, "Time for a Change", *Manifesto, Elections* 1992.

political leadership, including the Left leadership is derived. Very much over 90 percent of the Left leadership throughout the region is drawn primarily from the professional and intellectual strata of the middle classes as was already indicated in Table 2.4 in chapter 2. Even among the Marxist and Revolutionary Left such as the PPP and WPJ which claim to represent the masses and working classes, no peasants or workers could be found among the upper echelons of the party leadership, even though a minuscule few members of these majority classes (usually less than 5 percent) became parliamentary representatives for the PPP in Guyana at various intervals in the country's political history (see Table 6.1 for PPP class based parliamentary representation between 1953 and 1992).

The intellectual-professional stratum of the middle classes, therefore, dominates the Caribbean political elite, particularly the leadership of the Left. This dominance is readily demonstrated in the distribution of Cabinet posts over the years throughout the English-speaking Caribbean, as earlier reflected in Table 2.4 in chapter 2. Similarly intellectual-professional dominance could be gleaned from a cursory observation of the leaders of the major Left parties throughout the region during the 1970s and 1980s, who by virtue of their occupational background have been prominent members of these relatively privileged classes. Table 6.2 reflects this trend.

Three factors centrally explain the rise to prominence of the professional-intellectual stratum among the Caribbean political elite and Left leadership. First, their special metropolitan training or educational experience exposed them not only to foreign radical and revolutionary ideology, but also to knowledge, skill and practice in political organization and agitation. Secondly, their higher educational levels enable the development on the part of this group of an exemplary capacity for articulating the grievances of all classes in the society, as well as for crafting relevant propaganda for successful political mobilization. Thirdly, the relative

Table 6.2   Occupational background of Caribbean Left party leaders: 1980s

Country	Party	Leaders	Occupation	Ethnicity
Grenada	NJM	M. Bishop	Lawyer	African
		B. Coard	Academic	African
Guyana	PNC	F. Burnham	Lawyer	African
		D. Hoyte	Lawyer	African
	PPP	C. Jagan	Dentist	East Indian
	WPA	E. Kwayana	Teacher	African
		W. Rodney	Academic	African
		R. Roopnarine	Academic	East Indian
Jamaica	PNP	M. Manley	Politician	Mixed
		P.J. Patterson	Lawyer	African
	WPJ	T. Munroe	Academic	African
Trinidad and Tobago	ULF	B. Panday	Lawyer	East Indian

absence of a strong indigenous and entrenched capitalist class in the relatively non-industrialized Caribbean creates the opportunity for the middle class professionals and intellectuals to fill a void in the political leadership structures without serious class competition. The coincidence of these groups with specific racial or colour-caste identifications in the Caribbean socio-political spectrum exposes the Caribbean political elite to a complex variety of conflict situations involving both class and ethnic-racial dimensions – a situation which facilitates foreign engineered divide-and-rule policies, particularly in multi-ethnic societies such as Guyana, Trinidad and Tobago, and Jamaica. What in essence we are witnessing in the Caribbean context is the entrenchment of a power elite whose major sources of strength reside not in the indigenous masses of the Caribbean but outside the region in the metropolitan corridors of economic and political influence.

Intra-elite power or hegemonic struggles represent perhaps the most significant aspect of this multi-dimensional conflict situation in the English-speaking Caribbean. The consequence of these hegemonic or power struggles is either political violence or dictatorial repression. Elite instigation of political violence, for instance, is witnessed in the periodic mutual elimination contests between armed rival ethno-political groupings in which political organizational manipulation directed from the highest levels of party leadership is most evident particularly at election times throughout the region. Examples are legion in this respect:

Guyana 1962-64, 1992; Trinidad and Tobago 1957, 1961, 1970; Jamaica 1976, 1980; and Grenada 1976, 1979,1983. It is also seen in the frequent co-optation of spontaneous mass agitation and protest by organized, partisan political leadership, as in the cases of the anti-IMF mass riot in Jamaica (1985) where the PNP and WPJ intervened to lead the activities, and the general strike in Guyana (1989) interceded by both the PPP and WPA, for similar reasons.[2]

Dictatorial repression represents attempts to suppress opposition (usually Left) political forces and mass protest by the use of the state apparatus or private 'thug' armies, as well as tendencies within political parties to stifle dissent or purge ideological deviations. The notorious examples in this respect are the Gairy regime and the use of the 'mongoose' squad in Grenada during the 1960s and 1970s, the Burnhamite regime and the Rabbi thugs in Guyana during the 1970s and 1980s, the Seaga JLP regime with the alleged aid of foreign paid mercenaries in Jamaica between 1976 and 1980, and the Coardist led Revolutionary Military Council (RMC) regime briefly in Grenada in 1983. While, however, the state centred coercive approach is more frequently employed by the Right against the Left and masses in the society at large, the Left political leadership more frequently employs repressive tendencies against dissent and ideological deviations within the party. The examples here are the PNP purges of Marxist elements in 1952 (involving the inner circle), then in the early 1960s (involving the Young Socialist League), and again in the 1980s involving D. K. Duncan and others; and the PPP purges of the ultra Left in 1956 involving Sydney King, Martin Carter, Rory Westmaas and others, and again during the 1960s involving both B. H. Benn and his associates, and particular members of the Progressive Youth Organization (PYO).

The repression of mass protest takes several forms including the break-up of opposition political meetings as in the case of the unleashing of thug violence against WPA and PPP public meetings in Guyana in the 1970s and particularly in the 1980s, or of Gairy's 'mongoose gang' against NJM organized public protest in Grenada during the 1970s, often at the cost of several human lives and casualties. It takes the form further of official manipulation and rigging of elections as in the cases of both the Gairy regime in Grenada and the Burnham regime in Guyana. Mass repression equally takes the form of what could be termed ethno-political vendettas as in the case of JLP supporters organizing to prevent PNP supporters from burying slain PNP members in a cemetery adjacent to a JLP stronghold in Kingston.[3] The Caribbean masses, however, are not simply malleable and mindless subordinates of middle class control. Their capacity for independent action is demonstrated in their usual cynicism about politicians, often in ideological nihilism, and more frequently in their preferences for ethno-political or racial loyalties despite the often strenuous class conscious appeals of the Left political leadership, or the multi-racial (or ethnic neutrality) appeals of the more nationalist or Rightist middle class political leaders.

In consequence the elite-mass gap fosters the vulnerability of Caribbean political systems to foreign intervention, penetration and control. What make this vulnerability probable are: (a) the military and economic weaknesses of Caribbean states and political elites in relation to the foreign powers, (b) the dependence of the political elite on foreign financial and legitimizing support, and (c) the relative isolation of the more militant (i.e., the anti-imperialist Left) section of the political elite from the Caribbean masses. Measurement of the elite-mass gap follows several related lines of approaches including observation of mass perception of or response to elite demands for mobilizational support, as well as the reciprocal responses of the elite to mass demands for inclusion or economic benefits and entitlement. Existing electoral statistics and survey data indicate the degree of mass responses to elite political demands throughout the English-speaking Caribbean, while observed distinctions between elite rhetoric or promises on the one hand and their record of fulfilment or political practices on the other, attest to the level of elite efficacy or responsiveness *vis-à-vis* the Caribbean masses.

ELITE NEGLECT OF THE MASSES

The preoccupation of the Left leadership with the pursuit of centralized political power and foreign material and legitimizing support predisposes this group to either neglect the masses or utilize them as subordinate objects of mobilization rather than as allied partners in the struggle for change and social transformation. At a more critical level, elite neglect of the masses manifests itself in terms of exclusion of the latter from the reward structures of the organized Left movement itself. This mass exclusion is usually the result of the quest for vanguard status on the part of the Left leadership, particularly that of the more radical and revolutionary Left. Above all the neglect of the masses is reflected in the lack of systematic theory about mass involvement in revolutionary struggle with respect to the Third World and Caribbean experience. Apart from the objective circumstances which make mass work difficult, crucial evidence of mass neglect could be gleaned not only from the observations of independent writers on the subject, but more importantly from the available self-criticisms of significant Left leadership personnel across the region.

Exclusion of the masses from participation in the hierarchy of the party or state is more likely with the smaller, less endowed political organizations, than with the larger traditional parties in the Caribbean political process. However this exclusion is usually not deliberate, as the policies and objectives of small Left parties like the WPJ, WPA, and NJM otherwise indicate, but largely dependent on the circumstances such as lack of relevant resources or sufficient personnel, and the need to marshal the limited resources and time at their disposal in physical survival strategies. Yet in some crucial respects the lack or loss of mass support and following is due to the parties' own fault. For example, stringent restrictive rules introduced by the WPJ and NJM for the attainment of membership status within the respective parties – long waiting periods, onerous dues, security surveillance, intensive study programmes, preference for non (religious) believers, martial type discipline – served to discourage not only membership applications but even active support from the broad masses of the population.[4] For the WPA in Guyana the problem of mass support tends to be not so much the membership admission criteria which are simple and less onerous, but rather in their limited resource capabilities, the restricted urban bias of their mobilizing efforts, and the apparent specialization of the party for periodic electioneering campaigns. For these reasons membership and national popular support for these radicalized Left parties remained rather minuscule: the NJM having no more than 300 members at any time between 1979 and 1983,[5] while the WPJ argued that if its membership criteria had been less restrictive the party membership would have increased by more than 200 percent between 1978 (the time of its first congress) and 1981.[6]

Another aspect of mass neglect by the Leftist political elite is the tendency to subordinate the masses to the status of what Elean Thomas of the WPJ termed "foot soldiers" for the party's programmes and objectives. In a letter to a WPJ self criticism congress she put it this way:

our approach . . . was and still is too bureaucratic. We did not allow enough space for working people to come to us and fully benefit the Party with their experience. In practice many working people had to walk miles for months before they could get into Applicant membership; and once in the party we made them into foot soldiers, despite the fact that some of them were coming to us with more political experience than many of our leaders.[7]

Beyond this possible tactical error on the part of the WPJ, a certain degree of contempt for the masses has been developed in some other Leftist quarters. Bernard Coard, for example, second most prominent leader of the NJM in Grenada, and his close associates in the height of the most serious crisis facing his party and government in 1983, and after the cold-blooded execution of the first and most charismatic leader, Maurice Bishop, by the military directorate of the party led by the said Bernard Coard, had this to say about the Grenadian masses: "even if it takes 10 years, the masses have to understand."[8] And one of Bishop's former colleagues, George Louison, observed about Coard: "Bernard felt that if the masses demonstrate for weeks upon weeks, they are bound to get tired after a while and get hungry and go back to work. He said (Eric) Williams did it in 1970, Gairy did it in 1974, and it could be done again."[9] It is no doubt an extension of this Coardist contempt for the masses why Coard and the militarist faction of the NJM proceeded in 1982 to unilaterally disarm the masses by dismantling the people's militia when Bishop who established it was temporarily out of the country.[10]

Much of the neglect and subordination of the Caribbean masses stem from the pervasive drive among the more radicalized Left towards the creation of vanguard parties of one or other variety. Even reformist parties like the PNC with a history of a very fickle relationship with Marxism, had opted for a vanguardist position during the late 1970s and early 1980s. Such vanguardist positions, however, would seem to be more closely adhered to by the more radicalized and revolutionary parties like the NJM, the WPJ, and the PPP. These latter parties adopted the Leninist style of vanguardism which insists upon hard discipline, a single party monopoly outlook, ideological conformity, secrecy of central committee decisions, and security consciousness on the part of the general membership. Needless to say this vanguardist outlook runs counter to some of the most fundamental traditional practices in Caribbean political culture, including tendencies toward cutting corners, skirting rules, what are called liming and mamma guying reflecting the relatively slow, easy pace and comical sides of Caribbean life, and cultivating the art of political ridicule as means towards overcoming both economic hardships and political repressiveness whether from internal or external sources.[11] For this reason tensions, contradictions and conflicts, even violent confrontations are bound to emerge in attempts to institutionalize vanguard party politics in the English-speaking Caribbean.

VANGUARDIST POLITICS

There are three basic types of vanguardist politics among the Left in the Caribbean context: (i) exclusive elitism, in the sense of cultivating secretive hard core and dominant political leadership operating independently or in spite of the masses, (ii) expectant mass spontaneity, in which a relatively more mass sensitive leadership organizes itself in anticipation of co-opting future mass spontaneous activities, and (iii) elite organic leadership of mass movement, which suggests the organization of efforts to bridge the elite-mass gap through elite facilitation of the development of leadership directly from the working and subordinate classes of the political system. Examples of exclusive elitism in the region go back to the guerilla movements of Latin America, following the Cuban revolution of 1959, which inspired the development of the now discredited 'foco' theories of Régis Debray and Che Guevara, suggesting that the sole, single-minded and determined guerilla group can eventually win over the masses to its side after winning a series of sporadic battles against the established military forces; thus it is possible for guerillas to indefinitely win victories independently of mass support.[12] In the context of the English-speaking Caribbean, the Coardist faction in the NJM echoed this foco approach in its insistence upon determined, dedicated and disciplined leadership for the development of a highly regimented and militarized political organization independent of the will of the Grenadian masses.

Burnham's approach to 'bullying' the masses in Guyana during the heyday of his regime falls within this exclusive elitist category. However, unlike the Coard faction in Grenada, Burnham and the PNC recognized the historical importance of mass involvement in the revolutionary political process. At the same time, however, Burnhamist vanguardism, much like the Coardist approach, became preoccupied with martial discipline and the elimination of political opposition.[13] Its approach to mass mobilization was extremely commandist. Beyond his typical anti-democratic tendencies, Burnham fostered elitism by encouraging a cult of the personality of Burnham himself as the 'Comrade Leader', while party members were indoctrinated into believing that the leadership 'does no wrong'.[14]

A marginal case of exclusive elitism was that represented by the WPJ which, although seriously interested in mass agitation, participation and support, insisted upon a disciplined, dedicated, and vigilant leadership core. The WPJ itself had no significant mass following, although it hoped to influence PNP mass constituencies – a situation which brought the WPJ into serious conflict with the PNP and led to further alienation of much needed mass support for this vanguard party. The WPJ in essence falls somewhere between the elitist model and the second level of vanguardism which relates to systematic organizational preparation for possible future mass spontaneous agitation or uprising. The supportive involvement of the WPJ in the 1985 anti-IMF 'gasolene' riots in Kingston was an indication of action within this second level of vanguardist politics. But perhaps the more compelling cases of leadership in anticipation of mass spontaneous action were NJAC in Trinidad and Tobago, the WPA in Guyana, and the Movement for a New Dominica (MND). What these parties have in common is their strong advocacy of what are called variously people's parliament' or 'people's assembly' representing mass democratic participation in grass roots self organizations. The typical example here was NJAC's experience with mass discussion and debate at what is famously known as 'the university of Woolford Square', its encouragement of political 'rap and liming' sessions, and its frequent invitations to address spontaneous generated meetings of the unemployed, the farmers and workers throughout Trinidad.[15]

The problem with the 'people's assembly' idea is that its implementation does not necessarily eliminate the tendencies towards political centralization and elitism as far as leadership of the movement is concerned. The strenuous efforts needed towards mass mobilization by parties without significant mass support, or of masses without adequate political consciousness, often end up producing highly centralized and demagogic or charismatic leadership. Both Daaga, leader of NJAC, and Rodney, one of the principal WPA leaders, fit this demagogic or charismatic type of leadership image. Secondly, the parties that have had the resource capability to implement the 'people's parliament' idea, such as the NJM and PNC, succeeded mainly in creating highly bureaucratic structures with a top-down (or directive) administrative approach, and without any form of decision-making or policy creating authority given to the masses themselves; in fact in both cases what were regarded as 'masses' were invariably reduced to party supporters only.

Yet a third group of Left political organizations advocates a more organic style of vanguard leadership of mass movements. This group includes the PPP of Guyana, the ULF of Trinidad and Tobago, and the Socialist Workers Party (SWP) of Dominica. The experience of the SWP defines the situation of this group. As Bill Rivière put it:

The SWP undertook . . . to develop a political organization led, though not manned exclusively by politically conscious elements of all classes and strata. In a sense, the goal was a mass party led by a vanguard, rather than a strict vanguard of the Leninist type. The perceived role of that political organization was the co-ordination of independent struggles waged by various social forces into a centralized popular movement seeking state power as the basis of remolding society. It was certainly not anticipated that these sectional struggles would occur spontaneously. On the contrary, they were to be initiated and sustained by mass organizations consciously assisted in their emergence by the League.[16]

The PPP in Guyana is, without a doubt, the strongest and most durable Left political organization in the history of the English-speaking Caribbean. Its revolutionary activism, crafted in the early 1950s, pre-dated the Cuban revolution by almost a decade. Originally a nationalist mass movement, the PPP moved relentlessly to an orthodox Marxist-Leninist position, particularly after suffering a series of setbacks and defeats at the hands of British colonialism and American hegemonic interventionism during the 1950s and early 1960s. Its march toward Marxist-Leninist vanguard status commenced in 1969 after the Burnhamite regime's blatant rigging of the national elections the year before, was interrupted briefly in 1975 with its declaration of critical support for the PNC on advice from an international socialist conference in Havana the same year,[17] but peaked in 1985 when it declared itself a full-fledged communist party. By 1989, however, this party retreated to a more moderate social-democratic position mainly to secure the help of foreign capitalist powers to withdraw their traditional support from an increasingly discredited Burnhamite regime. Such foreign support came in 1992 when the Commonwealth Secretariat, the Carter Center in Atlanta, and other independent mediatory groups intervened to protect the Guyana elections from further ruling party manipulations. The PPP proceeded to win the 1992 elections.

Throughout its career the PPP has had the most consistently successful association with the popular masses as compared with the record of any other Left political organization anywhere in the Caribbean. Its mass involvement included agitational work with trade unions, religious organizations, farmers associations, and civic movements, while its propaganda work involved the use of its own newspapers, periodicals, pamphlets and films or videos.[18] But at the same time, although this party is almost guaranteed mass support based on ethno-political loyalty patterns in Guyana, there are still several factors which tend to inhibit satisfactory levels of mass commitment and involvement in PPP prospective struggles. First, the thrust towards mass involvement did not lead to any dilution of the essentially middle class elitist character of its leadership hierarchy. For example , the central committee of the party, without much variation over the years, consisted of over 90 percent of personnel drawn mainly from the professional, intellectual, and commercial stratum of the middle classes, while elements drawn into the leadership from the working and subordinate classes were either minuscule or non-existent.[19] Secondly, despite massive efforts, the party leadership often complained that membership in the party, particularly from the lower classes, was far below satisfactory levels.[20]

The ULF experience in Trinidad and Tobago is similar to that of the PPP in that both parties have relied on leadership stemming from the professional/intellectual stratum of the middle classes, cultivated direct links with the mass base, particularly the trade union movement, wrestled with racial biases in their mobilization efforts, and suffered ideological reversals in the wake of defeats in the competition for political power. However, the ULF attempted to go beyond the PPP in its promise to institutionalize grass roots deliberative assemblies similar to the people's parliament advocated by other radical Left organizations such as the WPA, NJAC, and the NJM. Called the Conference of Shop Stewards and Branch Officers (or COSSABO), the ULF programme of grass roots and mass democratic participation involved the linking of street blocs, regional districts and national congresses as the basic units of democratic deliberations.[21] Despite the fact that the ULF never had the opportunity to implement these approaches, the promise here was definitely more fundamental and far reaching than the mass mobilizing practices of the PPP which were confined to bottom house meetings, the establishment of workers committees at places of employment and the like.[22]

Competition in electoral and parliamentary struggle has forced the ULF to discard or compromise most of its ideas on mass oriented strategies in favour of alliance with middle class groupings. In its contest of the 1976 elections the ULF made several elitist mistakes which most probably cost the party a lot of mass support at the polls. First, the ULF mistook trade union support for mass support by campaigning only in those areas of its trade union strength.[23] Similarly, this party largely ignored the African (traditionally PNM) constituencies, relying mainly on its East Indian support base – about 60 percent of the party's membership was East Indian.[24] Serious mass work on the African population in Trinidad and Tobago was definitely needed, since the primarily African dominated trade union component of the ULF coalition, the OWTU, was perceived by the black population at large as being a kind of aristocracy of labour earning much more than the average wage of the rest of the Trinidad work force.[25] Thirdly, the ULF abandoned its original COSSABO or grass roots mobilizational approach in favour of campaigning on the more traditional constituency basis, and so lost a lot of mass votes in areas such as the North where COSSABOs were not established.[26] It is clear, therefore, that the ULF, not unlike the more conventional parties in multi-racial Caribbean electoral systems, fell prey to pressures toward ethno-political mobilization strategies.

ETHNO-POLITICAL MOBILIZATION

Another major problem in Caribbean political culture which tends to preserve the elite-mass gap is the pervasiveness of racial, ethnic and tribalistic (in short ethno-political) forms of political affiliations and mobilizations. Ethno-political mobilization refers to the dependence of major political organizations on the traditional 'strong-hold' constituencies based on racial, ethnic, religious, clientelistic, and neighbourhood types of loyalties as an indispensable resource or weapon in the struggle for political power. As such, ethno-political rivalries, conflicts and violence are usually expressed periodically, but become most acute at election time in Caribbean political systems. Episodes of violent conflicts often result from the organized political rivalries between East Indians and Africans in Guyana and Trinidad, between loyalist neighbourhood constituencies in Jamaica, and between the state and religious-cultural communities such as the Rastafarians and the Black Muslims in Dominica and Trinidad respectively. Ethno-political violence is equally reflected in the degenerative use of private thug armies or 'death squads' whether by the state or political party, in order to control, neutralize, or eliminate political opposition.[27]

The Left political parties which are involved in this degenerative form of politics at various levels are: (a) at the racial-ethnic level, the PPP and PNC in Guyana, as well as NJAC and ULF in Trinidad and Tobago, (b) at the tribalistic or clientelistic level, the PNP and, marginally at least, the WPJ of Jamaica, and (c) at the religio-cultural level, YULIMO in St Vincent, LSW in Dominica, and not least the NJM in Grenada, each with close ties to the Rastafarian movement. Among the approaches taken by these Left parties, which tend to accentuate the elite-mass gap, the most important are: (i) failure to mobilize beyond their own specific ethno-political strongholds at election time, (ii) use of a zero-sum approach to eliminate ethno-political rivals in the contest for power, (iii) purges and splits within the party largely along ethno-political lines, and (iv) increasing authoritarian control within the party or state, based on ethno-political criteria of inclusion and exclusion.

As regards the failure to mobilize beyond ethno-political strongholds, the ULF neglect of PNM African dominated constituencies in the 1976 Trinidad and Tobago elections. PPP and PNC neglect to field candidates or seriously campaign in each other's strongholds in various elections in Guyana between 1957 and 1992, and WPJ confinement to local government elections while skillfully avoiding JLP strongholds in Jamaica, are cases in point.

Tribalistic mobilization patterns are reflected in the typical zero-sum contests between PNP and JLP garrison type constituencies in Jamaica, very similar to the ethnic mobilization patterns of the PNC and PPP in Guyana over the years. Similarly in Trinidad and Tobago ethno-political rivalry was reflected in the attempts by Bhadase Maraj of the sugar workers union to prevent George Weekes of the OWTU from mobilizing the sugar workers, even at the request of the disgruntled sugar workers themselves, during the late 1970s.[28] Purges and splits within the party do the same thing as ethno-political mobilization, of restricting or contracting the mass base for party recruitment. These ethno-political contractions are often considered necessary to augment the power of particular political leaders over the party itself. The classic historical purges and splits and ideological transitions within Caribbean Left political organizations, are reflected in Table 6.3.

Several of those original ideological factions within the Left soon degenerated into race based or ethno-political alliances with a relatively more moderate or independent ideological agenda. Both the Burnhamist faction within the PPP in Guyana in 1955 and the ULF-NAR transition in Trinidad and Tobago in 1985 follow this trend. Others were either totally transformed (e.g., YULIMO to MNU in St Vincent) or disappeared entirely from the political landscape (e.g., Coardist NJM in Grenada, URO in Trinidad and Tobago, and the WPVP in Guyana). While explanations for the splits and purges range from underlying ethnic tensions[29] to irreconcilable ideological differences,[30] evidence seems more strongly to suggest that the pertinent explanation lies in the inextricable combination of foreign influences or pressures and the ambitious quest for political power among domestic politicians, parties and movements. Undoubtedly this foreign linked power quest reinforces the typically elitist characteristics of Caribbean Left political leadership. Both the Burnhamist split within the PPP in Guyana in 1955 and

Table 6.3:   Purges and splits within major Caribbean Left parties 1952-1992

Country	Party	Date of Rift	Description
Jamaica	PNP	1952	Ideological faction: Marxist circle purged
		1955	Rejection of Democratic-Socialist platform
		1961	Forced resignation of Radical Left caucus
	WPJ	1989	Resignation of moderate leaders
		1992	Dissolution of party
Guyana	PPP	1955	Split by Burnhamist moderate faction
		1956	Resignation of ultra-Leftist faction
		1976	Defection of key leaders to PNC
	PNC	1992	Purge of Hamilton Green faction
Trinidad and Tobago	ULF	1977	Withdrawal of Shah faction
		1985	Absorption of leaders within moderate ANR
Grenada	NJM	1983	Usurpation of leadership by militarist faction

the Coardist coup within the NJM in Grenada in 1983 represented the most outstanding examples of this power elitist trend.

Foreign involvement in the Burnhamite PPP split in 1955 is already well documented, the main suggestion being that the British imposed Robertson Commission of Inquiry into the suspension of the British Guiana (Waddington) Constitution of 1953 precipitated the split by pitting a 'moderate' Burnham against a radical extremist Cheddi Jagan as leader of the party.[31] Later events – in particular the foreign (British and American) support for the Burnhamist PNC in its bid to violently overthrow a subsequent Jagan government in the 1960s – would seem also to confirm this foreign collusion with Burnhamite power ambitions.[32] However, with respect to the Grenada case, such foreign influence could as yet only be inferred in the Coardist NJM coup in 1983. Circumstantial evidence suggests not only the prevalence of CIA activities at the time, but that there were probably 'moles' within the leadership hierarchy of the NJM.[33]

That power ambition characterized both the Burnhamist and Coardist splits within their respective parties is borne out by the shrewd observations of their close colleagues. Burnham's sister, Jessie, had characterized him as having, since early childhood, a penchant for selfish ambition, acquisitiveness and domination.[34] His colleagues within the party had also observed that Burnham voiced his dissatisfaction with chairmanship of the party and would settle for nothing less than leader, a position already held by Jagan.[35] In the case of Coard, one colleague observed a tendency to reprimand high ranking leadership personnel within the party and government, while another accused Coard of attempting since 1978 to establish a power base within the party.[36] Another colleague observed that Coard had in one instance favourably compared himself with such authoritarian Caribbean political leaders as Eric Gairy and Eric Williams in terms of their skill in repressing the Grenadian and Trinidad masses respectively.[37] In addition, both Burnham and Coard cultivated close relationships with the military, the former declaring himself commander-in-chief, the latter surreptitiously increasing the pay of the army to gain their support when the official commander-in-chief, Maurice Bishop, was out of the country.[38]

The quest for personal power would seem to be an imbedded peculiarity of Caribbean political culture, and characteristic of both Rightist and Leftist politics in the region. The Burnhamist and Coardist outlooks represent the most outstanding examples of this characteristic among the Left, and correspond equally to the extreme authoritarian styles of Rightist political personalities such as Eric Gairy of Grenada, Eric Williams of Trinidad and Tobago, and Alexander Bustamante and Edward Seaga of Jamaica. Approximating this type of authoritarian leadership style among the Left were Cheddi Jagan's responses to what was often perceived to be ultra-leftist dissidence within the PPP during the 1960s,[39] and what was revealed by the charges leveled at Trevor Munroe by a plethora of resignees from the WPJ during the 1980s.[40] The possible exceptions here are Michael Manley of the PNP in Jamaica and Basdeo Panday of the ULF in Trinidad and Tobago, both of whom seemed to adhere more closely to the Westminster democratic tradition.

POLITICAL EDUCATION

Another aspect of the elite-mass gap among the Caribbean Left is the elitist tendency associated with political education programmes. Here we have the issue of an elite within the Left leadership either exempting themselves from the programmes, or invariably assuming the role of educators and teachers of the mass following who in some instances endure long and laborious hours of study. The fact that the mass following, including the unemployed, workers and farmers usually have comparatively lower levels of literacy, and have to absorb usually complex Marxist and other Leftist literature, serves to further compound the problem. Moreover, the usually foreign and internationalist orientation of the literature often contributes towards the further alienation of the masses who are usually more eager to learn about more localized national or Caribbean experiences and issues. Ultimately, the asymmetries associated with leftist political education projects serve to further accentuate the usually problematic gap between theory and practice.

The major Left parties which boasted of well developed political education programmes were, in order of the magnitude and extensiveness of these programmes, the PPP and PNC in Guyana, at the top of the list, the WPJ and NJM at the second tier, NJAC and the ULF of Trinidad and Tobago, at the third level, and the rest of the Left political organizations with little or no political education programmes at the bottom of the list. The magnitude of these programmes is determined by the level of expenditure and human resources utilized in these programmes, as well as the degree of priority accorded them on the strategic agendas of the respective parties. Both the PNC and PPP have by far devoted the most massive amount of resources and effort towards political education programmes in their political mobilization and ideological strategies. PNC efforts included production and distribution of a widely circulated party organ, the *New Nation*, the establishment of an ideological school, the Cuffy Ideological Institute, national policy public sector education programmes, and scholarships to ideological colleges in friendly socialist countries, such as Nico Lopez in Cuba, and the Kivu Koni Cooperative college in Tanzania.[41]

The PPP, although not privy to state funds as the PNC was during the 1970s and 1980s, nevertheless closely approximated the PNC in the extent of its political education efforts. Marxist-Leninist ideological training, for example, was conducted at the PPP ideological institute, Acabre college, during the 1960s and 1970s, while scholarships for the more advanced training were obtained by that party mainly from the Soviet Union during those periods. The work of the PPP ideological school was further supplemented by "area classes, study groups, discussion circles, talks on specific topics, setting up of small libraries and seminars".[42] Meanwhile the party's propaganda organ, the *Mirror*, even during the most repressive years of the Burnham regime, maintained a steady flow and circulation throughout the country.

Smaller parties like the WPJ and NJAC have also had significant mass political education campaigns. The WPJ itself boasted of having "done a great amount of work in building up the consciousness of the working people".[43] The main instruments of WPJ political education were radio and TV broadcasts, ideological newspapers and theoretical organs such as its periodical, *Struggle*, and a variety of independent pamphlets.[44] NJAC also boasted "our wide range of publications, booklets on economic analysis, political analysis, history, historical figures; the national newspaper of the organization, *Liberation*; the many area papers and special bulletins have been the most dynamic and continuous stream of mass re-education in the society."[45]

The typical asymmetrical relationship between educators and masses was reflected in the rejection of a proposal that PNC government ministers and certain higher officials attend political education indoctrination courses,[46] as well as proposals for appointment by the ULF of education officers only from the higher levels of the party leadership hierarchy.[47] But perhaps the most significant indicator of this class asymmetry is the conspicuous absence of members of the lower classes from editorial boards of party periodicals and propaganda organs.[48] The content of the programmes also reflects or precipitates much of the distance between the Left intellectual elite and their mass following. As Walter Bryan of the WPJ noted, much of the critical issues rooted in a more localized Caribbean context such as religion and black nationalism, were either nonexistent or relegated to secondary levels of importance in the WPJ (and most probably the typical Caribbean Left) political education curriculum.[49]

The problem of the elite-mass gap is further compounded by the apparent failure of the intellectual elite to take into account the level of literacy of the targeted masses. This problem is reflected in the massive drop-out rates in these programmes, stemming not only from the stringent study requirements demanded by most of these programmes,[50] but more importantly the impatience of the masses with long drawn out debates about abstract theoretical formulae.[51] The response of a working class man to an article contained in the Left periodical, *Abeng*, bears this out. He wrote as follows:

Like most of what is written in *Abeng*, I have a hard time to follow what he is saying because of a whole heap of big words and high sounding phrases used. For a majority of us black people who just barely pass through primary school, the *Abeng* is hard to read . . . words like 'bourgeois', 'monopoly'. . . phrases like 'archaic power structure' . . . confuse me and only make me feel to put down the paper.[52]

Three issues arise from this type of contradiction, all of which tend to further dramatize the power of the leadership elite over the masses. The first is what could be termed the Procrustean bed, or vice-like, effect of Marxist-Leninist theory and socialist ideology on the overwhelmed mass public, in the sense that there is an apparent forcing of theory down the throats, so to speak, of the masses. The second is what appears to be in effect intellectuals speaking only to themselves since much of the theoretical underpinnings are graspable only at their level of training and preparation. The third is the probable exclusion of the rich experiences of the masses from playing a necessary part in the educational content and curriculum.

Nothing dramatizes the theory-praxis gap more than the dilemma which faced the New World movement in the 1960s, and twenty years later the Tapia House movement in Trinidad and Tobago. The issue was how a professional intellectual class can become relevant to the practical problems of underdeveloped, dependent and often oppressive societies such as those in the Caribbean. New World's response to this dilemma was to choose to remain solely as educators, rather than become embroiled in practical political activism. Lloyd Best, one of the founders of New World, was concerned that involvement in agitational activism would not only debase the profession but more importantly prevent intellectuals from fulfilling their specific mission which is to disseminate ideas.[53] Best's later creation, Tapia House, in Trinidad and Tobago, was dedicated principally to influencing "a cultural revival, a moral resurgence . . . then all the rest will follow in economics and politics, in education and sport".[54] In defending Tapia's decision to stay out of the political protest movement in 1970 in Trinidad and Tobago, Best had this to say: "we cannot risk destroying more than we create . . . ", and further, that the 1970 Black Power uprising "must be reinforced by its own thought must be informed by its own ideas".[55]

Not surprisingly, Best's typically idealist position provoked a great deal of tension within the New World movement, which Best himself had acknowledged.[56] Norman Girvan, also alluded to what he termed "heated controversy" over the issue within the movement, the result of which, according to Girvan, were failures to establish suitable communication links and relevance with the masses, or to provoke any kind of thinking from New World mass audiences due to the "academic presentation of the material or lectures", while most of the teach-ins promoted by New World ended up becoming what Girvan termed "intra-elite dialogue".[57] Much of the elitist failures of New World were carried over into Tapia House which, according to a shrewd leftist observer "was based on a classless nationalist perspective, organized and directed by professionals", while, according to the same source, the Tapia movement made no attempt "to deal with the struggle of the working class".[58] At the same time, however, New World's and Tapia's failure to communicate with the Caribbean masses was not unlike the experience of other Caribbean Left political movements that were largely preoccupied with abstract ideology which distanced their elite leadership from the mass public they claimed to represent, and so accentuated the mass alienation from leftist political projects as a whole.

MASS ALIENATION

Mass alienation from the Caribbean Left political leadership, particularly since the 1980s, is reflected in marginal or dwindling electoral support and negative mass perceptions of the Left as revealed for example in voting patterns and a variety of social surveys throughout the region. Another critical factor reflecting or producing negative mass support for the left in the English- speaking Caribbean is what appears to be the general absence in these parts, of civil society in the classical sense of the term. In those very few instances where the Caribbean Left obtained sizeable electoral mass support (e.g., the PPP, PNC and PNP) the explanation had less to do with the traditional class or ideologically based mobilizational efforts characteristic of the left than with other non-class consid-erations such as race, ethnicity, tribalistic or clientelistic politics, and regime coercion.

As we have seen in earlier chapters electoral support for the Left throughout the English-speaking Caribbean remains rather low – in general not exceeding 5 percent of the general voting population. The best performance of certain parties like NJAC, and the WPA did not exceed 1 percent; for the WPJ it was 2 percent, while the ACLM obtained only about 4 percent of the votes in Antigua's national elections in 1980.[59] Performance slightly above this level came from Left parties like the DLM which obtained 11 percent of the votes in the 1980 Dominica elections, the ULF in Trinidad and Tobago with 10 percent voting support in the 1976 Trinidad and Tobago elections, and the combined Left in St Vincent and the Grenadines attracting approximately 15 percent of the votes.[60] The pre-1979 NJM might have exceeded this modest level of performance in its association with the Alliance party which gained 48 percent of the votes and 6 out of 15 parliamentary seats in the 1976 Grenada elections.[61] The much bigger picture which begs further explanation is the acquisition of well over 40 percent of the national votes by major Left parties in the region, such as the PPP, the PNC, the PNP, and the more recent case of the victory of the UNC, successor to the ULF, in the 1995 Trinidad and Tobago national elections. For a general picture of where the various Left parties fall in the electoral outcome in various Caribbean states, see Table 6.4.

Table 6.4:   Best electoral performance of Left parties in the English-speaking Caribbean; Average from 1944 to 1992

Country	Percentage range of votes: by various parties			
	0-5 %	6-20 %	21-40 %	Above 40 %
Antigua	ACLM			
Grenada	MBPM		NJM (AP)	
Guyana	WPA			PPP
				PNC
Jamaica	WPJ			PNP
Trinidad and Tobago	NJAC	ULF		
	WFP			
Dominica		DLM		
St Vincent			UPM	

Sources: Various documents including *Caribbean Dialogue*, NACLA, *Report on the Americas*, and *Caribbean Contact*

Table 6.5   PPP/PNC racial voting patterns, 1953-1968

Year	Ethnic constituency party support: percentage*		
	PPP East Indian	PNC African	Other Mixed
1953	100	–	50
1957	100	50	16
1961	100	77	27
1964	100	100	15
1968	81	100	15

*An ethnic constituency is defined in terms of at least 75 percent of a specific racial group residing in that particular electoral constituency; calculations are based on census statistics and those from the various election reports between 1953 and 1968.

The Guyana and Trinidad electoral polarization along ethno-political lines reflects the tenacity of racial/ethnic loyalties, and the difficulty of political parties in mobilizing on the basis simply of class or ideological commitments. Table 6. 5 gives an example of the close racial voting pattern for the two main Left parties in Guyana, the PPP and the PNC in various elections between 1953 and 1968. It is mainly at the level of the political elite where greater flexibility exemplified in cross racial party defections and floor crossings is observable.[62]

In Jamaica the existence of a more racially homogeneous society does not necessarily preclude the prevalence of ethno-political voting patterns exemplified through tribalistic or clientelistic loyalties to the two main contending parties, the PNP and the right-wing JLP. For example, while both the 1972 and 1976 elections results in Jamaica closely mirrored the popular strengths of the JLP (45 percent) and the PNP (55 percent) on average, there was a significant difference in the class composition of the 1976 votes compared to those of 1972. While in 1972 the PNP's support from the primarily working class (more urbanized) areas amounted to about 55 percent, in 1976, at a time of increased economic recession and hardships, this support was increased to 68 percent.[63] Meanwhile the middle class votes swung from the PNP to the JLP by a margin of some 10,000 votes (representing in fact a swing by some 375 percent) in the 1976 elections.[64] What this differential in class related votes suggests is that both the middle and working classes operate quite independently of each other as far as political and ideological commitments are concerned, and further that the degree of middle class switch of loyalty towards the right tends to be far greater than is the case with the masses and working class population. In the 1976 case in Jamaica this is reflected in a 13 percent swing on the part of the working classes to the PNP, as compared with a 375 percent swing of middle class support to the right-wing JLP. It suggests, further, that the mobilization efforts by the middle class leadership of the various parties, tend to have a greater impact on the middle classes themselves than on working class support.

Opinion surveys also reveal that the Caribbean masses tend to be alienated from the rather aggressive political styles of the major contending parties. In the Jamaican case, for example, Carl Stone attests to the general popular cynicism about Jamaican politics in general among the Jamaican masses, particularly in relation to the leadership of the two main rival parties, the PNP and the JLP.[65] This cynicism was particularly acute between 1980 and 1983 as reflected in the rapid decline of popular support for the two parties: PNP support declining from an estimated 48 percent of the electorate in 1976 to about 35 percent by 1980; and JLP popular support plummeting from 50 percent in 1980 to 38 percent by early 1983.[66] According to Stone it was a cynicism particularly among the youths who happened to be the strongest supporters of the PNP and the Left.[67] Stone's analysis of the reasons behind this mass alienation is instructive:

The essential pragmatism of the majority classes based on the impulse to survive harsh conditions entraps them into a power game controlled by the middle class patrons and power brokers. Revolutionary class developments are extremely unlikely to develop as long as these political power structures remain intact and are defended by dependent class formations among the poor for whom politics is a matter of personal survival.[68]

Similar mass cynicism or alienation was observed in Grenada as reflected in a CANA poll conducted in 1984. According to this poll most (46 percent) of the post invasion Grenadian masses were overwhelmingly preoccupied with economic survival issues such as unemployment, rather than with political questions such as the national leadership vacuum of which only 17 percent of the population showed any definite interests or concerns.[69] Leftist politics in particular fared badly at these polls, with only 10 percent showing favourable disposition towards the MBPM. At the same time, original NJM leaders like George Louison and Ken Raddix received only 5 percent and 6 percent favourable ratings respectively.[70] Quite significantly, though, the leftist MBPM gained its highest favourable responses from the two constituencies, St John's (20 percent) and St Mark (16 percent), where the issue of unemployment was regarded as the most pressing national problem.[71]

What we are probably witnessing in the Caribbean context is the as yet unrecognized existence of what could be termed spontaneous vanguard groups in the form of specialized but scattered working class or under-class constituencies which traditionally support Left parties and politics, while the masses in general remain largely conservative or apathetic. This is particularly the case of geographically concentrated populations like the St Mark and St John's constituencies in Grenada, specific regions in Kingston and St Andrew in Jamaica, and industrially based populations such as the sugar belt in Guyana and Trinidad and Tobago. Other marginal forms of these spontaneous vanguards are the rather embryonic, localized assemblies such as the type of grass roots movements the COSSABOs of the ULF were supposed to represent, or the spontaneous groups that were formed throughout the Trinidad countryside during the 1970 uprising, prior to the interventions by NJAC.

These groups are considered spontaneous creations in that they come into existence by their highly sensitive response to specific political, economic or social issues that affect them, without necessarily having the benefit of clear-cut leadership personnel from within or outside the group. At the same time, however, these largely spontaneous groupings represent vanguardist entities in two senses at least: (a) being among the first elements to feel the brunt of negative economic impact these groups are forced into self-mobilization ahead of 'representative' organization, and (b) in the absence of strong, self-conscious, relatively autonomous civil society in the Caribbean, these groups usually occupy (by default at least) the antiestablishment leadership role in the community or society. As regards their spontaneity, examples include (i) the 1970 black power uprising in Trinidad and Tobago where a variety of citizens and grass roots groupings spontaneously emerged in different parts of the island prior to the intervention of NJAC, (ii) the 1985 anti-IMF 'gasolene' riots in Kingston, Jamaica, which erupted prior to the mobilizing intervention of both the PNP and the WPJ, (iii) the anti-IMF bauxite and sugar strikes in Guyana which, like the 1985 Jamaica riots, preceded the organizing interventions of the trade unions (GMWU and GAWU) and dissident political parties (WPA and PPP), and (iv) the massive 1981 popular uprising in St Vincent against repressive legislation on the island.[72]

The weakness of Caribbean civil society is exemplified by the failure of civic movements such as the Guyana Association for Reform and Democracy (GUARD) which emerged in 1989 for the express purpose of protesting both the harsh economic conditions and the political dictatorship in Guyana. GUARD started with a bang – a spontaneous public response in support of the 1989 anti-IMF general strike – and petered out a few months later in a whimper, with the leadership of the movement eventually giving its endorsement to the PPP, the conventional left-wing party GUARD leaders had initially opposed, in its electoral campaign towards the 1992 elections. GUARD's rather artificial ties to the localized, grass roots communities, were strongly reflected in the composition of its leadership personnel drawn mainly from urbanized, middle class sources. The institutional bases of support for the movement were essentially the established (Roman Catholic and Anglican) churches. GUARD's failure was due to several closely interrelated considerations: (a) the leadership soon abandoned its autonomy or independence of traditional partisan politics by entering candidates for contesting national elections, thereby transforming itself into another among many competing parties, (b) because of its highly contrived and politicized nature, the leadership split along the same lines of the traditional PPP-PNC and GAWU-NAACIE rivalries in the Guyana political process, and (c) its mass appeal was geographically limited to specific sections of the city of Georgetown, while the rural countryside remained largely unmoved by the movement.

The failure of GUARD underscores the relative absence of a strong civil society in Guyana, and indeed throughout the Caribbean. Such an absence of autonomous, civic conscious, constantly self-mobilizing communities or collectivities means that an important bridge is lost between the power conscious leadership elite and the popular masses in the region. What remains, therefore, is a serious and pervasive chasm between the two, reflecting the possibly inevitable polarization of forces which seems endemic in peripheral capitalist societies. The Caribbean Left, therefore, unlike the Left in much of Latin America, was unable to tap a significant source of their power to intervene on behalf of the masses, a factor which undoutedly impaired their mobilizing potentialities and capacity to eventually bridge the problematic elite-mass gap.

CONCLUSION

The typically middle class character of the Leftist leadership in the English-speaking Caribbean manifests itself in the increasing elitist tendencies in the political mobilization practices of Leftist parties and movements, and the consequent alienation of the masses and subordinate classes from such leadership orientations. This elite-mass gap, as it were, tends to have negative implications for the legitimacy of the Leftist movement as a whole, while it renders the Leftist leadership particularly vulnerable to external (foreign) destabilizing pressures. Within the movement itself isolation of the leadership from the masses facilitates the tendencies towards factional splits and purges which are usually more devastating than helpful to the movement. One of the main reasons why this elite-mass gap within the Left attracts foreign fissiparous pressures is that it facilitates the traditional divide and rule policies which subordinate the domestic population to foreign penetration and control, and so cater to the exploitation of domestic resources by international capital.

The disintegrating consequences of these external pressures manifest themselves in three basic forms of responses by the Leftist leadership elite: (a) the militarization psychosis in the form of increasing military spending and mobilization, in the interest of strengthening military defenses against perceived threats from either internal or external sources, (b) the 'Trojan Horse' effect in the sense that specific local groups and factions are often used as a kind of proxy to facilitate penetration of external (foreign) political, economic and military forces, and (c) the ultimate transformation of the political and ideological orientation of dissident groups in keeping with the prevailing international hegemonic trend. The more specific dynamics of these foreign destabilizing forces will be examined more closely in the following chapter.

7

Destabilization and Disintegration

When in his last moments facing a firing squad, Maurice Bishop cried "my God they have turned their guns against the people," his remarks symbolized the vast distance the vanguard leadership elite had traveled away from the Caribbean masses. The fact also that on that fateful October day in 1983 many from the Grenadian masses were killed along with Bishop and his Cabinet colleagues by the Coardist led military regime, dramatized the depth of antagonism between the leadership and masses in the Caribbean political context. The events further demonstrated how elite contempt for the masses can ultimately lead to the total destruction of the movement itself. This chapter is concerned with the linkage between, on the one hand, the factors, both domestic and foreign, which determine the elite-mass gap, and on the other, the disintegration or reversal of the Caribbean Left movement as a whole.

More specifically, this chapter is concerned with the interconnection between the overall weaknesses of the Left leadership elite, and the levels of militarization, political violence, organizational disarray, and ideological transformations involving particularly Left political movements in Caribbean political systems. One of the objectives here, therefore, is to demonstrate the interrelationship between elite-mass contradictions, the vulnerability of the Caribbean political elite to external manipulation, and the rise and development of right-wing ideological and political forces in the region. Ultimately, the interaction of these contingent forces spelt the dissolution of the Leftist core projects in the region.

The dissolution of the Caribbean leftist project took several forms, the most critical of which were evidenced by (a) splits and purges within parties, and attendant Left/Right ideological struggles in Caribbean societies as a whole, (b) patterns of political violence reflecting both elite competitiveness and mass disenchantment with the failures of middle class political leadership, and (c) militarist tendencies on the part of a significant section of the Left leadership, reflecting apparent paranoia against the possibilities of foreign military interventions, and destabilizing mass upheavals. These three factors are closely inter-related in that they share certain common characteristics including middle class dominance in the structure of political leadership, the involvement of some level of foreign influence, and increasing subordination of the masses.

It must be recalled that the openness of the Caribbean leadership elite to international influences renders such political leadership vulnerable to foreign pressures to conform to the dominant ideological system. Such vulnerability increases relative to the lack of control of domestic resources and population by the political elite. In peripheral capitalist societies like the Caribbean, therefore, such lack of domestic control is usually manifested in foreign ownership of domestic resources. As such, whatever semblance of real power resides with the domestic elite, including the intellectual stratum and the Left leadership, is derived more from their associations with outside influences and supports, than with purely domestic factors. The particular type of international pressures meted out to the domestic political elite are often related to the hegemonic pursuits of international actors which tend to combine economic, political, and ideological demands with threats of military sanctions against domestic forces in peripheral states.[1]

Most of the pressures from developed capitalist powers are meted out not against or amongst themselves, but *vis-à-vis* poorer countries.[2] Part of the response of the domestic political elite in these poorer countries including the Caribbean, to these international hegemonic pressures, is to attempt to augment their own strength and dominance at the cost of further subordinating the masses of the population. As far as the impact on the Left is concerned, this process involves a fateful cycle of (a) foreign pressures, (b) elite isolation, (c) coercive mass mobilization, (d) increasing subordination of the masses, (e) further elite isolation and vulnerability, (f) increased probability of foreign intervention, leading ultimately to, and (g) the possible disintegration of the Left forces.

A most recurrent example of disintegration of Left forces is reflected in party splits and purges. The most prominent instances of these splits and purges in the Caribbean context, as already discussed in Chapter 6, are: (i) the 1952 purge of the Marxist inner circle from the PNP in Jamaica, (ii) the 1955 split in the PPP in Guyana, and (iii) the 1983 debacle in the NJM and the Grenada revolution. Other relatively less significant intra-Left splits or purges throughout the region include the 1988 spate of resignations from the WPJ in Jamaica, the 1992 expulsion of the Hamilton Green faction from the PNC in Guyana, the withdrawal of the Raffiq Shah elements from the ULF coalition in Trinidad and Tobago in the late 1970s, and the series of dissolutions and recombinations involving Left parties in other Caribbean territories, such as YULIMO (MNU) in St Vincent, the DLM in Dominica, and the URO in Trinidad and Tobago.

Close observation of major splits in Left parties throughout the region reveals similar interlocking trends. These similarities relate to a consistent pattern of foreign or international involvement in the events, escalating levels of ideological struggle and contestation, and equally devastating consequences, primarily in the forms of dilution or destruction of the Leftist project, and increasing rightward ideological shifts. While the international involvements into these splits related mainly to Western hegemonic responses to cold war struggles and what were perceived to be immanent communist threats of expansion into the region, the ideological involvement demonstrated extreme levels of polarization between Right and Left political forces both within the party and throughout the society as a whole. What is particularly noticeable in this regard is the apparent organic interconnection between hostile international forces and the rise and development of organized right-wing politics throughout the region.

FOREIGN INVOLVEMENT

The evidence which demonstrates international involvement in these events remains sketchy, and in some instances more indirect and circumstantial than in others. The 1952 PNP events, however, strongly suggest that the purges of the 4-Hs and the Marxist inner circle were motivated largely by cold war concerns of the more conservative leaders of the party, Norman Manley and H. Glasspole. Anti-communist cold war hysteria was whipped up mainly by the Jamaican media, particularly the *Daily Gleaner* newspaper which had singled out the Marxist elements for special attacks not only for what was said to be their 'Godlessness', but more particularly for their denigration of the glories of the British empire.[3] Within the PNP, cold war anticommunism was imported by the top leadership to discredit and ostracize the Left. According to Richard Hart, one of the founders of the inner circle, the PNP leaders associated the members of the circle with "a lot of terrible things the Russians were doing".[4]

Another intrinsic issue within these cold war propaganda concerns was the influence of the British TUC on the more conservative leadership of the PNP which was encouraged to disassociate the Jamaican TUC (sponsored by the PNP) from the communist sponsored World Federation of Trade Unions (WFTU), in favour of the Western sponsored International Confederation of Free Trade Unions (ICFTU) founded in 1949. The fact that the anti-WFTU position was defeated within the party by one vote in 1949 angered the right sufficiently to spur them into seeking the expulsion of the Left from the party. The 1952 PNP congress provided the occasion for this sudden surprise move as Hart saw it.[5] The moment was appropriate since the cold war had heated up to the highest of levels with the US involvement in the Korean war which pitted communism against capitalism on a world scale.[6] The cold war toll on the Jamaican Left in 1952 was not only a split within the PNP, but a split within the Jamaican TUC as well, initiated by Manley and Glasspole.[7]

Foreign influence in the 1955 PPP split in Guyana was evident in several respects. First, the British-imposed Robertson Commission of Inquiry into the 1953 suspension of the British Guiana Constitution inspired the split by pitting what the commission perceived to be a "moderate" Burnham against a "radical extremist" Cheddi Jagan.[8] Not only were the foundations laid for serious ideological discord between moderates and "communists", but the Commission further inspired racial divisions within the party, and indeed in the Guyanese society as a whole, by suggesting the existence of irreparable tensions and animosity between East Indians and Africans.[9] Further evidence of foreign facilitation of rightist triumph in Guyanese politics during this period was the secret British financing of the right-wing trade union, the Manpower Citizens Association (MPCA) to undercut the PPP sponsored union, the GIWU, as competitors for workers support in the sugar industry.[10] During this period, also, the British financed and cultivated a rival right-wing party, the NLF, to help frustrate the electoral ambitions of the PPP.[11]

Probable foreign influences were also involved in the extremely self-destructive ideological rifts in the NJM in 1983. *Covert Action Information Bulletin* has alluded to the possibility of CIA involvement not only in Grenada just prior to the fateful 1983 events, but directly within the leadership hierarchy of the NJM and PRG regime itself.[12] Both the US Consular Services and offshore medical school in Grenada were said to have been implicated in either initiating or facilitating the deadly events. The evidence seems to suggest that secret information from within the Central Committee of the NJM was routinely passed on to the CIA and other US agents so much so that the Pentagon was said to have known of the impending coup against Bishop two weeks in advance of the events. At the same time the coincidence and strong similarity of pattern between these events and the CIA inspired military coup against Salvador Allende and the Alliance Party in Chile in 1974 were indeed very striking – a pattern involving infiltration of the movement, pitting moderate against extremist leaders, indulgence in smear anti-Left propaganda, and financing rightist forces particularly within the military.[13] The *Bulletin* also suggested that the Coardist military elements were used and then finally double-crossed by the US agencies.[14]

It is not altogether surprising that the Coardist elements in Grenada might have been double crossed by US operatives, since this follows a general pattern of creating or fostering entirely new right wing forces by foreign hegemonic interests after using elements within the Left to destroy the Left movement itself. This pattern is observed throughout the Caribbean. In the 1952 PNP case, for example, it was not so much the Manley wing that benefited from the anti-Left purge, but the right wing JLP which was supported by foreign interests to win the next elections. Again in the Guyana case the Burnhamist faction received only minimal international support, while it was rightist parties such as the NLF and later the UF that gained the bulk of British and American support toward enhancing their chances of winning national elections. Similarly in Grenada following the 1983 fiasco the Coardist RMC was soon rudely brushed aside and superseded by the creation of new right-wing forces, in particular the NNP, with massive material support from foreign, mainly US sources.[15]

It is significant how these foreign involvement in Caribbean conflict situations serve the interests of the divide and rule strategies initiated by earlier colonial authorities. Attempts to destroy the Left are perhaps the most devastating consequence of such foreign initiated divide and rule strategies. This tendency is reflected also in the patterns of domestic political violence and militarization throughout the region. Such patterns are also instructive not only as regards the prevalence of foreign involvement, but equally in terms of the domination by elite leadership, highly politicized confrontations involving Right/Left ideological polarization, and the increasing subordination of the Caribbean masses in the process.

PATTERNS OF POLITICAL VIOLENCE

The various party splits in themselves have resulted in different types and levels of political violence, each reflecting different dimensions of ideological conflict and struggle. While, for example, the 1952 PNP split was a precursor to the later PNP/JLP ideological and political, and often violent struggles, the 1955 PPP split directly inspired later violent ideological and political conflicts between the PPP and the PNC. Meanwhile the 1983 fiasco in Grenada was itself a process involving the highest levels of political violence including, as in the Guyana case of 1963-64, foreign military intervention. The primary trend among these experiences is the initiation of political violence by the partisan leadership elite via mass mobilization with the ultimate objective of capturing political power. That intra-elite contestation represents the dominant trend in political violence in the English-

Table 7.1   Levels of organization in Caribbean political violence 1980-1989

Country	Level of Organization: No. of Events					
	Political	Business	Labour	Other	None	Total
Antigua	–	–	–	1	–	1
Grenada	4	–	–	1	–	5
Guyana	6	–	1	–	–	7
Dominica	4	–	1	–	–	5
Jamaica	6	1	6	–	–	13
St Lucia	1	–	–	–	–	1
St Vincent	–	–	–	–	1	1
Trinidad and Tobago	–	–	3	–	1	4
Total	21	1	11	2	2	37
%	57	3	30	5	5	100

Source: Compiled from *Latin American Regional Reports*, Caribbean, 1980-89.

speaking Caribbean is reflected in the extent of contending political organizations in the events, as suggested in Table 7.1.

As Table 7.1 suggests, the greater proportion (over 50 percent) of political violence events involved conflictive political organizations as opposed to the more spontaneous mass events (which constituted only about 5 percent of total events). Going beyond the tables, one finds a significant level of Right or Left ideological and political conflict in the political violence process. The specific types of violence aimed against the Left, for example, were significant for their high levels of extremity. Such anti-Left violence ranged from the breaking up of political meetings and marches, to bombings, assassinations and armed coups. The 1981 break up of a WPA meeting by a combination of police and PNC thugs in Guyana, the bombing of an NJM rally in St Georges, Grenada, the following year, leaving three people dead, the assassinations of Walter Rodney in 1980 and Maurice Bishop in 1983, and the army coup attempt in Jamaica against the Michael Manley PNP government in 1976, are cases in point. But perhaps the most extreme case of anti-Left violence in the English-speaking Caribbean was the combined strategy of armed guerilla tactics, bombings, assassinations, and arson by foreign inspired right-wing forces against the pro-Marxist PPP government during the 1963-64 period.

Table 7.2   Foreign involvement in political violence events: Caribbean countries, 1980-89

Country	Numbers and Levels of Events*			
	Non-violent protests	Violent protests	State repression	Total
Antigua	0	1	0	1
Dominica	2	2	1	5
Grenada	1	3	1	5
Guyana	2	2	3	7
Jamaica	8	5	0	13
St Lucia	1	0	0	1
St Vincent	1	0	0	1
Trinidad and Tobago	3	1	0	4
Total	18	14	5	37
No. Foreign involved	7	10	0	17
% Foreign involved	39	71	0	46

*Non-violent protest = anti-government demonstrations, marches, strikes
Violent protest = riots, armed attacks, casualities
State repression = mass arrests, states of emergency, police violence

Source: Compiled from *Latin American Regional Reports*, Caribbean, 1980-89.

Foreign involvement in these events were also evident. The CIA, for example, was very much involved in the 1963-64 events in Guyana, and implicated in the bombings and other insurrectionary efforts in Grenada during the early 1980s. Also, foreign finances were involved in the 1976 army coup attempt in Jamaica, as well as for the cultivation of Charles Johnson's private army aimed at assisting the coup plotters against Michael Manley's Democratic Socialist, PNP government. Both political and civic organizations (mainly trade unions and religious bodies) were involved in these political violence activities throughout the region. The notorious roles of the MPCA and TUC in violent subversion in Guyana, as well as of the Roman Catholic and Anglican churches in destabilizing the PPP government in the 1960s, are already well documented. In this regard the AFL-CIO and its international secretary, Serafino Romouldi, as well as prominent US church personalities were notable foreign instruments in this deadly fray.

Additionally, a significant proportion of political violence events involved some level of foreign intervention, as suggested in Table 7.2.

Table 7.2 demonstrates the relatively high percentage of foreign involvement in political violence events in the English-speaking Caribbean between 1980 and 1989. What is also significant is that the greater percentage of foreign involved participation in these events comprised the higher level events (over 70 percent) as compared with about 29 percent of foreign involvement in relatively non-violent (lower level) political protest activities. The examples here of higher level violence involvements represent events such as the 1981 mercenary military expedition mounted by US based groups including the KKK, to seize the island of Dominica, the 1980 River Antoine guerilla attacks against the Maurice Bishop NJM government in Grenada, and of course the US military invasion of that unfortunate island three years later. Foreign influences in non-violent protest activities included such events as the IMF provoked general strike in Guyana in 1989, and the 1985 expulsion from Antigua of US based churchmen who were said to have been plotting a coup against the Bird government.

One consequence of the violent attempt to destabilize the Left in the region is the tendency toward militarization particularly on the part of the Left leadership itself. This militarization tendency is usually directed against possible hostile foreign intervention and mass political upheavals. The PRG of Grenada, for example, was particularly concerned about the possibility of foreign invasion from forces utilizing unfriendly neighbouring territories,[16] while Guyana cited threat of border incursions from neighbouring Venezuela. For these reasons the strength of the military in Leftist controlled states – e.g., Grenada under Maurice Bishop, and Guyana under Forbes Burnham – tended to be far out of proportion to the needs of the respective countries, or in relation to military strength of neighbouring territories in the English-speaking Caribbean. Additionally, the type of weaponry purchased by the police in the major Leftist controlled states in the region overwhelmingly concentrated on weapons of crowd control which aimed at the masses of the population. Table 7.3 suggests these trends.

The very association of the Left with military build-up has been very costly to these groups in terms of the destruction of their leadership as well as transformation of the movement as a whole. The tragic deaths of both Walter Rodney and Maurice Bishop have been associated with their cultivation of close ties with the military in their respective countries. At the same time top leadership of the PNC boasted of having infiltrated the leadership hierarchy of the WPA through the utilization of Guyana Defense Force personnel.[17] The WPA in turn is convinced that the high ranking GDF officer, Gregory Smith, who infiltrated the party was a principal source of Rodney's death.[18] Since Rodney's death the WPA underwent drastic ideological transformations, from Marxism-Leninism at its inception in 1979,[19] to what it called an "independent Marxist" position during the 1980s, and eventually to what it refers to today as "Rodneyism", reflecting a more multi-racial

Table 7.3   US arms sales to Caribbean police forces, 1976-1979

Country	Gas Grenades & Projectiles	Gas Guns	Canisters Mace	Rifles/ Guns & Revolvers	Ammunition (1,000 rounds)
Antigua	116	–	–	–	–
Bahamas	421	–	–	–	–
Belize	310	–	–	–	26
Guyana	4,000	–	–	–	–
Jamaica	2,550	32	100	750	247
St Kitts	30	–	–	–	–
St Lucia	50	–	–	–	1
St Vincent	50	–	–	–	–
Trinidad and Tobago	200	–	18	7	–

Source: Michael T. Klare and Cynthia Arnson, *Supplying Repression, US Support Authoritarian Regimes Abroad*, Washington D.C.: Institute for Policy Studies, 1981, pp. 58, 59.

and nationalist-humanist orientation. The high degree of alienation of the WPA from the Guyanese masses was undoubtedly reflected in its less than one percent showing at the polls during the 1992 Guyana elections.

Bishop's death in Grenada in 1983 also represented a similar attempt to import military tactics and discipline within the midst of the leadership hierarchy of the New Jewel Movement. In the end it was the military that summarily executed Bishop and several of his close cabinet colleagues. Several among the Grenadian masses who supported Bishop, and marched with him to Fort Rupert, were also killed in the fray. Like the WPA, also, the NJM, following Bishop's death, underwent significant transformation both ideologically and politically: the party split into two sections, one section becoming the more moderate MBPM which contested the 1984 Grenada elections and obtained five percent of the votes; the other, remnants of the Coardist RMC which retained the title of NJM, disappeared from the political landscape in the 1990s.

In Jamaica, military involvement in political destabilization was exemplified in the 1976 attempted coup by elements within the Jamaica Defense Force in association with Charles Johnson's private army against the PNP democratic socialist government. These events tied in closely with right-wing political violence unleashed by the Seaga led JLP. Herb Rose, a high standing official within the JLP exposed the sinister plot which prompted his resignation from the party.

According to Rose, the objectives of the JLP were to (a) establish an armed underground using weapons far more powerful than those used by the Jamaican police force, (b) selectively assassinate rival political leaders, and (c) unleash extreme violence among the Jamaican population.[20] The result was several people killed, including a minister of the PNP government. But what was even more significant than these sinister objectives was Rose's further disclosure that the plan was inspired and financed by a combination of CIA sources and Jamaican businessmen in Canada.[21] It is important, therefore to look more closely at the deadly role of foreign financing of political destabilization throughout the English-speaking Caribbean.

FINANCING DESTABILIZATION

The foreign financial factor has usually been pivotal in the engineering of political destabilization in the Caribbean. The variety of sources of these foreign finances for destabilization include hegemonic and globally powerful capitalist states like the United States and Britain, private business interests such as multi-national corporations, international trade union connections like the AFL-CIO, and covert institutions such as the CIA and its various front organizations. Usually, the funds are channeled through rightist political, social, or religious groupings to subvert or destabilize leftist tendencies and movements

Perhaps the most outstanding case of foreign financing for destabilization in the English-speaking Caribbean, judged by both the volume of funds and the intensity of the violent outcome, was the 1963-64 spate of political-cum-ethnic disturbances in Guyana. The CIA and US State Department spent a total of (US) $1.2 million to help finance an 80-day general strike against the pro-Marxist Jagan government, resulting in large scale, race based insurrectionary political violence with a death toll of hundreds, and property damage costing tens of millions of dollars.[22] The AIFLD, and British trade unions also contributed together between 50 and 70 thousands of dollars per week to Guyanese trade union leaders to help sustain the strike.[23] Jagan on the other hand suggested that the sum was closer to $100,000.00 per week.[24] The cost of the operation was said to be as much as the entire annual budget of the AIFLD, the Latin American arm of the AFL-CIO.[25] So important was this foreign financial support that without it, as Jagan himself remarked, "the strike would have collapsed in a couple of weeks".[26]

That the trade union movement was regarded as pivotal to the destabilization efforts in Guyana, was reflected in the fact that during the period leading up to the 1962-64 events the AIFLD spent the sum of $60,000.00 to train in the United States a group of Guyanese trade unionists in subversive strategies. These trainees were then sent back to Guyana at a pay of about $250.00 per week to aid the anti-government strike activities of the Guyana TUC.[27] For these purposes, also, an official of the Public Service International personally paid out of his own funds the sum of $100,000.00 as strike benefits.[28] Between 1958 and 1961 most of the funding for TUC activities in Guyana came from foreign sources. In 1961, for example, foreign funding amounted to about 70 percent of the entire TUC budget.[29] The great bulk of the foreign funding of the TUC strikers and labour leadership was paid through the International Affairs Department of the American Federation of State, County and Municipal Employees which the *New York Times* concluded was run by the CIA through a front, paper organization called the Gotham Foundation.[30]

If the leadership of the trade union movement had been the key proxy elements in foreign instigated destabilization of the Left in Guyana, it was the leadership of right-wing political parties which facilitated a similar 'Trojan Horse' effect in Jamaica. The main party involved in this anti-Left project was the JLP which received massive amounts of financial support from CIA and other foreign sources to carry out its systematic campaign of violence and terror against the democratic socialist PNP government and its supporters in 1976. In that year alone the JLP was alleged to have received (US) $18 million from the CIA sources alone, and additional funds from multi-national corporations operating in Jamaica.[31] In addition the JLP leadership was the beneficiary of seventeen high ranking CIA advisors to assist in this campaign.[32] The strategy involved the projected spending of (US)$25 million within the Jamaica Defense Force (JDF) to carry out a coup, the employment and payment ($1000.00 per week) of 30 gunmen in each polling division to assassinate PNP leaders and supporters, supportive funding from local businessmen to train JLP youths on US soil, and even within the JDF, for the development of a private army, and the purchase or rental of a fleet of bullet proof cars to conduct guerilla type operations. This strategy would seem to have had its toll during the 1976 elections when fifteen front line PNP supporters were killed.[33]

In the following election year, 1980, the JLP continued its violent destabiliza-tion campaign with further financial assistance from foreign sources. Two US based organizations, the Friends of Free Jamaica, and the Jamaica Freedom League which was closely connected to Cuban exile groups in Miami, were prominent among these foreign financial sources for the JLP at this time.[34] The CIA connection of the Jamaica Freedom League was its bank, the Bank of Perrine, which, according to a *Covert Action Information Bulletin* report, was closely linked to Castle Bank of the Bahamas, "the CIA's major financial institution in Latin America".[35] In the 1980 Jamaica elections, the JLP went on to defeat the Michael Manley democratic socialist party and government by a wide margin.

Beyond foreign financing for destabilization efforts in Guyana and Jamaica, the Eastern Caribbean islands represent something like a hot-bed of similar foreign intrigues. To be recalled here is the assertion by Bob Woodward that US$100,000.00 was received by the Dominican Prime Minister to help create an atmosphere of legitimacy for US troops to invade neighbouring Grenada in 1983.[36] Much more was spent by the US to help the earlier creation of the Organization of Eastern Caribbean States (OECS) as a regional security organization against the possibilities of further leftist advances which were viewed as threatening to the democratic stability of the region.[37] A further foreign financed rightist advance into the region was the establishment in Antigua in 1982, of a Voice of America radio transmitter under the direction of Charles Z. Wick who was said to have controlled a budget of $750 million to broadcast US propaganda material throughout the Eastern Caribbean.[38] So important is the weapon of anti-Left propaganda to the United States that in 1983 alone almost two-thirds of the United States Information Service (USIS) annual budget was ear-marked for building radio transmitters for its regional programmes.[39]

Foreign financing for destabilizing leftist programmes and movements throughout the Caribbean has been most significant since it provides resources for the Right which were always far superior to whatever resources the Left can muster from international or domestic sources. The real consequence of such foreign funding is, apart from the possible physical destruction it engenders, to further isolate the leadership elite from the masses by making the former less immediately dependent on the latter for the success of the movement or process. It is as a result of this kind of isolation from the masses that intra-elite competitiveness and conflicts tend to escalate leading ultimately to the destruction or transformation of the movement itself. But such destructiveness is usually never complete, particularly as far as the general level of leftist consciousness among particular sections of the masses is concerned. If covert methods such as secret foreign funding for the Right are not sufficient to complete the destructiveness of the Left, then one remaining more overt approach utilized by foreign hegemonic powers to help the completion of the process is direct military intervention.

FOREIGN MILITARY INTERVENTION

Regional security and defense groupings such as the Regional Security System (RSS) among the Eastern Caribbean states interpret 'security' to cover a much broader spectrum than the traditional border defense, sovereignty and territorial integrity issues, and often reaches out towards the repression of the Left political forces within a conventional cold war perspective. These objectives are usually evident in (a) the close linkages between these bodies and foreign hegemonic and military interests, (b) the strategies and tactics used in conjunction with foreign hegemonic forces to demonstrate comparative military prowess, (c) the nature and distribution of foreign military aid to particular Caribbean territories, and (d) the selective targeting, for elimination or incarceration by intervening military forces, of Left leadership in particular.[40]

Other regional security and defense arrangements had similar objectives of fighting cold war battles within Caribbean territories, with the effect that hegemonic interests mainly of foreign capitalist states were advanced. The October 1982 Memorandum of Understanding, for example, signed by Dominica, St Lucia, Antigua, St Vincent and Barbados, which proposed the formation of a regional defense force, was motivated by an interest in protecting these states from the possibility of another Grenada type revolution in these islands or anywhere in the region. Such a possibility seemed to have been reflected in the rise of strong leftist political developments in two of these signatory islands, Dominica and St Vincent, at the time.[41] According to a NACLA report, this proposed security arrangement to have been headquartered in Barbados, "served to integrate the US more closely into the security of the Eastern Caribbean".[42] Similarly in 1985 another security arrangement signed between Barbados and Trinidad was particularly concerned with the possibility of increasing terrorism and what they called "the techniques of subversion" in the region; for this reason a 120-man regional police force was proposed "to deal with any internal armed threat to an elected government".[43] By its terms such an arrangement seemed to be arraigned not only against mercenary military expeditions like the KKK inspired attempted coup against Dominica in 1981, but equally against internal coups like the one in Grenada in 1979. As such these security arrangements opened the door for the repression by a regional police force, of internal dissent and popular mass protest within particular Caribbean territories.

These regional security initiatives make Caribbean states very receptive to foreign military aid. The larger proportion of foreign military aid given to the Caribbean aims at buttressing relatively conservative or right-wing regimes against the possibilities of Leftist incursions in the state or the region as a whole. This particular trend is very noticeable in Table 7.4 which gives a breakdown of US military aid to the region between 1950 and 1979, and suggests that relatively conservative regimes like that of Eric Williams in Trinidad and Tobago received three times as much Economic Support Funds (ESFs), (US $29.7 million) as received by more leftist regimes like Guyana ($9.6 million), or twice as much as obtained by the democratic socialist regime of Michael Manley of Jamaica ($12.1 million). ESFs are subsidies received by what are viewed as threatened pro-US regimes from the Economic Support Fund, formerly known as the Security Supporting Assistance Program, of the US Military Aid to Foreign Governments programme.

Table 7.4　US military aid to Caribbean governments, 1950-1979

Country	Type of military aid (US$million)					
	MAP	FMS	EDA	IMET	ESF	Total
Cuba	8.6	0	5.5	2	0	16.1
Dominican Republic	21.7	3	3.9	10.6	209.2	248.4
Guyana	0	0	0	0	9.6	9.6
Haiti	2.4	1.2	0.2	1.3	47.7	52.8
Honduras	5.6	12.5	2	8.4	1.6	30.1
Jamaica	1.1	0	*	*	11	12.1
Nicaragua	7.7	8	5.2	11.5	8	40.4
Suriname	0	0	0	0	1	1
Trinidad and Tobago	0	0	0	0	29.7	29.7

Legend
MAP = grants of arms, equipment, services
FMS = credits for purchases of US arms
EDA = deliveries of surplus US arms
IMET= International Military Education and Training Programme
ESF = security support for threatened pro US regimes
* = a few thousand dollars

Source:　Michael T. Klare and Cynthia Arnson, *Supplying Repression, US Support Authoritarian Regimes Abroad*, Washington D.C.: Institute for Policy Studies, 1981, pp. 113

While, also, US military aid to the Manley PNP regime in Jamaica had at one stage sunk to zero during the 1970s, the figures dramatically climbed to over $8 million by 1986 in support of the succeeding right-wing JLP regime led by Edward Seaga.[44] This anti-Left dimension of US military aid to the Caribbean is further reflected in the Caribbean Basin Initiative (CBI) inspired by the Reagan administration's cold war fight against the Sandinista government of Nicaragua, and other Leftist regimes and movements throughout the region. Although the CBI was originally intended as a Marshall Plan type economic deal for heavily indebted countries in the region, the bulk of the aid package went towards the propping up of military security matters, while at the same time most of the military portion of the aid was ear-marked for right-wing regimes in the region, such as El Salvador and Jamaica. Leftist regimes like Grenada, Guyana and Nicaragua were totally left out of the CBI aid package.[45]

Table 7.5   Foreign military and covert interventions in the wider Caribbean, 1953-1989

Country	Date	Private/ Mercenary	British	US	Other
Guyana	1953	–	X	–	–
	1963/64	–	X	X	–
Jamaica	1976	X	–	X	–
	1980	X	–	X	–
Grenada	1983	–	–	X	–
Dominica	1981	X	–	–	–
Trinidad and Tobago	1970	–	–	X	X
St Vincent	1984	–	–	X	–
Dominican Republic	1965	–	–	X	–
Haiti	1993	–	–	X	–
Panama	1989	–	–	X	–

The "Type/Source of foreign interventions" header spans the Private/Mercenary, British, US, and Other columns.

Foreign military manoeuvres in the region also reveal similar anti-Left tendencies. During 1980 alone US warships made at least 125 calls to 29 Caribbean seaports.[46] Also, most of the manoeuvres during the 1980s, such as the 1981 Ocean Venture operations, simulated US military invasion of Leftist 'enemy' states like Grenada in the region.[47] US hegemonic interests were equally served by sub-imperialist powers in the region such as Venezuela whose war ships were noticeably busy around Port-of-Spain during the 1970 Black Power uprising in neighbouring Trinidad and Tobago. Similar Venezuelan incursions on the borders of neighbouring Guyana during the 1980s served as sharp reminders that powerful capitalist powers would not tolerate the development of future Cubas at their very doorstep.

Direct foreign military intervention in the region also follows the cold war logic of containing or destroying left-wing movements and trends. Table 7.5 gives a breakdown of the volume of foreign military intervention in the wider Caribbean region between 1953 and 1989.

Some of the most prominent examples contained in the statistics in Table 7.5 include: (a) the intervention of British troops into Guyana both in 1953 and the 1963-64 periods aimed in each instance at putting down the democratically elected pro-Marxist PPP government, (b) the 1965 US military invasion of the Dominican Republic to put down the newly elected leftist Bosch government, (c) the 1983 invasion of Grenada by a combination of US and surrogate Caribbean troops to oust the remnants of an already decapitated leftist party and government, and (d) the 1989 US invasion of Panama to oust a renegade Noriega military regime that in its last days demonstrated a great deal of political independence of the US decision making process.

Foreign military intervention in conjunction with elite isolation from the Caribbean masses contributed significantly to the ultimate disintegration and ideological retreat of the Caribbean Left. Following the US invasion of Grenada, for example, a McCarthyite witch-hunt atmosphere developed among Caribbean ruling circles leading to expulsions of Cuban diplomats from Jamaica under Seaga, and Suriname under a military dictatorship, as well as a prominent Guyanese journalist, Ricky Singh, from Barbados under the right-wing Tom Adams' regime.[48] As early as 1970 the leaders of the Black Power uprising in Trinidad and Tobago were startled by the threatening manoeuvres of US and Venezuelan war-ships steaming towards Port-of-Spain; and in 1984 the US battleship *Iowa* lurked outside the shores of Martinique in readiness for any 'emergency' during the conduct of the St Vincent elections at the time.[49]

In general, therefore, it would seem that the reasoning behind foreign (particularly US) military interventions in the Caribbean envisions the security of the region as infinitely tied in with the containment of Leftist influences and the consequent support for the development and entrenchment of Rightist political forces throughout the region. This particular perspective was manifested in the US creation and support of the right-wing NNP following the Grenada invasion in 1983, even to the point of attempting to rig the future national elections in favour of this new party.[50] It is therefore important to look more closely at the variety of foreign inspired efforts towards the cultivation of these rightist forces to replace Leftist influences in the region.

CULTIVATING THE RIGHT

Continual propping up and reinvention of the Right in the Caribbean has been the traditional preoccupation of foreign powers, beginning with colonial authorities since the inception of modern electoral politics in the 1950s, and coinciding eventually with the postwar assertion of US hegemonic interest in the region. The mushrooming of pro-colonialist-capitalist parties such as the NLF and the UF in Guyana, in the 1950s and 1960s respectively, represents early examples of right-wing politics cultivated by British colonial policies in the region. Meanwhile, parties such as the JLP in Jamaica and the PNM in Trinidad and Tobago, developed right-wing ideological orientations in accordance with colonialist demands for ideological conformity with international capitalist interests.

The JLP, for its part, was helped in winning the 1944 elections through persist-ent British inspired propaganda against the rival Norman Manley's democratic socialist party, the PNP. The American observer of the 1944 elections reported that "the character of the attack on Manley by the island's press was similar to that directed against Tugwell and the Popular Democratic Party in Puerto Rico, and God, communism and the British Empire were all dragged in for the final as-sault."[51] Similarly, Eric Williams' PNM in Trinidad and Tobago, although coming into being in 1956 as a vibrant anti-colonial nationalist party, was willing to compromise with the Americans on the Chaguramas naval base issue, at the cost of sacrificially purging prominent Leftists such as C. L. R. James from the party in 1962.[52] From then on, the party's rapid move to the Right was a foregone conclu-sion.

Resulting, therefore, from the combined British and American efforts, the dominance of right-wing forces becomes entrenched in the political systems of the English-speaking Caribbean. At the same time, however, both these foreign hegemonic powers relied on a highly exaggerated cold war psychosis to inform their policies with respect to Caribbean security issues. The Reaganite conception of the domino theory, for example, to the effect that leftist successes anywhere in the region will inevitably lead to the establishment of Soviet-Cuban beachheads on American doorsteps, turned out to be largely unjustifiable. Within this domino perspective, consequently, the Grenada revolution of 1979 was supposed to spawn a plethora of socialist states and revolution everywhere throughout the Eastern Caribbean and beyond. This did not happen. On the contrary, the 1980s witnessed a flurry of right-wing activities and political dominance among OECS countries of which Grenada is a part. National elections in St Vincent and St Lucia in 1989, and Dominica and Antigua in 1980 saw almost a landslide in favour of right-wing political parties in the respective Caribbean states, while the Left's percentages of the votes ranged from 4 percent in Antigua to an equally low 11 percent in Dominica.[53]

This tendency toward Rightist political dominance in the English-speaking Caribbean is reflected, for instance, in Ivelaw Griffith's schema evaluating power distributions among 36 ideologically distinct parties throughout 12 different English-speaking countries.[54] The prescribed ideological distinctions among these 36 parties range from 'Capitalist-Conservative' and 'Capitalist-Reformist' at the rightist end of the ideological spectrum, to 'Socialist-Reformist' and 'Social-ist-Radical' at the leftist end. Along these lines, fully 85 percent of the ruling parties (in 10 out of 12 states) were capitalist (or rightist) oriented, while only about 15 percent of those which occupied power positions (in 2 of 12 states) were classified as 'Socialist-Reformist' and zero percent as 'Socialist-Radical' or Marxist. The Left, therefore, despite all the 'domino' prognostications of the Reagan administration, were quite under-represented, to say the least, in the corridors of power through-out the English-speaking Caribbean during the 1980s and beyond.

The period following the 1983 US invasion of Grenada witnessed a new level of cold war reaction resulting in foreign powers deliberately setting up right-wing governments and political organizations in specific states throughout the region. The Grenada case was particularly noticeable in that the New National Party (NNP), a tripartite coalition created to consolidate US victory over the ousted Leftist NJM regime, was born out of a secret meeting held on St Vincent's Union Island in August 1984 attended by a prominent US government representative and the Prime Ministers of Barbados, St Lucia and St Vincent.[55] US officials were even prepared to go as far as rigging the 1985 elections in Grenada to ensure that their creature, the NNP, obtained the majority of votes. According to a NACLA report a specially assigned US embassy official named Tierney who had " put the factions of the NNP together' and was "the brain behind it", had "accepted direct respon-sibility for the fraud with the election ballots".[56] The report further indicated that "Tierney admits that special ballots were brought in from Georgia . . . already marked with special chemicals. The votes cast by Grenadians didn't show up."[57]

The ultimate setback for the Caribbean Left, stemming from external or inter-national sources, is rooted in the phenomenon of structural adjustment imposed during the 1980s on debt dependent Third World, including Caribbean states by IMF and World Bank conditions. The conditionalities imposed by these major international economic institutions insist on: (a) curtailment of working class demands such as higher wages and full employment, (b) strengthening of export oriented market strategies, (c) shifts towards privatization and divestment of state owned enterprises, and (d) maintenance of ideological conformity to a liberalist-capitalist international outlook, all on pain of economic squeeze or sanctions. Needless to say, these strategies conduce towards the curtailment of leftist activities which are usually stimulated by working class strength, collective rather than individualistic efforts, and anti-imperialist ideological perspectives.

Within this rather restrictive framework allowed for the Left by structural adjustment conditionalities, the Right by contrast tend to flourish. The Seaga JLP government of Jamaica between 1980 and 1988, was indeed one of the chief political (although not necessarily economic) beneficiaries in the region, of these IMF inspired structural adjustment policies. The recently recognized fact, however, that these same IMF imposed strategies tend to foster greater economic dispari-ties, immiseration and impoverishment, as well as accompanying popular unrest, among the Third World, including the Caribbean, masses,[58] would seem to create definite space for probable future rekindling of the Leftist momentum in these parts.

8

Ideological
Impact

The development of left-wing politics in the Caribbean, as elsewhere, hinged most significantly on the role of ideology in the process of change. The Caribbean experience in this respect raises crucial issues having both theoretical and practical implications. Among the most pertinent issues are: (a) the sources of ideological differences and how they relate to the classification of different ideological movements; and (b) the effects of these different lines of ideological commitments on the conduct and outcome of leftist political practice. In other words, we are interested here, in relation to the Caribbean experience, in the very general question of how alternative ideologies and movements occur in the context of an already dominant and aggressive overarching ideological system, and the extent to which these occurrences have any permanent or lasting significance and impact.

Antonio Gramsci raised the same set of questions, and further lamented the fact that there is a dearth of theory attempting to explain this crucial problem. "What must be explained", Gramsci put it, "is how it happens that in all periods there co-exist many systems and current of philosophical thought, how these currents are born, how they are diffused, and why in the process of diffusion they fracture along certain lines and in certain directions".[1] Similar questions have been raised much earlier by Marx, Weber, and much later by Manheim.[2]

The more practical impact of ideology has also been the focus of wider attention far beyond the Caribbean context. It represents, in fact, one basic dimension of the wider issue of the usually problematic relationship between theory and practice, in particular the question of the extent to which theory or ideology plays an independent determining role in influencing the nature and direction of political practice. Reciprocally, it also has implications for understanding the relationship between ideology and class, particularly whether class position influences the choice of ideological commitment and orientation. Or, it is possible that the autonomous existence of a body of ideological and theoretical formulations can contribute to the creation and development of particular political groups and movements.

A critical theoretical tradition of scholarship within which these questions are centrally located is largely lacking in the English-speaking Caribbean. Existing studies about ideological formations and movements or those expressing particular ideological orientations have either failed to explain ideological divergences,[3] or are too uncritical about the role of particular ideologies in the Caribbean political process.[4] Nevertheless, Caribbean political practice has certainly given rise to questions about the demarcating lines between Right and Left political movements and tendencies or, more importantly, between reformist, radical and revolutionary orientations and movements.

Caribbean Marxist scholarship, for example, tends to focus on the dominant ideological pattern, which in the Caribbean case is represented by capitalism, and its ramifications in terms of perpetuating the politically dominant classes.[5] What would seem to be needed, however, is an investigation not simply on how ideology buttresses the power position of the ruling classes but, more importantly, on: (a) how ideological deviations from the prevailing order emerge within peripheral Third World states; (b) the impact of internal and external pressures on both class and ideological fragmentation processes; and (c) the potentialities of each type of class or ideological formation for bringing about meaningful changes in the political system as a whole.

The significance of this approach for understanding the recurrent difficulties which faced the various political unification attempts in the Caribbean, such as the problematic NAR in Trinidad and Tobago, and the PCD in Guyana, each comprising ideologically distinct components, can hardly be disputed. In this way, also, we can better explain the continual vacillating tendencies on the part of parties like the PNC in Guyana as far as its ideological commitments are concerned, or the sudden extremism of a once-dormant Coardist faction within the radical New Jewel Movement of Grenada. Further, within this particular perspective, we are better placed to understand why the hegemony of the US-sponsored (capitalist) ideological system persists in the hemisphere, and the continual fragmentation and failures of alternative ideological projects.

SOURCES OF IDEOLOGICAL DIFFERENTIATION

Within Caribbean social science scholarship, the issue of political ideology has been specifically addressed by only a small section of Marxist and neo-Marxist scholars. As such, much of the economic determinism of the classical Marxist tradition creeps into the explanation of the origins of ideological perspectives and movements in the region. The recurrent identification of economic hardships, or crises in the international capitalist system, as directly or exclusively responsible for the radicalization of significant sections of the Caribbean population is a case in point.[6] Additionally, this explanation tends to complement the general thesis of the dependency theoretical tradition that the increasing proletarianization of the Third World masses through their immersion and subordination within the international capitalist system, leads to their inevitable radicalization.[7]

These essentially reductionist arguments on the part of Caribbean and Third World Marxist-oriented theorists might be true up to a point. However, they do less than justice to the full import of Caribbean political reality and trends. For they cannot fully explain why, for example, the Caribbean radicalization process is usually initiated and led by middle class rather than the relatively more economically depressed working class elements, as is noted in the early development of radical movements in the region, nor why the Caribbean working classes tend to be largely conservative on very crucial political and economic issues. In Jamaica, for example, Stone concluded that as much as 40 percent of what he termed "the majority classes", preferred to surrender Jamaican sovereignty in preference for US statehood, and the figures are much higher, to as much as 60 percent, for the more working class-based JLP supporters.[8] The explanation for this trend, according to Stone, is rooted in what he termed the "essential pragmatism of the majority classes" which are entrapped in the politics of survival.[9]

The radicalization that developed within the Caribbean political process is essentially a middle class phenomenon. Political leadership of the Left movement and the struggle toward the creation of political parties and the attainment of political independence stemmed, as was observed in the earlier chapters, from middle class personalities, particularly the intellectual and professional elements of these classes. And such radicalization of the middle class could be attributed to factors beyond economic considerations, such as exposure to foreign-based ideologies like Soviet Marxism which influenced the leadership of parties such as the PPP and WPJ, and Labourite socialism, which influenced the PNP and PNC, imported mainly by West Indian students who studied in London, Paris, New York and other metropolitan centres. We noted, too, that returned veterans from World War II were foremost in the creation of political organization in several countries in the region and several, such as Rory Westmaas of the PPP in Guyana and

Cipriani in the early Trinidad labour movement were notable radicals among these. Momentous international political and ideological trends such as the rise of Black Power in the USA also had a significant and far reaching impact on the Caribbean middle class leaders of Left political movements such as NJAC of Trinidad, NJM of Grenada, and the WPA of Guyana. We also noted earlier the significance of the Russian, Chinese and Cuban Revolutions in influencing the ideological developments of the more radical and revolutionary of these political movements in the region.

The Caribbean example, therefore, should contribute to the enrichment, if not the revision, of the classic Marxist explanation of the phenomenon of ideological developments in the region since it lends credence to other rival theories, such as de Tocqueville's suggestion that revolutionary developments are usually initiated by the upwardly mobile classes which might be suddenly frustrated in their climb to the summits of power,[10] and also that of Lyford P. Edwards and Alvin Gouldner that it is the transfer of the allegiance, or alienation, of intellectuals which is the main precipitant of revolutionary trends.[11] As such, the 'economic hardship' thesis by itself is inadequate since it equally explains the process toward conservatism currently taking place in the world political arena.[12]

Intellectuals indeed have played a key role in initiating and influencing the development of radical and revolutionary trends in the English-speaking Caribbean. The rise of the New World Group during the 1960s, which concentrated on the development of radical scholarships and encouraged direct intellectual participation in the formulation of public policy, was a remarkable case in point. Other later developments such as the Ratoon Group in Guyana and Abeng in Jamaica in the 1970s were also notable examples of intellectual involvement in attempting to influence the course of Caribbean political developments. A strong commitment to partisan politics was also characteristic of some of these groups as in the case of Ratoon constituting an intrinsic part in the creation of the WPA party during this period. Prominent intellectuals also formed part of the top leadership of such radical and revolutionary Caribbean parties as the NJM in Grenada, WPJ in Jamaica, the PPP in Guyana, and the early formation of the ULF in Trinidad and Tobago.

The 'middle class upward mobility' thesis is powerful, although not necessarily sufficient in its capacity to explain not only the origins of radical politics in the English-speaking Caribbean, but the tendencies toward ideological fragmentation and disintegration within particular Left political organizations and movements in the region. C. L. R. James' contention that the Caribbean middle classes are: (a) deliberately cultivated by external forces for political domination and control and thereby subjected to external influences and trends; and (b) basically conflictive, unstable and with inherent tendencies toward vacillation,[13] is indeed very ingenious, as it definitely sets the stage for understanding the ideological fragmentation phenomenon in the Caribbean. A contributing factor also relates to the structural differentiation of these classes into a variety of fractions – that is, professional, intellectual and mercantile fractions of the Caribbean middle classes. Additionally, the existence of a liberal democratic political framework allows ample political space for conflictive maneuvers and multiple ideological commitments. However, it is the very artificial, fragmented and conflictive nature of the ideologically and politically hegemonic middle classes that gives rise to the sharp ideological disparities which typify Left politics in the English-speaking Caribbean. The tragic splits in the PPP in 1955 in Guyana, and in the ULF in Trinidad and Tobago, the exceedingly violent rupture of the NJM in 1983 in Grenada, and not least the ideological vacillations of the PNP in Jamaica and the PNC in Guyana are recognized as the logical extension of this phenomenon of middle class disunity, ambivalence and ambition in Caribbean politics.

The variety of Left movements and political organizations which encapsule the Caribbean radical and revolutionary tradition tend, therefore, to be largely weak and fragile, reflecting, no doubt, the weaknesses of class forces in general and the centrifugal tendencies of the middle classes in particular. Their classification into reformist, radical and revolutionary tendencies represents only one possible dimension of the political differentiation and fragmentation process. However, these characterizations are based not only on ideological grounds, but more fundamentally on orientation toward political practice. In terms of their viability and long-term survival capacity, however, another form of classification might be more pertinent, that is, the Gramscian classification between "organic" movements which are more strongly class-based, born of historical necessity and, therefore, more permanent, and "conjunctural" movements "which appear as occasional, immediate, almost accidental", and, therefore, tend to be more transient.[14] Ideologies which are more conjunctural than organic tend to be "arbitrary, rationalistic, or willed".[15] Caribbean Left movements, it would appear, tend in general to be more conjunctual than organic, hence, their tendencies toward internal conflicts, disintegration and eventual marginalization or disappearance.

COURSE OF IDEOLOGICAL CHANGE

The historical development of Leftist ideology in the English-speaking Caribbean followed a somewhat zig-zag and sometimes contradictory path. What began as a definitely pro-labour working class commitment of the Left movement in the 1940s, had by the late 1980s developed into a clearly pro-capitalist programmatic stance. Yet it was not simply an opportunistic shift, but a rather pragmatic

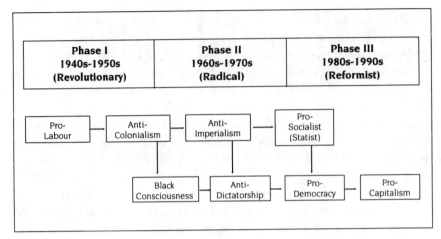

Figure 3   Phases of Left ideological development in the Caribbean, 1940-1990

reconstitution of the movement in the interest of its own survival. Those few Leftist groups that have changed merely for tactical or opportunistic reasons, such as the WPVP in Guyana and the ULF in Trinidad, or doggedly resisted change, as in the cases of the NJM in Grenada and the WPJ in Jamaica, failed to survive. In general, however, the Caribbean Left have today come to represent something like a synthetic fusion of broadly contradictory ideological positions, involving the inter-relationship between a class-conscious, state-centric, and socialist orientation on the one hand, and a race-conscious, anti-dictatorial, democratic-capitalist position on the other. Figure 3 illustrates this trend.

As Figure 3 suggests, the emphatically pro-labour and class-conscious phase of the Caribbean Left appeared in their earliest beginnings during the 1940s and 1950s. The left-wing of the PNP (in particular its Marxist 'inner circle'), and the PAC, which produced the Marxist PPP in Guyana in 1950, were the prime examples of this labour-centred, confrontational phase of the movement. At the time, the Caribbean Left sought either to control existing labour movements such as the Guyana and Jamaica TUCs, or to develop trade union organizations of their own, such as GAWU out of PPP efforts. Although, of course, the race issue featured during this period in the works and programs of such significant Caribbean Left intellectuals as C. L. R. James who championed a Left Pan Africanism and the need for a Black vanguard to lead the world working class revolution,[16] and also in the Garveyist influences among the earliest PNP leadership including its Marxist 'inner circle' members,[17] such race consciousness was nevertheless considered to be subordinate to the basic class struggle. In fact, it was the period in which the Caribbean Left placed overwhelming emphasis on the class confrontational theories and strategies contained in the classic Marxist texts of Marx, Engels, Lenin and Stalin.[18]

The second phase of the ideological development of the Caribbean Left came during the decolonization period, that is, during the 1960s and 1970s. It was a period characterized by both anti-colonialism directed against European colonial powers and anti-imperialism directed against the United States in particular. Black consciousness became more pronounced during this period, not only because of stimulation from the Black Power movement in the United States, but more importantly because it was perceived as organically tied to a particular radicalized conceptualization of imperialism as 'white racist' oppressiveness of the black Caribbean masses.[19] This Black conscious anti-imperialism also coincided with a vociferous anti-dictatorial struggle against the new post-colonial rulers such as Eric Gairy in Grenada, Forbes Burnham in Guyana, and Eric Williams in Trinidad and Tobago, who assumed a strong state-centred and authoritarian approach to political control. While their anti-imperialist position impelled the second phase Left movements to embrace socialism as the only alternative to capitalism, their anti-dictatorial position led them naturally to espouse greater democratization of the political process. It was a period, too, when many Left political organizations such as the PNC, the PNP and the NJM, controlled state power, thereby augmenting the forces advocating the more statist approaches to socialist transformation in the region.

The significance of the creative nexus between race and class in conjunction with the anti-dictatorial thrust in the ideological development of this period was introduced mainly by NJAC in Trinidad and Tobago and the WPA in Guyana. This was reflected in NJAC's efforts to mobilize black and East Indian working classes against the established black PNM political leadership which was seen to be in league with white imperialism, and the very creation of the WPA by Africa-conscious Marxist leaders like Eusi Kwayana and Walter Rodney. Unlike the first phase ideological developments, the leadership of this period tended to be inspired not only by European ideological influences, but mainly by the works of Third World revolutionary intellectuals and leaders such as Mao Zedong, Che Guevara, Amilcar Cabral, and Frantz Fanon.[20] Thus, the narrower Europeanized conceptualization of working class leadership within what was then perceived to be an increasing capitalist industrialization trend throughout the Western world, was replaced, particularly among the Radical Left, by a broader conceptualization of mass movement embracing not only workers, but the peasantry, the lumpen proletariat, and the lower echelons of the middle classes, as being the more relevant forces for revolutionary change under Caribbean conditions.

A third phase in the development of Caribbean Leftist ideology was ushered in during the 1980s and continued into the 1990s. This period is best characterized

Table 8.1 Changes in ideological orientation of major Caribbean Left parties

Ideological Commitments	Changes over time				
	1950s	1960s	1970s	1980s	1990s
Marxist-Leninist	In. Circle (PNP) WIIP	PPP	PPP WPJ WPVP	WPJ NJM	–
Marxist (Ind.)	PPP	WFP	WPA PNC NJM ULF	PPP WPA	
Social Democratic	PNP	PNC	PNP		WPA
Liberalist-Nationalist	PNC	PNP		PNP ULF PNC	PPP
Conservative					PNP PNC
Dissolved	Inner Circle	WIIP	WFP	WPVP NJM	ULF WPJ

by the Left's reversion to an emphasis on Westminster democratic practices, particularly in the wake of selective repression under unscrupulous Caribbean dictatorial regimes, and especially in the aftermath of the violent NJM fiasco and subsequent US military intervention in Grenada in 1983. However, much of this return to Westminster democracy was given justification in Marxist terms, particularly through the works of Rosa Luxemburg and some aspects of Marx and Engels' writings. While the early Marxist classics praised the advent of universal suffrage and free elections in nineteenth century Britain as a potentially revolutionary opportunity for the working classes,[21] Roza Luxemberg railed against statist repression of the creative potential of radical Leftist groups and individuals.[22]

From a pro-Westminster position it became relatively easy to make the transition to the reformist pro-capitalist position that characterizes the Caribbean Left today. All the elements of pro-Westminster and pro-capitalist tendencies among the Caribbean Left are there: (a) accent on the rule of law and the protection of private rights and property; (b) legitimizing the divorce between state and market forces; (c) the elevation of market and privatization policies; (d) accent on civil and human rights; (e) advocacy of foreign capital investments; and (f) support for the rapid development of an indigenous entrepreneurial class.[23]

Table 8.1 gives a breakdown of the changed ideological positions of the various Caribbean Left political parties over the years between 1952 (begining with the PNP) and 1992 (ending with the dissolution of the WPJ). The highlights of these changes include most prominently rejection of its democratic socialist platform in 1955 and Communist and left-wing support in 1980, PPP's Marxist-Leninist commitment in 1969 and advocacy of 'critical support' for the reformist PNC in 1976, PNC's radical nationalism in 1971, cooperative socialism in 1975, brief championing of Marxism-Leninism in 1989, and finally staunch advocacy of the neo-liberalist structural adjustment policies in the 1990s. Also included here are WPA's abandonment of its initial Marxist revolutionary platform of 1979 in favour of the more moderate 'Rodneyist' political orientation in 1992, ULF's absorption in the more reformist NAR party in 1985, and NJM's self destruction and eventual supercession by the more moderate MBPM following the 1983 fiasco.

The 1980s also saw the rise of new social movements fostered by both a growing popular demand for greater voice in the more dictatorial Caribbean states, and an increasing mass protest against economic hardships occasioned by mounting international debt and stringent conditionalities imposed by international lending institutions like the IMF and World Bank. In Guyana during the late 1980s, the most prominent of these social movements was GUARD which was created out of a concatenation of diverse forces including the established churches, a section of the trade union movement (FITUG), human rights organizations (e.g., the Guyana Human Rights Association – GHRA), business associations, and opposition political parties and intellectual groupings. In Trinidad and Tobago, the NAR, which briefly controlled state power in the 1980s, was formed out of a similar convergence of oppositional political and social forces including the ULF, several Leftist trade unions and the more rightist Organization for National Reconstruction (ONR).

On a wider Caribbean plane, but with considerable influence within Caribbean states, is the work of the CCC, which played a dynamic role in the development of these social movements. The CCC is also vociferous in championing political democracy, human rights and both national and regional sovereignty. At the ideological level, these new social movements were influenced by a combination of liberalist economic theory and liberation theology. They sought individual rights, social justice, and political stability within an economic structure driven by market and privatization strategies. They opposed both the traditional reformist parties and the more extreme Marxist parties, yet were amenable to tactical alliances with both leftist and rightist forces opposed to dictatorship and economic mismanagement anywhere in the region. However, unlike the more consistent organic alliances between the new social movements and the Left in Latin America, the relationship between their Caribbean counterparts and the Caribbean Left has been rather tenuous and transient. GUARD, for example, moved from rejection of Marxist groups such as the PPP, to the demand for tactical alliances with them, to finally a complete withdrawal from Guyanese politics. The interest in forming alliances with these liberalist social movements led much of the Caribbean Left to further retreat from class to embrace mass centred politics, and to make corresponding compromises regarding capitalist market and privatization strategies.

CHARACTERISTICS OF CARIBBEAN LEFT IDEOLOGY

What is most peculiar about the ideological expression of the Caribbean Left is that it reflects a history of attempts to reconcile seemingly contradictory forces and orientations – between race and class, dictatorship and democracy, violence and non-violence, and ultimately, middle class leadership and working class struggle. Admittedly, these contradictions also existed among the Left in North and Latin America, but their levels of reconciliation tend to be uniquely different in the Caribbean context.

The conceptualization of the role of race within a Leftist ideological perspective, for instance, differs significantly among the Caribbean Left as compared to what obtains among the Left in North and Latin America. In the USA socialist ideological development prior to World War II reflected strong racist overtones particularly since blacks were excluded from the movement. Class interests here were interpreted in the narrowest of terms to mean white working class interests.[24] Even Stalin's 'Black Belt' thesis promulgated by the Comintern ostensibly to assist the American Black struggle, meant in effect the physical separation of Blacks and Whites in America.[25] In Latin America, because of the heavy economism in Leftist ideology there, the concept of race played a relatively minimal role in the analysis of class struggle, except, perhaps in Guatemala where consciousness of the plight of the indigenous population has been incorporated in the programmatic platform of the Leftist guerilla movement.[26]

In the Caribbean, however, race soon moved to a very prominent role in the definition of working class interests within Left ideology, whether it was the black vanguardism of C. L. R. James, or 'Black Power' among the Radical Left during the 1960s, or race as a tactical advantage in winning elections in the cases of the PPP and PNC in Guyana. It was not only an attempt to elevate the hitherto disadvantaged and oppressed Black masses to centre stage historically and internationally, but to recognize that in the Caribbean, as in Africa, Blacks are in fact the majority of the population, and should therefore be in the command seats of political decision making. The level of success so far attained by the Left in this attempt does reflect the complexity of this problematic of reconciling race to working class ideology since Caribbean politics manifests oppression and class divisions within the black race itself. A second problematic in this respect is the artificial colonialist-inspired divisions between Blacks and other non-white Caribbean races, notably the East Indians and Amerindians in countries such as Trinidad and Guyana. The effort by Walter Rodney to lump together Blacks, East Indians and Amerindians into the singular oppressed category, as opposed to the more endowed and privileged white and near-white few (including Chinese and Portuguese),[27] did not help very much to stem the apparently increasing tide of racial animosity, and recriminations among these disadvantaged groups themselves. Caribbean Left ideology, therefore, falls short on this racial reconciliation issue, not only in view of its inability to grasp or resolve the increasing tensions between the different disadvantaged groups, but equally because it fails to shed light on how black-controlled states can attain real power in the international system, or how to resolve the issue of black elite oppression of the black masses in the Caribbean and elsewhere.

Another contrast between Caribbean Left ideology and that of its counterparts in North and Latin America is in the nature of the struggle for democracy against dictatorship. Although in North America questions are often raised among the Left about the restrictive nature of American democracy, there was still no particular experience of struggle against dictatorship in the classic sense of the term, as is most dramatically exemplified by, say, military and personalist dictatorships throughout Latin America during the 1960s and 1970s. While in North America there was no real dictatorship, in Latin America there was no real democracy. In the Caribbean, however, the Left conceptualization of, and struggle against dictatorship was made all the more difficult because the Caribbean region as a whole, particularly the English-speaking Caribbean, is often characterized as an example *par excellence* of real working democracies in the Third World. Yet major political leaders and heads of states throughout the post-colonial history of the English-speaking Caribbean behaved more like personalist dictators than democrats in dealing with both their own parties and the nation at large. These included Alexander Bustamante in Jamaica, Eric Williams in Trinidad, Eric Gairy in Grenada, Forbes Burnham of Guyana and Edward Seaga of Jamaica. This peculiar political culture of dictatorship within democracy had forced the Caribbean Left, much earlier than other regional Left movements, to theorize the ideal nature of democracy – to demand, that is, a more inclusive and extensive structure and form of democratic participation and decision making – at a time when most of the Latin American Left seemed to have trained their attention on the violent overthrow of dictatorships and the immediate imposition of statist forms of socialism.

The dilemma of dictatorship within democracy in the English-speaking Caribbean further led the Caribbean Left to pursue a strategy toward change that incorporated the use of existing democratic processes which uniformly eschew the use of violent methods (excepting the isolated instances of the NUFF guerilla activities in Trinidad and the NJM coups in Grenada in 1979 and 1983). This near-uniform conclusion led the Caribbean Left to confront the third dilemma of how to reconcile non-violent struggle with the increasing degree of repressive violence that was trained against them by dictatorial states and foreign forces. Unlike the Caribbean Left, the Latin American Left were split on the issue, with a significant proportion of the latter embracing and employing armed guerilla struggle.[28]

As in the case of the American Left, the Caribbean Left settled for the more non-violent methods such as characterized by Martin Luther King's conceptualization of the strategy of the American Civil Rights Movement. For the Caribbean Left, however, the high point of the struggle was conceptualized in terms of the use of the general strike and, not unlike civil rights tactics, various forms of boycotts including boycott of parliament. The level of conceptualization of violence or non-violence in Caribbean Left ideology, however, did not keep pace with the actual use of violence at particular moments in their struggle for change. Such violence might be relatively spontaneous (e.g., Rastafarian violence in the Eastern Caribbean) or forced upon the Left by circumstances beyond their control (e.g., destabilization violence in Guyana and Jamaica), and not necessarily theorized as a necessary part of Left strategy in the region. In fact, given the extent and frequency of political violence events in postwar Caribbean history, the greater proportion of which was initiated by rightist and foreign forces, the whole notion of the significance of a violent strategy was undertheorized by the Caribbean Left.[29]

And yet a critical theorizing by the Caribbean Left of this violence issue might have provided the necessary justification for their *de facto* adherence to the non-violent approach. Firstly, the history of violent struggle in the Caribbean has had extremely negative consequences for the masses in particular. Not only was youthful and energetic leadership stemming organically from these classes totally eliminated by the overwhelmingly more powerful state apparatus and foreign forces, as in the case of NUFF in Trinidad during the 1970s, and the assassinations of Rodney and Bishop in the 1980s, but Caribbean societies have been most likely irretrievably divided, as in the cases of recurrent ethnic-political (including tribalistic) violence in Trinidad, Guyana, Suriname and Jamaica. Secondly, almost invariably the use of violence by the Left has given rise to the systematic elite justification of both institutionalized or politicized racism and increasing militarization and state repressive tendencies throughout the region.

There is, however, much in the Caribbean Left ideological developments that compare more positively with similar developments in the hemisphere. The first observation here is that commitment to particular forms of ideology does influence political behaviour, making ideology relatively autonomous of the economic base and an independent determining element in the social process. Hard core Leninist and Stalinist influences were instrumental not only in the creation of the first set of leftist movements in the region during the 1940s, but directly shaped the vanguardist, principled and relatively doctrinaire behaviour patterns of these groups ranging from the Marxist 'inner circle' in Jamaica, the Political Affairs Committees, and the PPP in Guyana, to the Coardist faction of the NJM, and the leadership of the WPJ in Jamaica. At the same time, however, there was no necessary one-to-one correspondence between particular types of ideologies and particular classes, despite the claims of many groups that Marxism necessarily corresponds to the interests and aspirations of the working classes, while the middle classes in general were supposed to be reactionary and capitalist oriented. The Caribbean experience has shown, on the contrary, that significant sections of the middle classes tend to be the more revolutionary elements of the population compared to significant proportions at the subordinate classes who display relatively more conservative tendencies.

This 'ideology of the middle classes' in the Caribbean is somewhat complex. On the more enlightened side it champions some of the finer virtues of liberal democracy, such as the rights of the individual, and the unhindered freedom to pursue whatever is humanly possible. However, on the more problematic side, individual rights become for the middle classes a kind of 'possessive individualism', or the highly aggressive pursuit of private property and political power. It cherishes consumption (particularly of foreign goods) over production, eschews the work ethic and harbours an inherent distaste for manual labour. Further, the ideology of the Caribbean middle classes complements the dominant capitalist ideology of the metropolitan ruling interests. What is peculiarly Caribbean about it is that it reinforces its extreme competitive instincts with careful cultivation of the role and image of the cunning 'smartman' who sees the ability to take shortest cuts or to outwit opponents as synonymous with efficiency, and a flair for demagoguery as a neat substitute for knowledge of scientific principles.

Undoubtedly, this kind of ideological orientation influences middle class political practice which is couched in terms of arbitrariness, and authoritarian tendencies in leadership styles at the domestic level, and pacifism or resignation at the international levels. This kind of schizophrenic tendency is most aptly demonstrated in the Coardist responses to the Grenada crisis situation in 1983.

While the Coardist faction was quick to repress mass protest aimed at defending Maurice Bishop with extremely violent measures, the entire Coardist leadership fled without a fight in the face of the invading US army following these events.[30]

The Caribbean working classes, on the other hand, have so far been unable to develop any particular ideology of their own, despite the efforts of some middle class intellectuals to theorize, with the aid of Marxism, the interests of these disadvantaged elements of the population. But much still needs to be done as far as the development of both organic working class intellectuals and more appropriate theory of working class potentialities is concerned. Within this ideological vacuum, middle class values and ideological orientation are naturally infused among the working classes. The result of this contradiction is that sizable proportions of the working classes become apathetic, or escape into humour, cynicism or self-ridicule, even in the face of serious political crises such as violent repression, official corruption, economic scarcities and the like. This predilection to escape the impact of middle class influence is an indication that the Caribbean workers' lack of militancy is based not on satisfaction with capitalism as was suggested about the American working classes,[31] but in fact, the very opposite. Stone had intimated the prevalence of a similar escapist tendency on the part of the Jamaican masses caught in the teeth of officially-sponsored political violence;[32] the Guyanese masses, too, demonstrate the same escapist behaviour patterns in the wake of massive electoral political manipulations.

How the Caribbean Left handled this contradiction between middle class militancy and working class ideological apathy also leaves much to be desired. Their basic approach is to deny the existence of the often demonstrative conservatism of the Caribbean working class, and to imagine that this class is all that Marx said about it: revolutionary, militant, defiant and class conscious. At the same time, the middle classes as a whole are subjected to severe criticism and condemnation by the Left. There is indeed much to justify the Left criticisms of the middle classes, but such criticisms are usually based on a forgetfulness of their organizational capabilities, that the progressive elements and the Left itself stemmed from this class, and that much of the political advances in the Caribbean were derived from the consistent efforts of this class. Those among the Caribbean Left who recognize this dilemma seek to resolve it through activism at the trade union level as well as efforts toward political (particularly Marxist) education specifically for the working classes. But the trade union themselves often became tools of middle class and foreign interests, while the political education efforts foundered in part because of lack of support from the very Leftist leaders who advocated it in the first place.

What is, therefore, most needed for the development of Left ideology in the Caribbean is a concentrated analysis and critique of the Caribbean working classes as a complement to the relatively embryonic critique of middle class politics in the region. This intellectual effort will undoubtedly set the stage for a more comprehensive understanding of the potentialities of the relevant classes for initiating and arranging relevant changes in Caribbean political systems. Such an understanding based on a critique of the working classes is not necessarily incompatible with Marxism.

THE IMPACT OF MARXISM

The aftermath of the Grenada fiasco of 1983, in particular led many prominent leftist activists and intellectuals to question the very significance of their ideological commitments, particularly Marxism. Many contended that the Grenada 1983 fiasco was simply the culmination of the series of inevitable failures of the Left throughout the history of Caribbean political development, resulting from what were perceived to be inherent flaws in Marxist and Marxist-derived ideological systems. C. Y. Thomas, for example, railed at the tyrannical and violent potentialities of Marxism-Leninism which ultimately blinded the Grenada leaders to the importance of electoral democracy and what Thomas termed 'due process', and therefore destroyed the Grenada revolution.[33] Don Robotham, in his letter of resignation from the WPJ in Jamaica, also complained of similar tyrannical and repressive possibilities in the Marxist-Leninist ideology which dominated the WPJ leadership hierarchy.[34]

Trevor Munroe, too, admitted that Marxism-Leninism was partly responsible for the dogmatism followed by the Coardist faction in Grenada, and the authoritarian leadership style of his own party, leading to both the destruction of the NJM and the spate of resignations from the WPJ. He saw this inherent flaw in Marxism-Leninism as the principal reason for the complete rejection of this particular ideology by the Jamaican and Caribbean masses.[35] On the political Right the perception of the Left is that the Marxist ideology to which the latter are significantly committed predisposes them to essentially violent approaches to political change, and therefore justifies the use of repressive violence against them whether by the state or foreign destabilizing sources such as the US State Department or the CIA. Thus, the Marxist ideology is accused by both Left and Right political forces for being anti-democratic, authoritarian and violent and therefore inherently self-destructive.

Certainly the practices of some of the Leftist groups which adhere to Marxism give the impression that the critics are correct in their categorization of Marxism in this way. What, of course, legitimizes this negative perspective of Marxism are instances such as the Pol Pot violent extremities in Cambodia and the anti-democratic character of failed Marxist states such as the Soviet Union and Eastern Europe. Also at the theoretical level, the Marxist insistence that class conflict is the motor of history, that the working classes demand revolution and that the dictatorship of the workers' state is justifiable, give much credence to the rather negative perception of the Marxist ideology as an agent of destructive social change. But when one looks closely at the Caribbean experiences of the Marxist-inspired Left struggles, many of these charges that the perceived problems stem from the intrinsic fallacious nature of the Marxist ideology seem to have missed the source of the problem.

A case has already been made out to show that most of the problems and failures of the Caribbean Left have been due to objective factors, external causes and mistakes in theory and strategy. On the other hand, many of their strengths in organization, popular mobilization, resilience, and political and social impact seems to have been stimulated by the nature of their particular ideological commitment, particularly their commitment to the Marxist goal of egalitarianism, national liberation, self-determination and socialism. Among the objective factors contributing to the failure of the Caribbean Left, as we have seen, are the inertia imposed by the hegemonic stranglehood of global capitalism, the destabilization efforts of international capitalist states, particularly the US, against Leftist states and movements, problematic and vascillating middle class leadership, and the miscalculation by the Caribbean Left about both the nature of the capitalist system and the level of commitment and consciousness of the Caribbean masses. Not only was the strength of the capitalist system underestimated (as the consistent successes of destabilization demonstrated), but the willingness of the Caribbean working people to support Leftist causes was definitely overestimated by the Caribbean Left (as the low votes for and isolation of the Left showed).

In fact, the problem of the Caribbean Left was more a crisis of leadership than of ideology *per se*. Weaknesses in Left leadership stemmed not only from the limitations imposed by their typically middle class orientation, but also from a very narrowly focused and self-serving reading of Marxism – a reading which focused on power and control over people rather than a more democratic involvement of the masses at all levels in the political process. In a word, the Caribbean Left failed to separate Marxism, which could be interpreted as more humanistic, from Stalinism or Leninism, which pretended to be more scientific and flawless. Gordon Lewis was, therefore, correct when he said that Leninism, with its emphasis on iron discipline and clandestine organization, is fundamentally different from the classic Marx, and more relevant to the nineteenth century repressive condition of Czarist Russia than to the condition of the postwar Caribbean or anywhere else for that matter.[36] Lewis further contended that the dogmatism, rigidity, intolerance and contempt for the masses displayed by such leaders as the Coards and their henchmen in Grenada stemmed from this essentially one-sided reading, making Leninism or Stalinism synonymous with Marxism.[37]

But, unlike the critics' position, it does not always follow that Marxist influences inevitably or even generally foster undemocratic or authoritarian practices among Leftist leaders or organizations in the region. The Caribbean region is replete with Leftist leaders and organizations who were influenced to a greater or lesser extent by Marxism, and whose democratic commitments and examples can hardly be challenged, let alone surpassed. Left political organizations such as the PPP under Cheddi Jagan in Guyana, the PNP under Michael Manley in Jamaica, the Alliance Party under Salvador Allende in Chile during the 1970s, the WPJ, the WPA of Guyana and not least, the ULF under Panday in Trinidad during the 1980s, are prime examples of parties with excellent records of commitment to democratic politics at the national level.

The fact that many Left political parties in the region lacked democracy within their own structures – whether in the form of PPP censorship of its radical left-wing in the 1960s; or the PNP's ousting of its own left-wing in the 1940s and again in the 1980s, or the WPJ's dictatorial leadership – does not mean that these anti-democratic tendencies are only confined to Left parties or the result of their Marxist commitments. This within-party authoritarianism affects Rightist parties as well, and sometimes to greater extremes than practiced in Left parties, as in the cases of Eric Williams' domination of the PNM in Trinidad, or Edward Seaga's arbitrary control of the JLP in Jamaica, or Eric Gairy's total monopoly of GULP and politics in Grenada during the 1960s.

A similar argument could be used to dismiss the criticism that the Marxist Left is invariably violent because of their Marxist commitment. In the first place, the records indicate that the Right has been much more violent against the Left than vice versa,[38] while the basic strategy of the Left toward change had been largely non-violent, relying more on demonstrations, strikes and boycotts than on armed confrontation. Of course, there are exceptions to this general rule as in the cases of NUFF's sporadic guerilla activities in Trinidad and the NJM's internal violence in 1983. Rightist violence, on the other hand, ranged from assassinations and gang-like executions on the one extreme to urban guerilla warfare and active involvement in foreign mercenary and military interventions on the other. Rightist parties like the UF in Guyana and the JLP in Jamaica were perhaps the most notorious examples of use of such foreign-supported violent techniques against the Left; while it was a consortium of Rightist parties, including the BLP of Barbados led by Tom Adams, the Freedom Party led by Eugenia Charles of Dominica, and Seaga's JLP in Jamaica that instigated the US military intervention in Grenada in 1983.[39]

To deduce from Marx's notion of class conflict being the motor of history that violent, armed confrontation is the invariable tactic of the Left is indeed very far-fetched, since violent revolutions do not occur all the time throughout history.

This perspective about inevitable Marxist revolutionary violence reflects an extremely narrow and negative reading of Marx. Indeed, one of the strengths (and also the weaknesses) of Marxism is that it is amenable to contextual interpretation, which means that one has to take account of the prevailing local circumstances as a guide to understanding and implementing relevant political practices. At the same time, however, this apparent relative flexibility of Marxism tends to justify any kind of (even contradictory) interpretation which lend legitimacy to those who wish to follow the narrower, negative and violent path. What could be asserted, however, is that the post-colonial Caribbean conditions do not (up to the 1980s, at least) seem to warrant such an emphasis on violent revolutions, which can indeed become self-defeating if not assuredly suicidal.

Fortunately, the narrow negativism of the Caribbean Left in their reading of Marxism did not descend to the extreme hopelessness and despair engendered by such latter day theoretical developments as post-structionalist and deconstructionist debates emanating from Western European Left quarters. This is so despite the Caribbean Left's experiences of continual failures amidst a perennially hostile and inhospitable political and economic universe – that is, despite the compatibility of their experiences with post-structuralist notions of an ever-increasing and permanent domination over the progressive forces by an all pervasive and omnipotent *status quo*.[40] The capacity for residual hope among the Caribbean Left is indeed reflected in the apparent determination and capacity to survive, in their evidential resilience, and in their persistent self-perception as being relevant agents of meaningful change. It is in this sense that a more positive reading of Marxism can help buttress the spirit of guarded optimism that is required for any struggle against immense and overwhelming odds.

9

Conclusion:

The Future of Left

Wing Politics

The Caribbean Left, notwithstanding their nearly half-a-century of active political existence, are today waging a desperate struggle for survival as a significant political force in the region. Yet, despite their fluctuating historical fortunes, they have been able to make some indelible impact on Caribbean politics, particularly with respect to the infinite struggle towards increasing democratization of the Caribbean political process. But, whether the Left will be able eventually to realize their ultimate objectives of fundamental social and political transformations depends heavily on their capacity to transform the usually skeptical working classes, and to utilize to their advantage the typically hostile geo-political environment dominated as it is by US hegemonic interests. The primary issue for the Left, therefore, is how to successfully transform their conditional viability into a relatively more independent capacity for maneuver, if their ultimate and far-reaching objectives are ever to be realized.

Two factors are of considerable importance in helping the Caribbean Left attain relatively independent viability. First, the very perpetuation of steep inequalities under the existing and dominant socio-economic conditions facilitates the generation of a periodic counterculture which fosters the emergence and development of leftist protest movements. Secondly, the strong adherence and commitment of these movements to an ideology advocating fundamental change gives them some kind of spiritual and psychological ammunition against the very inhibiting and conservative essence of the existing political and social order.

Nevertheless, these facilitating factors tend to be weak at this stage in the historical development of the English-speaking Caribbean, relative to the overwhelming forces which operate to the disadvantage of left-wing political developments in the region. The combined impact of an intransigent conservative political culture and a hostile geo-political environment has undoubtedly contributed to obvious disintegrating patterns within Caribbean Leftist movements. Yet, neither of these two opposed tendencies is totally decisive as far as the future development of Caribbean left-wing politics is concerned. A kind of uneven dialectic would seem to be at work in the Caribbean situation to transform the very factors aimed at undermining or destabilizing the Left into factors which tend to facilitate the resilience of the movement as a whole.

A closer look at the Caribbean experience of left-wing political struggles reveals that the discerned disintegrating tendencies affecting the Left represent more specifically an increasing rightward shift of Left forces, with the reformist elements becoming more conservative, while the radical and Marxist-Revolutionary Left becoming more reformist or moderate in their ideological perspectives and practical approaches towards power and change. Disintegration of the Left movements in the Caribbean does not, however, mean the total disappearance of the particular pro-Leftist constituency on which their support, however small, was initially-based. It means most probably the absorption of part of these pro-Left constituencies within what remains of the transformed Left and the dispersal of the rest within Caribbean civil society. The general tendency, however, is toward a rightward shift, in which case radicals become more reformist and moderate than revolutionary, particularly in the wake of both pressures to conform to the exigencies of Westminster electoral participation and prospects of externally-instigated destabilization. At the organizational level, this tendency is borne out by the experiences of the three most prominent Radical Left political organizations in the Caribbean: the ULF of Trinidad becoming absorbed within the more moderate NAR, the WPA of Guyana rethinking its original Marxist ideological position to announce recently that it is no longer Marxist, but Rodneyist and 'democratic republican', and, of course, the NJM of Grenada recombining after the 1983 fiasco to form the relatively more moderate political party, the MBPM.

The Revolutionary Left was not spared these disintegrating trends. The transformation of the PPP in Guyana to a more moderate, pragmatic and pro-western party is a classic example of the increasing disintegration of the Leftist revolutionary orientation which characterized this party from its earliest inception. Also, the spate of resignations from the leadership hierarchy of the WPJ in Jamaica, the subsequent dissolution of its Marxist platform, and the eventual transformation of the party into a relatively benign mass movement (renamed the New Beginning

Movement) parallel the PPP example of the disintegration of the Revolutionary Left in the region.

Disunity tends to be rather endemic among Left political organizations in the Caribbean, often leading to the deliberate refusal to develop any kind of communication between particular Left groups. Even when this problem is recognized and efforts are made to engage in constructive collaborative relationships, the result is usually a kind of 'dialogue of the deaf' between groups. This was particularly the case between movements across ideological boundaries such as between revolutionaries and radicals than, say, among different revolutionary Marxist groups. The Guyana examples of efforts between the PPP and WPA, between elements within the WPA and the WPVP, and between the PNC and the PPP, to develop such collaborative relationships have all collapsed because of ideologically-based disparties. For similar reasons, the prospects of the PCD ever getting beyond sporadic protest activities against the commonly targeted PNC regime proved to be illusory.

The political environment in the English-speaking Caribbean continually pressures left-wing political organizations and movements toward disunity and polarization. The demands of electoral competition, internal repression, threats of destabilization, and the absorptive capacity of international capitalism combined to produce the observed rightward shift of the Caribbean Left.

Although capitalism has had tremendous negative consequences for the Caribbean working classes – through impoverishment, exploitation, and violent subordination – there, nevertheless, seems to have been something akin to an absorptive capacity on the part of capitalist ideology, particularly in its international ramifications, which pulls even the disadvantaged working classes along its apparently irresistible path. What, then, constitutes this pull effect? The full answer to this important question remains a difficult puzzle. But there are some clues in the historical development of the relationship between international capital and the Caribbean working classes which need to be closely examined. Perhaps the most noticeable of these clues is the penchant for consumerism on the part of the Caribbean masses, particularly for foreign products. No doubt this foreign consumption orientation reflects a desire to escape from the very impoverished conditions which capitalism imposed on the peripheral working classes in the first place.

A second pull effect of capitalism is that the peripheral working classes, in their consistent quest to escape economic hardship, seek upward mobility within the very stratified and hierarchical capitalist system characteristic of Caribbean states. Already it has been argued, particularly in relation to developed capitalist states such as the United States, that the working classes' quest for upward mobility diffuses tendencies towards leftist agitation, and prevents or postpones the development of a meaningful leftist or socialist agenda. In the Caribbean context, the upsurge in the 1980s of an underground or 'parallel' market economy among typically working class elements anxious to shift into commercial merchandizing activities throughout the region, is a strong example of this diffusing quest for both upward mobility and escape from economic hardship, which at the same time buttresses the international capitalist classes.

Thirdly, capitalism holds the adherence of large sections of the Caribbean working classes by its promises of economic and material rewards to adherents, and threats of failure, hardships, or further immiseration to opponents. Expectations of becoming wealthy through business pursuits and property acquisitions have all been positive influences of capitalism on the collective consciousness of the Caribbean masses. The fact, however, that the capitalist reward structure is usually skewed in favour of the economically and politically dominant classes increases the predilections and pressures towards upward mobility within the system. In the Caribbean context, pressures towards conformity to the dominant capitalist ideological patterns are reinforced by: (a) widespread acceptance by Caribbean states of IMF conditionalities which invariably mandate the abandonment of socialist or Leftist projects in preference for privatization, free-market and anti-labour policies; (b) the ready availability of foreign capitalist financing for the more moderate or rightist political parties in Caribbean elections; and (c) the willingness of foreign capitalist powers to destabilize thriving alternatives or leftist programmes and movements. To a large extent, therefore, fear of defeat, destabilization, destitution and death characterizes the nature of popular adherence to the prevailing capitalist ideology in peripheral capitalist societies including the Caribbean. For these reasons, the co-optation or absorption of the Caribbean labour leadership by the dominant pull of capitalism becomes a foregone conclusion.

Above all, working class absorption within the capitalist hierarchy is facilitated by the general failure of the educational and consciousness raising functions of the more radicalized sections of the Caribbean middle classes. This failure in turn helps to consolidate the hegemony of the more liberalist and conservative section of the middle classes through their scrupulous use of the established ideological institutions – particularly churches and public schools – with significant advantages accruing to this section in terms of extended influence in the economic, political, and cultural spheres, thereby cementing their stranglehold over the Caribbean masses and subordinate classes. The Caribbean Left concentrated most of their resources and energy on the pursuit of state power to the relative neglect of hegemonic struggles to persuade and educate the Caribbean masses the legitimacy and acceptance of socialist and other leftist objectives.

Unification at the organizational level – i.e., a coalition of various existing Left political organizations – would seem to be much more feasible in the Caribbean context than to wait for the spontaneous moment when the working and subordinate classes will develop sufficient class consciousness to enable a more viable class unity. Given the weakness of class forces and the divisions among them in the Caribbean, the strategy based on spontaneous class unification outside of the existing political organizational framework would seem to be either an indulgence in wishful thinking, or a calculated tactic to avoid the possible sharing of power positions or resources. This expectation of spontaneous class unity was used, for instance, by the PNC as a means of rejecting the PPP's overtures toward the creation of a National Front government in the interest of furthering Left unity, anti-imperialism, and socialist development. The PNC had claimed that the National Front proposal represented unification only at the top, and not among the working classes themselves.

The question of the organization versus the spontaneous resolution of the unity problem facing the Caribbean Left is also related to the issue of the choice between political and militaristic or violent approaches to the resolution of problematic social issues. The PNC's rejection of a political solution to the Guyana problem, as encapsuled in the PPP's National Front proposals which were also supported by the WPA, was in effect a logical extension of its preference for the more coercive and militarized approach to cementing internal political and social conflicts. Similarly, the impatience displayed by the Coardist faction in dealing with Maurice Bishop at a sustained political level obviously resulted from its capability for imposing a military solution despite the usually disastrous political and social consequences of this approach. This penchant for a militaristic approach was also witnessed at the broader hemispheric or international level in the Reagan policy toward Central America, and his Caribbean Basin Initiative (CBI), with equally disastrous consequences.

The preference for the more coercive and militaristic approach to conflict resolution on the part of a significant section of the Caribbean and hemispheric political leadership has serious negative implications for development of Caribbean democracy itself. Democracy, in particular, would appear to be the greatest political casualty of the coercive-militaristic approach, as was witnessed during the 1980s in the widespread suppression of political dissent and genuine pluralism in the case of Grenada under the almost paranoid NJM, the deliberate distortion of, including military intervention in, the electoral process in the Guyana case, substituting considerations of national security for the promised extension in political participation as in the case of the FSLN in Nicaragua, and the displacement of prospective civilian rule by military rule as in the cases of Honduras and El Salvador in Central America. Above all these distortions of the democratic process in the region were invariably rationalized in terms of the threat of hostile forces, whether externally perceived as in the instance of US imperialism against the NJM of Grenada and the FSLN of Nicaragua, or internally generated as in the case of opposition political movements in Guyana, Honduras and El Salvador during the 1970s and 1980s.

Externally engineered destabilization, particularly from the dominant capitalist powers led by the United States, is always a factor to be reckoned with by Caribbean Leftist States and political movements which challenge the existing political and international *status quo*. In practical effect, such destabilization represented more an attempt to fight out the East-West (cold war) conflict on Caribbean soil, than to foster the development of Caribbean democracy and the stability of Caribbean political systems. For in the name of anti-communism, US-sponsored destabilization undermined regional democracies in Guyana under Jagan between 1953 and 1964, and Jamaica under Manley between 1972 and 1980, while it championed brutal dictatorships such as those of the Duvaliers in Haiti and Pinochet in Chile.

Certain factors, however, tend to catapult destabilization maneuvers into the realm of facilitating conditions for left-wing politics. These facilitating conditions derive from the very complex nature of class forces and relations in the Caribbean, and how these are played out in the equally complex process of change at both domestic and international levels of operation. Among these critical factors are the increasing class inequalities generated by the capitalist-dominated economic system, and political inequalities inherent in the typically neo-colonialist political system in the English-speaking Caribbean. These inequalities create the under-classes and counter-cultures from whence protests movements and political dissent emerge. In addition, the dependency relationship which characterizes Caribbean states *vis-à-vis* the dominant metropolitan capitalist centres, tends to radicalize the politically dominant middle classes in significant sections of peripheral states into developing sentiments and commitments toward anti-colonial nationalism or anti-imperialism. Thus, this radicalization process in the Caribbean significantly links the destinies of both the subordinate classes and crucial sections of the dominant (middle) classes.

The destabilization process tends also to further the complexities of the class situation through its instigation of sectional divisiveness and general political instability. In this regard, ethnic, racial and religious divisions cut across class forces as active agents in the determination of political behaviour and change. This intertwining of ethnic and religious elements in basic class relations further complicates the analysis of the political process in the Caribbean, and points to the need for the development of more rigorous theoretical insights into these complex processes. The cultural pluralist theories which purport to address specifically these ethnic and culturally related tendencies in the Caribbean are definitely devoid of the more fundamental economically-related tendencies underlying these processes. In turn, the orthodox Marxist analysis espoused by a significant section of Caribbean Leftism, seriously lacks insights into non-class and culturally-related elements in the determination of significant trends in Caribbean and Third World processes. Orthodox Marxist analysis, despite its potential for comprehensiveness and fundamental insight into specific social problems, has proved to be largely inadequate in its grasp of the complexities of the Caribbean conditions. To explain, for example, the intrinsic radicalism of specific elements of the hegemonic middle classes, as well as the contrasting conservatism of the Caribbean masses and subordinate classes, and other factors beyond the class issue, Marxist analysis itself will have to be significantly extended or even radically revised. Further, the consistent evidence of serious ethnic political conflicts in the Caribbean makes the lack of a Marxist theory of ethnic relations a serious omission in the spectrum of Marxist social science and the development of Marxist theory and analysis as a whole.

The failure of the Caribbean Left to develop a more adequate theory of race-class relations is due mainly to either their orthodox interpretation of Marxist theory, or their usually Utopian vision of socialism as being an absolutely egalitarian and peaceful universe where class and racial differences are finally resolved. This perceptual distortion is further compounded by their neglect to consult theoretical developments on the race-class problematic in Caribbean social science. A more adequate Marxist theory of race-class relations which can guide a more constructive or transformative political practice would provide answers to the following important questions: (a) What forces substitute as major agencies of change where, as in the Caribbean context, class forces are weak, ill-defined and fragmented? (b) How best to avoid the degeneration of class conflict into ethnic or racial and fratricidal violence in multi-racial societies like the major Caribbean societies? and (c) What constitutes the best state form for multi-racial Caribbean societies interested in socialist (egalitarian) transformations? In these respects, therefore, much thought must be given to displacing the earlier vanguardist notions of struggle which give privileged position exclusively to the working classes, with a focus on alliance politics and mass mobilization strategies, understanding the relationship between conflict, violence and cooperation so as to glean insights into conflict resolution, and modification or transformation of existing state forms to institutionalize the procedures for the reduction or containment of ethnic tensions or fratricidal conflicts – more probably a state involving a more decentralized democratic process of political participation and decision making which facilitates the hegemonic control by multi-racial mass-based political alliances.

Admittedly, there are serious problems in reconciling orthodox Marxist theory to the peculiarities of the Caribbean conditions. To challenge Marxism to undertake this reconciling task is an important issue on the current agenda of Left political movements (particularly the Radical Left) in the region. But for such a reconciliation to be adequate, it is necessary, first, to revise the orthodox Marxist assumptions about class structures and behaviour patterns which are more pertinent to the more industrialized capitalist contexts, and within this reformulation to specify the inevitable interconnection between class and ethnic-cultural divisions peculiar to the Caribbean and other Third World conditions. Secondly, within this more flexible class perspective, it is necessary to stress that the crucial labour processes are inclusive of a wider range of 'producers' beyond the industrial 'proletariat' in the strict Marxist explanation. In the Caribbean context, these productive classes embrace also aspects of the dominant classes, such as the self-employed artisans and service workers as well as the semi-peasant and casual workers on sugar plantations. Thirdly, a relevant social theory of political change and social transformation should recognize significantly the progressive and revolutionary potentialities of elements within the dominant middle classes, particularly the centrality of the role of significant sections of the intellectuals and professionals in initiating and influencing the process and directions of change in the Caribbean and Third World contexts.

A fourth factor of importance to the development of Marxist theory relevant to the Caribbean and the Third World relates to the relative degree of importance given to the different, but equally crucial, goals of the Left political movements. The priority given to the immediate realization of socialist transformation as the beginning of a transition stage toward the ultimate classless egalitarian society, for instance, would seem to be idealistic in the Caribbean context, given the continuing hostility of the geo-political environment despite the decline of the East-West ideological conflict situation, as well as the limited inclusiveness of the traditional Westminster type political culture. A revision of priorities to focus on: (a) deepening the process of democratization both within and beyond the party; (b) the democratic consolidation of political power by Leftist incumbents; and (c) the development of both the size, and the level of consciousness of the working classes, is therefore needed if Marxist theory is to be more relevant to the Caribbean conditions.

Another closely-related aspect of Marxist theory which comes under scrutiny in relation to the Caribbean experience relates to the problematic of the necessary unity of theory and practice. Marx's suggestion, for example, that such unity becomes possible only to the extent that theory becomes radical, should, in light of the Caribbean and Third World experiences, be extended to include the element of class relations in the equation. In the Caribbean circumstances the dominance of the typically factious and vacillating middle classes remains an obstacle to the successful bridge between radical theory and working class political practices. It would seem, therefore, that it is only to the extent that the Caribbean working classes gain control of political power that the possibility exists for any radical theory to successfully interact with and possibly determine the process of social transformation.

Several factors have already been identified as responsible for preventing the working and subordinate classes from gaining greater control of political power, the most obvious examples being the hegemonic control by the liberalist middle classes and the lack of organic leadership stemming from the working classes themselves. In addition, the working classes have not yet been sufficiently radicalized to demand any privileged right or access to Leftist leadership, while, ultimately, these disadvantaged classes have for too long been bogged down at subsistence levels and, therefore, in a consuming quest for economic survival. Nor yet is this quest for economic survival sufficiently translatable into trade union consciousness, let alone political consciousness, since only a relatively small proportion of the Caribbean working classes is unionized or directly involved in trade union activities.

The persistent failure of the Caribbean working classes to control political power, or the contradictions inherent in middle class governments purportedly operating in the interest of the working classes, gives rise to serious questions about the capability of the Caribbean Left to influence the course of political and social change. Given the serious disadvantages placed in the way of these movements, the prospects for the success of alternative political development will naturally depend on more self-conscious strategies which take into consideration the concrete conditions within Caribbean social formations. Above all, strategies toward the mobilization of the Caribbean masses are more likely to succeed if they are relatively flexible in their pursuit of class and political alliances, and continually maintain the closest links with the masses and grass-roots population. In ethnic plural societies in particular such strategies should be as far as possible non-violent so as to minimize the prospects of self-destructive ethnic communal violence. Secondly, success in this direction will further depend on the level of democracy which operates within the political organization or movement itself, since intra-party democracy is essential for the maintenance and development of democracy at the national level, as well.

The current situation in which the Caribbean Left is placed, *vis-à-vis* the particular class and ideological control of the political process, and *vis-à-vis* the more conservative contending political organizations, could well be described as that of pragmatic retreat. The progress which the Left has made particularly during the 1970s, not only in mobilizing or sensitizing larger masses of Caribbean people toward some variety of socialism or radical socio-economic changes, but also in controlling political power among a larger contingent of Caribbean states than at any previous moment in Caribbean political history, seems, within recent times to have been stymied by a combination of continual conflicts and fragmentation, as well as external anti-Left aggression and destabilization. However, these experiences have forced the Left to rethink many of their strategies and alliance patterns in the interest of their future viability and effectiveness. In the final analysis, the viability of the Caribbean Left is rooted in the ever-increasing constituency of a largely dissatisfied population within Caribbean and Third World political systems.

The viability of the Left in Caribbean and Third World contexts is of crucial importance to the long-standing Leftist project of the realization of socialist transformation under conditions of economic backwardness. Much depends on how socialism itself is perceived, whether as the struggle for economic equality and justice and elevation of the working classes to positions of political leadership at both party and state levels, or as the demonstrably failed practices among those states that purport to be bastions of socialism such as what was once the USSR, and its Eastern European counterparts. Socialism in the Caribbean cannot strictly follow the lines of these already-tried but flawed established systems, but must be based on the specific demands of the particular Caribbean conditions. It is the conditions, however, which are largely undetermined given the relative lack of appropriate research and theory which could guide successful political practices in these parts.

What, then, is the possible future of the Caribbean Left? The alternatives that seem to face these beleaguered Leftist forces involve varying levels of probabilities as follows: (a) the risk of total annihilation by engaging in violent armed conflict against overwhelming odds, a course of action that failed in the Latin American context; (b) a process of self-liquidation by acknowledging defeat and the impossibility of realizing egalitarian socialism in the teeth of a more powerful capitalist system; (c) pursuing the convergence thesis by recognizing the need for political compromises with forces inimical to working class interests; or (d) acknowledging the possibility of the pendulum effect in the alternating historical development of the Right-Left struggles for dominance throughout the twentieth century, in which case the expectation is that the pendulum might swing again in favour of the Left during the early stages of the twenty-first century. That interest in leftist struggles will re-emerge to prominence in the future is based on our assessment that the social problems – dispossession, dictatorship, and expectations of political and economic development – which precipitated the emergence and development of Leftist ideologies in the first place, have not disappeared, and are most likely to increase over time, particularly in the Third World, given the already observed negative consequences of structural adjustment policies influenced by liberalist-capitalist ideologies.

What then is required under the circumstances, if left-wing politics should survive or develop in a highly disadvantageous context? Firstly, it appears that the stage of the struggle for Left political efficacy is necessarily at the more theoretical or ideological level, particularly in this phase of retreat affecting the future development of leftist politics in these parts. It means, in short, a period of soul-searching and self-analysis even to the extent of rethinking their strategies and tactics, after a careful analysis of the geo-political context. Here both education and research play a crucial role, as indispensable tools in the struggle for the realization of necessary changes in Caribbean systems as a whole. The costliness to the Left of the struggle for power would seem to have relegated the movement to the realm of educational and ideological struggle where the use of propaganda weapons become the main arsenals in the hegemonic quest. It is within this context that the main thrust of the Caribbean Left should be the struggle for an agenda focusing on democratic openings to get their demands and aspirations placed on the mainstream political platforms, that is, to institute systematic pressures to influence public policy. This focus is ultimately a quest toward the greater or increasing legitimation of the Left in the consciousness of the Caribbean masses.

The chances of Left successes are enhanced to the extent that the struggle for change is defined more in terms of enhancing or deepening the democratic content of the Caribbean political processes than in terms of the immediate realization of the more statist goals in the name of socialism. Given greater democracy which eliminates official discrimination against left-wing participation in the political process, the Left will thereby have an equal opportunity to compete for the development of the political consciousness of the masses, and so be able to make some impact toward at least the ideological neutralization if not the complete conquest of the usually inhospitable Caribbean political culture.

Finally, the Caribbean Left should try to come to grips more closely with the significance and relevance of capitalism in the developmental process in these parts. Earlier Leftist preoccupation with what has been regarded as either the non-capitalist path to socialism, or the inevitability of the dependency-underdevelopment syndrome would appear to have underestimated the extent of capitalist penetration and its developmental and transformative potential in the region. At the very least, it should be recognized that capitalism has so far demonstrated its capacity to manage, if not totally resolve, its own self-generated crises, and so postpone if not totally prevent its own demise. Socialism, therefore, must be viewed as essentially an intrinsic critique of existing capitalism and the manifestation of capitalism's transformative potential, rather than an idealized theoretical construct, if the Left is to be able to play a meaningful role in its eventual realization.

Notes

Chapter 1

1. The only significant attempt within recent times to address this issue systematically in the context of the English-speaking Caribbean is Trevor Munroe's, *Jamaican Politics: a Marxist Perspective in Transition* (Kingston: Heineman/Lynn Reinner 1990). However, Munroe's analysis is confined to the Jamaican as opposed to the wider Caribbean experience.

2. See C.Y. Thomas, *Dependence and Transformation* (New York: Monthly Review Press 1974); Richard Jacobs and Ian Jacobs, *Grenada: the Route to Revolution* (Havana: Casa de Las Americas 1980); George Beckford and Michael Witter, *Small Garden Bitter Weed: Struggle and Change in Jamaica* (London: Zed Press 1980); Fitzroy Ambursley and Robin Cohen (eds.), *Crisis in the Caribbean* (New York: Monthly Review Press 1983).

3. See C.L.R. James, *Party Politics in the West Indies* (Port of Spain: Vedic Enterprises Ltd., 1962); Frantz Fanon, *The Wretched of the Earth* (Middlesex: Penguin 1963); Brian Meeks, *Caribbean Revolutions and Revolutionary Theory* (London: Macmillan 1993).

4. Soviet or Cuban military and financial aid to the English-speaking Caribbean was either negligible or non-existent during the 1970s and 1980s. See United States State Department, *Warsaw Pact Economic Aid Program in Non-Communist LDCs: Holding Their Own in 1986* (Department of State Publication 9345, Bureau of Intelligence and Research, August 1988); also, Timothy P. Wickham-Crowley, *Guerillas and Revolution in Latin America* (New Jersey: Princeton University Press 1992), 86, 90; NACLA, "Soviet collapse not so relevant", *Report on the Americas* 35, no. 5 (May 1992): 15.

5. Michael Manley, *Jamaica: Struggle in the Periphery* (London: Writers and Readers 1982); *Caribbean Dialogue* 2, nos. 5 & 6 (June 1976): 2-6, 14.

6. See Maurice Bishop, "In Nobody's Backyard", in *Maurice Bishop Speaks: the Grenada Revolution 1979-1983* edited by Steve Clark, (New York: Pathfinder Press 1983), 26-31.

7. This concept of 'impermissible world context' represents a slight modification of Brian Meeks' adaptation of Farhi's concept of the 'permissive world context' to the explanation of Caribbean revolutions, in that our conceptualization discerns a generally constant hostility to the Left coming from Western hegemonic quarters while at specific historical times this

hostility might be disguised, but hardly eliminated sufficiently to spell an open or permissive international environment; See Brian Meeks, *Caribbean Revolutions and Revolutionary Theory*; also Faridah Farhi, "State disintegration and urban-based revolutionary crisis: a comparative analysis of Iran and Nicaragua", *Comparative Political Studies* 21, no. 2 (July 1988).

8. Two such examples are the National United Freedom Fighters (NUFF) in Trinidad and Tobago, and the Working People's Vanguard Party (WPVP) in Guyana during the 1970s.

9. Author's interview with Cheddi Jagan, leader of the PPP, in 1989; see also, WPA *Manifesto: Justice, Opportunity, Security for a Multiracial Guyana* (Georgetown: Guyana National Newspapers Ltd., nd.,), 1; "There are many roads to Socialism – Dr Jagan", *Starbroek News*, 3 March 1990, 11, and 14 April 1990, 9.

10. Immanuel Wallerstein, *The Capitalist World Economy* (Cambridge: Cambridge University Press 1979); Andre Gunder Frank, *Latin America: Underdevelopment or Revolution* (New York: Monthly Review Press 1970); Samir Amin, *Unequal Development* (New York: Monthly Review Press 1976); George Beckford, *Persistent Poverty* (London: Oxford University Press 1972).

11. Samir Amin, *Empire of Chaos* (New York: Monthly Review Press 1992), 8.

12. Samir Amin, *Delinking: Towards a Polycentric World* (London: Zed Press 1985), viii.

13. Andre Gunder Frank and Maria Fuentes, "Civil democracy, social movements in recent world history", in *Transforming the Revolution: Social Movements in the World System* edited by Samir Amin et. al., (New York: Monthly Review Press 1990), 156.

14. See Christopher Clapham, *Third World Politics: an Introduction* (London: Croom Helm 1985), 168; also P. Chabal, *Amilcar Cabral: Revolutionary Leadership and People's War* (Cambridge: Cambridge University Press 1983), 24-25, 175-176.

15. Walter Rodney, *Groundings with my Brothers* (London: Bogle L'Ouverture 1969).

16. cf. Eric Ohlin Wright, *Classes* (London: Verso Press 1987).

17. C.L.R. James, *Party Politics in the West Indies*; Gordon K. Lewis, *The Growth of the Modern West Indies* (London: MacGibbon and Kee 1968); Carl Stone, *Democracy and Clientelism in Jamaica* (New Jersey: Transaction Books 1980); Paget Henry, "Political accumulation and authoritarianism in the Caribbean: the case of Antigua", *Social and Economic Studies* 40, no. 1 (March 1991).

18. See Carl Stone, *Democracy and Clientelism in Jamaica*; and Percy Hintzen, *The Cost of Regime Survival* (Cambridge: Cambridge University Press 1989).

19. C.L.R. James, *Party Politics in the West Indies*; Frantz Fanon, *The Wretched of the Earth*.

20. A good example of this intellectualizing trend was the New World Group which emerged in the English-speaking Caribbean during the 1960s. This group, initiated by several leading Caribbean intellectuals, including Lloyd Best, Norman Girvan, and George Beckford, produced several discussion periodicals, such as *New World Quarterly*, *New World Fortnightly* (Guyana), and *New World Weekly* (Guyana), and various special issues celebrating the independence of the ex-British colonies in the Caribbean.

21. See Lloyd Best, "Whither New World", *New World Quarterly* 4, no. 1(1968); and Norman Girvan, "Chairman's report

on New World Group, Jamaica, for period August 1967 to September 1968",
New World Quarterly, 4, no. 3 (1968).

22. See Gordon K. Lewis, "Grenada 1983:
The lessons for the Caribbean Left",
paper presented at the Conference on
the Grenada Revolution, 1979-1983,
University of the West Indies, St
Augustine, Trinidad, 24-25 May 1984.

23. Trevor Munroe, *Jamaican Politics*.

24. See Walter Rodney, *A History of the
Guyanese Working People* (Baltimore:
Johns Hopkins University Press 1981);
John G. Taylor, *From Modernization to
Modes of Production* (London: Macmil-
lan 1979).

25. See Robert Gilpin, *The Political Economy
of International Relations* (New Jersey:
Princeton University Press 1987), 65-
92; Robert O. Keohane, "The theory of
hegemonic stability and change in international economic regimes, 1967-
1977", in *Change in the International System* edited by Ole Holsti, et. al., (Boulder: Westview Press 1980); also,
Nicholas Abercrombie, et. al., *The
Dominant Ideology Thesis* (London: Allen
and Unwin 1980).

26. The relevant political economy litera-
ture on the Caribbean include:
George Beckford, *Persistent Poverty*; Nor-
man Girvan, *Foreign Capital and Eco-
nomic Underdevelopment in Jamaica*
(Mona: ISER 1971); also C.Y. Thomas,
*The Poor and the Powerless: Economic Policy
and Change in the Caribbean* (New York:
Monthly Review Press 1988); Jay Man-
dle, *Patterns of Caribbean Development: An
Interpretive Essay on Economic Change*
(New York: Gordon and Breach
Science Publishers 1982).

27. See Ronald H. Chilcote, and Dale L.
Johnson (eds.), *Theories of Development:
Mode of Production or Dependency* (Bev-
erly Hills: Sage Publications 1983).

28. Cheryl Payer, *The Debt Trap: The International Monetary Fund and the Third World*
(New York: Monthly Review Press 1974).

29. Arthur MacEwan, *Debt and Disorder:
International Economic Instability and US
Imperial Decline* (New York: Monthly
Review Press 1990); Cathy McAffee,
*Storm Signals: Structural Adjustment and
Development Alternatives in the Caribbean*
(Boston: South End Press 1991).

30. Antonio Gramsci, *Selections from the
Prison Notebooks* (New York: International Publishers 1978).

31. Robert O. Keohane, *After Hegemony,
Cooperation and Discord in the World
Economy* (Princeton: Princeton
University Press 1984), 44.

32. Keohane, *After Hegemony*, 45.

33. Gramsci, *Prison Notebooks*, 6, 7ff.

34. See Robert Bocock, *Hegemony*
(Sussex: Tavistock Publications 1986),
78, 106.

35. Antonio Gramsci, *Prison Notebooks*,
210, 211.

36. William I. Robinson, *A Faustian Bargain*
(Boulder: Westview 1992).

37. Gramsci, *Prison Notebooks*, 275-276:
a similar tautology is noticeable in
Unger's suggestion that one of the
reasons for the recurrence of alternative institutional schemes is that "no
set of institutional practices or con-
ceptions of social life ever wins a
complete victory"; see Roberto
Mangabeira Unger, *False Necessity:
an Anti-necessitarian Theory in the Service
of Radical Democracy* (Cambridge:
Cambridge University Press 1987),
221; see also Brian Meeks, *Caribbean
Revolutions*, 38.

38. W G Runciman, "The 'triumph' of capitalism as a topic in the theory of social selection", *New Left Review* no. 21
(March-April 1995), 34; also Robert
Bocock, *Hegemony*, 121.

39. Martin Staniland, *What is Political Economy?* (New Haven: Yale Universiy Press 1985)160.

40. See Jenny Pearce, *Under The Eagle: US Intervention in Central America and the Caribbean* (Boston: South End Press 1981), 111.

Chapter 2

1. Government of Great Britain, Colonial Office, *West India Royal Commission (The Moyne Report)*, Cmnd. 6607 (London: HMSO 1945), 57, 198.

2. Morley Ayearst, *The British West Indies: The Search for Self Government* (New York: New York University Press 1960), 36.

3. Ayearst, *The British West Indies*, 18.

4. See George Beckford, *Persistent Poverty* (London: Oxford University Press 1972); Jay Mandle, *Patterns of Caribbean Development: an Interpretative Essay on Economic Change* (New York: Gordon and Breach Science Publishers 1982); Lloyd Best, "Outline of a model of pure plantation economy", *Social and Economic Studies* September (1968).

5. George Beckford, *Persistent Poverty*; Brian L. Moore, *Race, Power and Social Segmentation in Colonial Society: Guyana After Slavery, 1838-1891* (New York: Gordon and Breach Science Publishers 1987); Ken Post, *Arise Ye Starvelings* (The Hague: Martinus Nijhoff 1978).

6. See John G. Taylor, *From Modernization to Modes of Production: a Critique of Sociologies of Development and Underdevelopment* (New York: Macmillan 1979).

7. See Walter Rodney, *A History of the Guyanese Working People* (Baltimore: Johns Hopkins University Press 1981); Sydney Mintz, "The question of Caribbean peasantries: a comment", *Caribbean Studies* 1, no. 3 (1961).

8. See Jay Mandel, *Patterns of Caribbean Development*, 43.

9. John G. Taylor, *From Modernization*, pp. 79, 80, 137, 197 and passim.

10. C.L.R. James, *Party Politics in the West Indies* (Port of Spain: Vedic Enterprises 1962); Gordon K. Lewis, *The Growth of the Modern West Indies* (New York: Monthly Review Press 1968).

11. A consensus seems to have emerged that these bodies form the main constituencies of the Caribbean working classes. See Walter Rodney, *A History of the Guyanese Working People*; C.Y. Thomas, *The Poor and the Powerless: Economic Policy and Change in the Caribbean* (New York: Monthly Review Press 1988); George Beckford and Michael Witter, *Small Garden Bitter Weed* (London: Zed Press 1980).

12. See Odida Quamina, *Mine Workers of Guyana: the Making of a Working Class* (London: Humanities Press 1981); Ivar Oxaal, *Report of the Demba Panel of Consultants on Community Attitudes and Their Effect on Industrial Relations* (Georgetown, 1966), 7ff.

13. See R.T. Smith, *British Guiana* (London: Oxford University Press 1962); Jay Mandel, *Patterns of Caribbean Development*; Manning Marable, *African and Caribbean Politics* (Verso Press 1987), 3.

14. See Anita M. Waters, *Race, Class and Political Symbols: Rastafari and Reggae in Jamaican Politics* (New Brunswick: Transaction Books 1989).

15. Franklyn W. Knight, *The Caribbean* (New York: Oxford University Press 1970), 143.

16. For a more comprehensive overview of Chinese immigration to Guyana, see Brian Moore, *Race, Power and Social Segmentation in Colonial Society*, 161-188.

17. For additional statistics on Portugese immigration to Guyana, see Walter

Rodney, A History of the Guyanese Working People, 33.

18. Brian Moore, Race, Power and Social Segmentation, 140 ff.

19. International Commission of Jurists, Report of the British Guiana Commission of Inquiry: Racial Problems in the Public Service (Geneva, 1965).

20. C.Y. Thomas, "State capitalism in Guyana: an assessment of Burnham's co-operative republic", in Crisis in the Caribbean edited by Fitzroy Ambursley and Robin Cohen (New York: Monthly Review Press 1983).

21. A survey of various issues of Caricom Perspectives for 1987, for example, reveals this fact.

22. C.L.R. James, Party Politics in the West Indies; Frantz Fanon, The Wretched of the Earth (Middlesex: Penguin 1963).

23. See Fitzroy Ambursley and Robin Cohen, Crisis in the Caribbean, 3.

24. C.L.R. James, Party Politics in the West Indies; Gordon K. Lewis, The Growth of the Modern West Indies.

25. cf. H.A. Lutchman, "Patronage in colonial society", Caribbean Quarterly 16, no. 2 (1970).

26. See C.Y. Thomas, "Perspectives on the future of the state in the Caribbean" (mimeo), Department of Economics, University of the West Indies, Mona, May, 1985.

27. See Richard Jacobs and Ian Jacobs, Grenada: the Route to Revolution (Havana: Casa de Las Americas 1980); also, Dessima Williams, "Grenada: from parliamentary rule to people's power", in Democracy in the Caribbean edited by Carlene Edie (Westport: Praeger 1994), 101.

28. See "Guyana: The faces behind the masks", Covert Action Information Bulletin no. 10 (August-September 1980): 21-24.

29. Carl Stone, Democracy and Clientelism in Jamaica (New Brunswick: Transaction Books 1980); Christopher Clapham, Third World Politics (London: Croom Helms 1985), 54-59.

30. See The Moyne Report, 378, 379 ff.

31. The Moyne Report, 381, 382.

32. See Ashton Chase, 133 Days Toward Freedom (Georgetown: New Guyana Company Ltd., 1954).

33. Janet Jagan, Army Intervention in the 1973 Elections in Guyana (Georgetown: New Guyana Company Ltd., 1973).

34. See "U.S. invasion of Grenada", Intercontinental Press 21, no. 22 (14 November 1983); Ellen Ray and Bill Schaap, "Massive destabilization in Jamaica: 1976 with a twist", Covert Action Information Bulletin no.10 (August-September 1980): 7-17; "Michael Manley under attack again", Covert Action Information Bulletin no. 7 (December 1979-January, 1980): 4-12.

35. Government of Trinidad and Tobago, Report of the Commission of Inquiry into Subversive Activities in Trinidad and Tobago, House Paper no. 2 (Port-of-Spain: Government Printer 1965).

36. Government of Trinidad and Tobago, "Industrial Stabilization Act 1965", Laws of Trinidad and Tobago, Act no. 8 (Port-of-Spain: Government Printer 1965).

37. Government of Great Britain, West India Royal Commission Report (The Moyne Report), 363.

38. The contest between the Manpower Citizens Association (MPCA) and the Guyana Agricultural and General Workers Union (GAWU) for recognition in the sugar industry in Guyana during the 1960s and 1970s is a case in point.

39. See Janet Jagan, Army Intervention; Lord Avebury, Something to Remember (Lon-

don, 1980); America's Watch, *Political Freedom in Guyana* (London, 1985); also PPP Statement (Press Release), 9 December 1985.

40. See Dessima Williams, "Grenada: from parliamentary rule to people's power", in *Democracy in the Caribbean* edited by Carlene Edie, 100-102.

41. For a useful survey of political violence in the Caribbean, see Neville Duncan, "Political violence in the Caribbean", in *Strategy and Security in the Caribbean* edited by Ivelaw Griffith (New York: Praeger 1991).

42. Michael Manley, *Jamaica: Struggle in the Periphery* (London: Writers and Readers 1982).

43. See Cheddi Jagan, *The West on Trial* (Berlin: Seven Seas Books 1972).

44. Richard Barnet, *Intervention and Revolution: America's Confrontation with Insurgent Movements Around the World* (New York: Meridian Books 1972), 181-211.

45. See Bob Woodward, *Veil: The Secret Wars of the CIA, 1982-1987* (New York: Pocket Books 1987), 322-337; also, "U.S. invades Grenada . . . Nicaragua next?", *Covert Action Information Bulletin* no. 20 (Winter 1984).

46. See Andrew Zimbalist and John Weeks, *Panama at the Crossroads* (Berkeley: University of California Press 1991), 136-155.

47. See Chris Searle, *Grenada: the Struggle Against Destabilization* (London: Writers and Readers 1983), 35 ff.

48. See Ken I. Boodhoo, "Suriname's military in control", *Caribbean Contact* (May/June 1990): 5.

49. About the seriousness of the drug problem in the wider Caribbean area, see Ivelaw Griffith (ed.), *Security and Strategy in the Caribbean*, 13-16.

50. See Cathy McAffee, *Storm Signals: Structural Adjustment and Development Al-*

ternatives in the Caribbean (Boston: South End Press 1991).

51. McAffee, *Storm Signals*, 26, 152, 154.

52. McAffee, *Storm Signals*, 37.

53. Levels of unemployment in the Caribbean during the 1980s ranged from 12 percent in Trinidad and Tobago, to 25 percent in Jamaica, 33 percent in Guyana, and between 40 and 50 percent in St Lucia. Jenny Pearce, *Under the Eagle: US Intervention in Central America and the Caribbean* (Boston: South End Press 1982), x, xi.

54. See, for example, "Dispute at Aroima" and "GAWU recognized after a year of struggle at CRM", *Combat*, Issue No. 2, 1992, p. 4.

Chapter 3

1. Antonio Gramsci, *Selections from the Prison Notebooks* (New York: International Publishers 1978), 327.

2. See Walter Rodney, *A History of the Guyanese Working People* (Baltimore: Johns Hopkins University Press 1981), 43.

3. Rodney, *A History of the Guyanese Working People*, 152.

4. Rodney, *A History of the Guyanese Working People*, 140-145.

5. Zin Henry, *Labour Relations and Industrial Conflict in Commonwealth Caribbean Countries* (Port-of-Spain: Columbus Publishers 1972), 22.

6. Ashton Chase, *A History of Trade Unionism in Guyana* (Georgetown: New Guyana Co. Ltd., 1964), 50 ff.

7. Chase, *A History of Trade Unionism*, 76.

8. Henry, *Labour Relations*, 36.

9. Chase, *A History of Trade Unionsm*, 75; William H. Knowles, *Trade Union Development and Industrial Relations in the British West Indies* (Berkeley: University of California Press 1959), 125.

10. Chase, A *History of Trade Unionism*, 73-75.
11. Chase, A *History of Trade Unionism*, 193.
12. Chase, A *History of Trade Unionism*, 123;
Knowles argued that the 1947 collapse of the CLC was due to cold war
pressures against the socialist and
communist unions that comprised
the movement, Knowles, *Trade Union
Development*, 125, 134; Richard Hart extends the explanation for the failure
of the CLC to the fact that Grantley
Adams, then-chairman of the CLC,
attempted to introduce anti-East
Indian racist perspectices into the
movement, thereby undermining its
legitimacy in multi-racial Caribbean
states like Guyana and Trinidad and
Tobago; see Trevor Munroe, *Jamaican
Politics: a Marxist Perspective in Transition*
(Kingston: Heineman/Lynn Reinner
1990), 123.
13. See George Padmore, *Pan Africanism or
Communism* (New York: Doubleday
1972); C.L.R. James, "Letters to Constance Henderson/Webb".
14. See Trevor Munroe, *Jamaican Politics*, 88
ff; also Ken Post, *Arise ye Starvelings*
(The Hague: Martinus Nijhoff 1978),
226-231.
15. See Harold Cruse, *The Crisis of the Negro
Intellectual* (New York, William Morrow
and Company 1967).
16. Trevor Munroe, *Jamaican Politics*, 96;
also, "Highlights of the Jamaica Progressive League's History", *Souvenir
Journal, Second Anniversary Celebration of
Jamaica Independence* (August 1962), 2-8.
17. Munroe, *Jamaican Politics*, 33. JPL demands included increased wages for
the working classes, localized ownership of sugar industries, land settle-
ment schemes, and outright peasant
ownership of land; see "Supplementary Memorandum of the Jamaica
Progressive League to the West India

Royal Commission, 1938", papers of
Egbert Ethelred Brown, Schomberg
Center, New York.
18. "Highlights of the Jamaica Progressive League's History"; Ken Post, *Arise
Ye Starvelings*, 222.
19. Rev. Ethelred Brown, "My recent visit
to Jamaica", *The Ambassador* 2, no. 2
(1952-53), 39.
20. W. Arthur Lewis, *Labour in the West Indies: The Birth of a Workers' Movement*
(London: Fabian Society 1939), 18-39;
William H. Knowles, *Trade Union Development*, 144 ff.
21. Government of Great Britain, *West India Royal Commission Report (The Moyne
Report)*, Cmnd. 6607 (London: HMSO
1945), 197, 198 and passim; also Zin
Henry, *Labour Relations*, 92.
22. See W. Arthur Lewis, *Labour in the
West Indies*.
23. Lewis, *Labour in the West Indies*.
24. "Highlights of the Jamaica Progressive League's History"; Trevor
Munroe, *Jamaican Politics*, 26-86; also
William H. Knowles, *Trade Union
Development*.
25. Francis Mark, *The History of the Barbados
Workers Union* (Bridgetown: Advocate
Commercial Printing, n.d.), 79 ff.
26. Lewis, *Labour in the West Indies*, 14.
27. Lewis, *Labour in the West Indies*, 21.
28. Henry, *Labour Relations*, 21.
29. Post, *Arise Ye Starvelings*.
30. Trevor Munroe, *Jamaican Politics*, 88, 89 ff.
31. Munroe, *Jamaican Politics*, 95.
32. See Ashton Chase, A *History of Trade
Unionism*, 132, 141; Cheddi Jagan, *The
West on Trial* (Berlin: Seven Seas Books
1972), 104; *People's Progressive Party, 21
Years, 1950-1971* (Georgetown, n.d.),
1; PPP, *History of the PPP* (Georgetown,
1963), 2, 3.
33. See Selwyn Ryan, *Race and Nationalism
in Trinidad and Tobago* (Toronto:

Toronto University Press 1972); and John Gaffar La Guerre, "Socialism in Trinidad and Tobago", *Caribbean Issues*, 4, no. 2 (August 1978).

34. Among the returned students and World War II veterans who constituted the early Left in the Caribbean were Richard Hart of the PNP 'inner circle' in Jamaica, and Rory Westmaas, Ashton C. Chase and Cheddi Jagan of the PAC in Guyana.

35. See *New World Quarterly* 4, no. 3 (High Season 1968): 1-6.

36. *New World Quarterly* 4, no. 3 (High Season 1968): 59-68.

37. *New World Quarterly* 4, no. 3 (High Season 1968): 1-6; Lloyd Best, "Whither New World?", *New World Quarterly* 4, no. 1 (1968): 1-6.

38. See Rupert Lewis and Trevor Munroe (eds.), *Government and Politics of the West Indies* (Kingston: Dept. of Government, University of the West Indies 1971).

39. *Moko* (October, 1968).

40. See *Abeng* (February 1969); and *Abeng*, (March 1969).

41. *Ratoon* (January 1974): 10 ff.

42. See CLAC, *Memorandum by the Civil Liberties Action Council (CLAC) to the United Nations Human Rights Commission on Violations of Fundamental Rights in Guyana*, 19 June 1970; also, People's Progressive Party Press Statement, "Admission of electoral fraud", 2 June 1973.

43. Richard Jacobs and Ian Jacobs, *Grenada: the Route to Revolution* (Havana: Casa de Las Americas 1980).

44. Some examples of leftist periodicals and newspapers in the English-speaking Caribbean during the 1970s and 1980s are as follows:

Political organizations	Country	Periodicals
1. **Reformist**	Guyana	*New Nation*
PNC		

Political organizations	Country	Periodicals
2. **Radical**		
ACLM	Antigua	*Outlet*
NJM	Grenada	*Free West Indian*
WPA	Guyana	*Dayclean/Open Word*
NBM	Trinidad	*Caribbean Dialogue*
3. **Revolutionary**		
PPP	Guyana	*Mirror/Thunder*
WPJ	Jamaica	*Struggle*

45. Editorial "Real threat to security of our region", *Caribbean Contact* (March 1981); see also "This hypocrisy about Cuba in Africa", *Caribbean Contact* (July 1978); Sherry Keith and Robert Girling, "The US response to Manley's 'democratic socialism' ", *Caribbean Contact* (September 1978).

46. See Robert Gilpin, *The Political Economy of International Relations* (New Jersey: Princeton University Press 1987), 298-301; Fitzroy Ambursley and Robin Cohen (eds.), *Crisis in the Caribbean* (New York: Monthly Review Press 1983), 83.

47. Michael Manley, *Jamaica: Struggle in the Periphery* (London: Writers and Readers 1982).

48. See Odida Quamina, *Mine Workers of Guyana: the Making of a Working Class* (London: Humanities Press 1987); Esui Kwayana, "The bauxite strike and the old politics" (Georgetown (mimeo) 1971).

49. See Hon. Michael Manley, Prime Minister of Jamaica, *Budget Debate Speech* (Kingston: Hansard, 12 May 1976), 4.

50. For an insight into the bauxite (alumina) trade arrangements between Jamaica and the USSR during the 1970s, see Michael Manley, *Jamaica: Struggle in the Periphery* 191.

51. Samuel Joseph, "Barbadian socialism, social democracy, or partnership with

imperialism", in MONALI, *Workers Unite: Against Imperialism* 1, no. 2 (April-June 1976): 5 ff.

52. See "Manley stays on as PNP turns right", *Latin America Regional Report: Caribbean* RC 81-08 (September 1981); also "Seaga stands to benefit from split in the Jamaican Left", *Latin America Regional Report: Caribbean* RC 82-08 (October 1982): 1.

53. See NJAC, *People's Declaration of Policy: for the Development of A New Trinidad and Tobago* (Port of Spain: Neracom, n.d.), 13 ff; WPA, *For A Revolutionary Socialist Guyana . . . (Draft)* (Georgetown, March 1979), 16 ff; *Caribbean Dialogue* 2, nos. 3 and 4 (April-May 1976): 21, 28, 29.

54. "ACLM: theses on liberation", *Caribbean Dialogue* 1, no. 3 (November/December 1975): 11-14; also, *Caribbean Dialogue* 2, nos. 5/6 (1976): 15.

55. Walter Rodney, *Groundings With My Brothers* (London: Bogle L' Ouverture 1969), 28-34.

56. Rodney, *Groundings With My Brothers*.

57. Rodney, *Groundings With My Brothers*.

58. WPA, *WPA Manifesto: For the Redemption, Reconstruction, and Rebirth of Guyana* (Georgetown, n.d.), 5.

59. *Caribbean Dialogue* 2, nos. 3 and 4 (April-May 1976): 11 ff; *Caribbean Dialogue* 2, no. 1 (January 1976): 2, 3; *Caribbean Dialogue* 3, no. 2 (February/March 1977): 27, 28.

60. See Lloyd Best, "The 'February Revolution' in Trinidad and Tobago", in Trevor Munroe and Rupert Lewis, *Readings in Government and Politics of the West Indies* (Kingston: UWI 1971), 213.

61. Walter Rodney, *People's Power: No Dictator* (Georgetown: WPA Publication 1979).

62. The WPVP was created out of a left-wing split in the PPP in the late 1960s; its original ideological position was Maoist in opposition to the pro-Moscow orientation of the Jagans in the PPP. Led by B.H. Benn and Victor Downer, the WPVP initially advocated the violent overthrow of the PNC regime and briefly participated in the formation of the WPA in 1979, but suddenly moved to the Right to embrace the pro-capitalist Liberator Party (LP). Out of this unlikely union was formed the very shortlived Vanguard for Liberation and Democracy (VLD) during the 1980s.

63. See Kojo Ramara (Renwick Rose), *Central Committee Report to the Second Annual Convention of* YULIMO (mimeo), n.d., 16 ff.

64. Trevor Munroe, *Programme: Workers Party of Jamaica* (Kingston, December 1978), 72.

Chapter 4

1. Walter Rodney, *People's Power: No Dictator* (Georgetown: WPA Publication 1979), 20.

2. ACLM, "Theses on liberation", *Caribbean Dialogue* 1, no. 3 (1975): 1.

3. See WPA, *For A Revolutionary Socialist Guyana* (Georgetown, March 1979), 14.

4. Cheddi Jagan, "Imperialist intrigue in the Caribbean", *Thunder* (January-March 1976): 14.

5. Jagan, "Imperialist intrigue in the Caribbean", *Thunder* (January-March 1976): 17-26.

6. Jagan, "Imperialist intrigue in the Caribbean", *Thunder* (January-March 1976): 10.

7. PPP, *National Unity for Democracy, Peace and Social Progress Report to the 22nd Congress*, 1985, 74.

8. ACLM, "Cable to Fidel Castro". The cable read: "Afro-Caribbean Liberation Movement and many in Antigua applaud and congratulate you and

people of Cuba for your support and participation in Angolan struggle. You and people have struck a mighty blow against aparthied and imperialism and therefore for world revolution," *Caribbean Dialogue* 2, no. 1 (January 1976).

9. *Caribbean Dialogue* 2, no. 1 (January 1976): 16, 17.

10. Canadian-owned multi-national corporations (MNCs), particularly the Royal Bank of Canada, were selected as specific targets of NJAC protest marches in 1970; for their typical anti-imperialist position, see NJAC, *People's Declaration of Policy: for the Development of a New Trinidad and Tobago* (Port-of-Spain, n.d.); see also NJAC, *An Analysis of the Economic System* (Port-of-Spain, October 1981), 5.

11. PPP, *For A National Front Government* (Georgetown, August 1977), 27 ff; also, PPP, *Political Programme: For Socialism in Guyana* (Georgetown, 1979), 33.

12. WPJ, *Programme: Worker's Party of Jamaica* (Kingston, December 1978).

13. PPP, *National Unity for Democracy, Peace and Social Progress*, 27.

14. See Jagan, "Imperialist intrigue in the Caribbean".

15. cf. PPP, *For A National Front Government*.

16. See Editorial, "The question of socialist strategy", *Caribbean Dialogue* 2, no. 2 (March, 1976): 1; also, *Caribbean Dialogue* 2, nos. 3 & 4 (1976): 27; also, *Caribbean Dialogue* 3, no. 2 (February-March 1977): 1.

17. *New World* (Guyana edition), 18 February 1966, 16.

18. See PNC, *Report, Third Biannual Congress* (Georgetown, 1979), 38.

19. PNC, *Report, Third Biannual Congress*, 109.

20. PNC, *Report, Third Biannual Congress*, 104.

21. *Guyana Chronicle*, 22 October 1977, 1; *Mirror*, 4 September 1977, 8.

22. WPA, "Text of election broadcast", Guyana Broadcasting Service, 23 November 1985.

23. WPA, Letter to Presidential Secretariat, 3 January 1990.

24. Walter Rodney, *People's Power: No Dictator*, 1.

25. See Janet Jagan, *Army Intervention in the 1973 Elections in Guyana* (Georgetown: PPP Publication 1973), 92.

26. Walter Rodney, *People's Power: No Dictator*, 16.

27. The Civil Liberties Action Council (CLAC) was created through the auspices of the PPP to protest PNC dictatorship, particularly the rigging of elections; see CLAC, *Memorandum to the United Nations Human Rights Commission On Violations of Fundamental Rights in Guyana*, June 1970.

28. *Caribbean Dialogue* 2, nos. 3 & 4 (1976): 38.

29. *Caribbean Dialogue* 2, nos. 5 & 6 (June-July 1976): 27.

30. Bill Reviere, "Ideology, mass work and political behaviour in the Commonwealth Caribbean: an exploratory study of Dominica", paper presented to ISER/Dept. of Economics-sponsored symposium in commemoration of the 20th anniversary of the 1970 February Revolution in Trinidad and Tobago, UWI, St Augustine, 19-21 April 1990, 6.

31. WPA, *For A Revolutionary Socialist Guyana*, 15.

32. WPA, *Manifesto: For the Redemption Reconstruction and Rebirth of Guyana* (Georgetown, n.d.), 5; also, WPA, "Draft Programme for the Democratic Republic . . .", Georgetown (mimeo), n.d.

33. WPA, "Draft Programme for the Democratic Republic . . .", 6.

34. See Cheddi Jagan, *The Truth about Bauxite* (Georgetown, 1971), 13, 14.

35. See C.Y. Thomas, "Comments on the Grenada crisis of 1983", *Intercontinental Press*, 15 October 1985.

36. Editorial, "Potentials and pitfalls of co-ops", *Caribbean Dialogue* 2, nos. 5 & 6 (June-July, 1976): 1.

37. See Cheddi Jagan, *The West Indian State* (Georgetown, 1972), 49.

38. *Caribbean Dialogue* 1, no. 3 (1975): 1.

39. WPA, *For A Revolutionary Socialist Guyana*, 13.

40. PPP, *For A National Front Government*, 1.

41. See C.Y. Thomas, "The non-capitalist path as theory and practice of decolonization and socialist transformation", *Latin American Perspective* 5, no. 2 (Spring 1978), 11-19.

42. Michael Manley, *Budget Speech Debate*, Hansard, 29 May 1974, 24.

43. WPA, "A new political system", Georgetown (mimeo), n.d.; also, Richard Jacobs and Ian Jacobs, *Grenada: the Route to Revolution* (Havana: Casa de Las Americas 1980).

44. Trevor Munroe, *Jamaican Politics: a Marxist Perspective in Transition* (Kingston: Heinemann/ Lynn Reinner 1990), 269.

45. Janet Jagan, *Army Intervention*, 45.

46. *Caribbean Dialogue* 2, nos. 3 & 4 (1976): 45.

47. See Harold Cruse, *The Crisis of the Negro Intellectual* (New York: Quill 1984), 143, 135 and passim.

48. C.L.R. James, Letters to Constance Webb, Schomberg Center.

49. Trevor Munroe, *Jamaican Politics*, 259.

50. See Phillip Reno, *The Ordeal of British Guiana* (New York: Monthly Review Press 1965).

51. See Leo Despres, *Cultural Pluralism and Nationalist Politics in British Guiana* (Chicago: Rand McNally 1967), 177-220.

52. Cheddi Jagan, *The West on Trial*.

53. See Walter Rodney, *Groundings With My Brothers* (London: Bogle-L'Ouverture Publishers 1969).

54. Trevor Munroe, *Jamaican Politics*, 263.

55. M. Zaharuddin, *From Self Destruction to Self Reliance* (Georgetown: PNC Publications 1973), 4.

56. M. Zaharuddin, *From Self Destruction*, 4.

57. Rodney, *Groundings*; NJAC, *People's Declaration of Policy*.

58. *Caribbean Dialogue* 2, nos. 3 & 4 (1976): 8.

59. WPA, *Argument for Unity Against the Dictatorship in Guyana* (Georgetown, 1983), 25.

60. NJAC, *People's Declaration of Policy*.

61. PPP, *For A National Front Government*.

62. *New World* (Guyana), 21 January 1966, 9.

63. Sydney King, "Observation on Jagan's Congress speech on 'The political situation' ", University of Puerto Rico, 1956.

64. Sydney King, *Next Witness* (Georgetown, n.d.).

65. Michael Lewis, "Letter from prison", *Caribbean Dialogue* 3, no. 1 (January 1977): 27-29.

66. See *Moko Review*, no. 1, 28 October 1968.

67. See Norman Girvan, "After Rodney – the politics of student protest in Jamaica", *New World Quarterly* 4, no. 3 (1968).

68. Although the PNC denied any culpability in Rodney's death, sections of the public and academia hold the view that agents of the PNC government were used in his assassination in 1980. See, for example, Robert Hill, "Walter Rodney: a brief biography", an introduction to *Walter Rodney Speaks* (Trenton: African World Press 1990), III, IV; also, "Guyana: the faces behind the mask", *Covert Action Bulletin* no. 10 (August-September 1980): 25.

69. See Trevor Munroe, *Report of the Central Committee to the Second Congress, Workers Party of Jamaica* (Kingston: WPJ 1981), 42, 43.

70. See WPA, *Argument for Unity Against the Dictatorship in Guyana*; also, PPP,

Strengthen the Party! Defend the Masses! Liberate Guyana! Report to the 21st Congress, 30 July -2 August 1982.

71. PPP, *For A National Front Government.*

72. WPA, "A new political system" (mimeo), n.d.

73. PPP, *National Unity for Democracy, Peace and Social Progress,* 27.

74. See Guyana Trades Union Congress, "Minutes of a Meeting of the Political Committee of the Guyana Trades Union Congress", 19 March 1985.

75. Shah has now retreated into relative political obscurity, although he is still active in trade union activities related to cane farming.

76. For some insight into the internal conflicts and transformations of the YULIMO, see Kojo Ramara (Renwick Rose), *Central Committee Report to the Second Annual Convention of YULIMO* (mimeo), n.d., 16 ff.

77. See John Patrick Diggins, *The Rise and Fall of the American Left* (New York: W.W. Norton 1992), 124 ff, 242 ff, 298 ff.

8. Characteristic examples of the more extreme right-wing violence against the Left in the Caribbean include the United Force (UF) initiation of violent insurection against the PPP regime in Guyana in 1962, 1963 and 1964; JLP guerilla violence against the Michael Manley PNP regime in Jamaica, 1976 and 1980; Eric Gairy's "mongoose gang" thug violence against the NJM in several instances between 1974 and 1979; and of course CIA-inspired violence against the PRG government in Grenada between 1980 and 1983; see *Report of the Inquiry into the Disturbances in British Guiana in February, 1962,* London: HMSO, 1962; *Grenada: Commission of Inquiry into the Breakdown of Law and Order and Police Brutality* (Duffus Commission), 27 February 1975

(Kingston 1975); "Fascism on the rise", *Caribbean Dialogue* 2, no. 2 (March 1976): 12 ff; "State repression and political prisoners", *Caribbean Dialogue* 3, no. 1 (January 1977); *Covert Action Information Bulletin* no. 10 (August-September 1980).

79. WPA, *For a Revolutionary Socialist Guyana.*

80. See Bonita Harris (ed.), WPA *Manifesto: Justice, Opportunity, Security For A Multiracial Guyana* (Georgetown: GNNL 1992).

81. See "PPP supports mixed economy, free press", *Stabroek News,* 23 March 1990, 11.

Chapter 5

1. Robert Barros, "The Left and democracy: recent debates in Latin America", *Telos* no. 68 (Summer 1986).

2. Michael Manley, *Jamaica: Struggle in the Periphery* (London: Writers and Readers 1982), 50, 51.

3. See Ivelaw Griffith (ed.), *Strategy and Security in the Caribbean* (New York: Praeger 1991); Anthony Bryan, J.E. Greene and Timothy Shaw (eds.), *Peace Development and Security in the Caribbean* (New York: St Martin's Press 1990).

4. Karl Marx, *Critique of Hegel's Philosophy of Right* (Cambridge, 1977), 121; John Hoffman, "Marxism, revolution and democracy", *Revolutionary World* 46/48 (1982): 79.

5. Carl Stone, "Ideology, public opinion and the media in Jamaica", *Caribbean Issues* 14, no. 2 (August 1978): 65.

6. See Jenny Pearce, *Under the Eagle: US Intervention in Central America and the Caribbean* (Boston: South End Press 1982), 111.

7. Carl Stone, "Ideology, public opinion and the media in Jamaica".

8. See Nelson W. Keith and Novella Z. Keith, *The Social Origins of Democratic Socialism in Jamaica* (Philadelphia: Temple University Press 1992), 273, 274.

9. See Manning Marable, *African and Caribbean Politics* (London: Verso Press 1987), 267; also *Caricom Perspectives* no. 27 (September-October 1984): 18.

10. See Eudine Barriteau, "The 1984 general elections in Grenada", *Caricom Perspectives* no. 29 (January-February 1985): 28.

11. See Selwyn Ryan, "Analysis of Trinidad and Tobago elections", *Caricom Perspectives* (January-March 1987): 13.

12. *Caribbean Contact* (December 1981): 9.

13. See Bob Woodward, *Veil: the Secret Wars of the CIA 1981-1987* (New York: Pocket Books 1987), 337.

14. See Carl Stone, *Democracy and Clientelism in Jamaica* (New Jersey: Transaction Books 1980).

15. Nicos Poulantzas and Ralph Miliband, "The problem of the capitalist state", in *Ideology in Social Science, Readings in Critical Social Theory* edited by Robin Blackburn (Bungay, 1972).

16. See Cheddi Jagan, *The West on Trial* (Berlin: Seven Sea Books 1972), 228-235; for press critique of Jagan and the PPP during the 1950s, see also, *The Daily Argosy*, 14 February 1955, and various other issues of the same paper between 12-14 February inclusive, 1955.

17. See "Tim Hector victorious at last", *Caribbean Contact* (February 1990): 2.

18. "CCC's 'no' to Grenada's invasion", *Caribbean Contact* (November 1983): 1.

19. Sources within FITUG suggest that the sum of $50,000.00 (US) was granted by the CCC to aid the 1989, anti-IMF-FITUC strike in Guyana.

20. See Cheddi Jagan, *The West on Trial*.

21. Tim Wheeler, "Jonestown and the CIA", *Daily World*, 23 July 1981.

22. Wheeler, "Jonestown and the CIA", *Daily World*, 23 July 1981, 11.

23. Wheeler, "Jonestown and the CIA", *Daily World*, 23 July 1981.

24. See "Guyana behind the mask", *Covert Action Information Bulletin* no. 10 (August-September 1980).

25. See Raymond T. Smith, *British Guiana* (London: Oxford University Press 1962); Leo Despres, *Cultural Pluralism and Nationalist Politics in British Guiana* (Chicago: Rand McNally 1967), 7.

26. See Trevor Munroe, General Secretary, WPJ, *Report of the Central Committee to the Second Congress* (Kingston: Vanguard Publishers 17 December 1981), 42 ff.

27. Munroe, General Secretary, WPJ, *Report of the Central Committee to the Second Congress*, 42.

28. PPP, *For A National Front Government*.

29. See *Latin America Regional Reports, Caribbean*, RC 81-07, 21 August 1981, 2.

30. *Stabroek News*, 24 May 1989, 1.

31. CLAC, *Memorandum to United Nations Human Rights Commission*, 14 June 1970; Janet Jagan, *Army Intervention in the 1973 Elections in Guyana* (Georgetown: PPP Publications 1973).

32. See Trevor Munroe, *Jamaican Politics: a Marxist Perspective in Transition* (Kingston: Heinemann/Lynn Rienner Publishers 1990), 112, 156-161.

33. WPA Press Release, "PNC Unleashes Savagery", 18 September 1981.

34. Richard Jacobs and Ian Jacobs, *Grenada: the route to revolution* (Havana: Casa de las Americas 1980)

35. *Latin America Regional Reports, Caribbean*, RC 81-06 17 July 1981.

36. *Caribbean Contact* (February 1990): 2.

37. Government of Trinidad and Tobago, *Report of the Commission of Inquiry into Subversive Activities in Trinidad and Tobago*, House Paper no. 2, 1965 (Port-of-Spain: Government Printery 1968).

38. *New World*, 22 August 1966, 16.

39. *New World*, 22 August 1966, 20.

40. United States Senate, *Hearings Before the Select Committee to Study Government Operations with Respect to Intelligence Activities and Covert Action in Chile* (Washington, D.C.: Government Printing Office 1976).

41. "Manley reveals Rightist plot", *Caribbean Dialogue* 2, nos. 5 & 6 (June/July 1976): 5; also Michael Manley, *Jamaica: Struggle in the Periphery.*

42. See Trevor Munroe and Rupert Lewis (eds.), *Readings in Government and Politics of the West Indies* (Kingston: UWI 1971), 208-210.

43. Data and information on the 1977 GAWU strike were gleaned from a series of Guyana newspapers, mainly *Chronicle* and *Mirror*, between September 1977 and January 1978.

44. *Guyana Chronicle*, 2 September 1977, 1.

45. *Guyana Chronicle*, 22 October 1977, 1; *Mirror*, 2 September 1977, 1.

46. *Guyana Chronicle*, 5 September 1977, 1.

47. *Caribbean Contact* (June 1985): 4.

48. *Mirror*, 2 September 1977, 1.

49. *Guyana Chronicle*, 3 September 1977, 1.

50. See Chris Searle, *Grenada: the Struggle Against Destabilization* (London: Writers and Readers 1983), 40.

51. "Jamaica: state of emergency", *Caribbean Dialogue* 2, nos. 5 & 6 (June/July 1976): 3.

52. *Mirror*, 1 July 1984.

53. Richard Barnet had estimated that the amount paid by the US Treasury to the anti-Jagan strikers in Guyana in 1964 was one million dollars (US), in contrast to the Jagan's estimate of 1.2 million; see Richard Barnet, *Intervention and Revolution: America's Confrontation with Insurgents Around the World* (New York: Meridian Books 1968), 282.

54. Bob Woodward, *Veil*, 325.

55. See United States State Department, *Warsaw Pact Economic Aid Programs in Non-Communist LDCs: Holding their Own in 1986* (Washington, D.C., August 1988); see also, "Soviet collapse not so relevant", NACLA, *Report on the Americas* 25, no. 5 (May, 1992), 15.

56. For a more extended discussion on the status of Cuba and Nicaragua in the transition to socialism during the 1980s, see Richard Harris, *Marxism, Socialism, and Democracy in Latin America* (Boulder: Westview Press 1992).

57. Timothy Wickham-Crowley, *Guerillas and Revolution in Latin America* (New Jersey: Princeton University Press 1992), 86-91.

58. Cheddi Jagan, *The West on Trial*; also Ashton Chase, *A History of Trade Unionism in British Guyana, 1900-1961* (Georgetown: New Guyana Company Ltd. 1964), 283 ff.

59. Cheddi Jagan, *The West on Trial.*

60. See "Jagan on Critical Support", *Caribbean Dialogue* 1, no. 3 (November-December, 1975), 17 ff.

61. See my "The Guyana 1985 elections in retrospect", *Bulletin of Eastern Caribbean Studies* 13, no. 4 (September-October 1987).

62. See Hilbourne Watson, "The Caribbean Basin Initiative and Caribbean development: a critical analysis", *Contemporary Marxism* no. 10 (1985).

63. Dion Phillips, "Caribbean militarism: a response to a crisis", *Contemporary Marxism* no. 10 (1985): 100.

64. Editorial, "The Prophet", *New World* (Guyana), 30 April 1965, 1-3.

65. *New World* (Guyana), 21 January 1966, 9.

Chapter 6

1. The working classes have often demonstrated their relative independence middle class mainly through their capacity to strike, or their usual alienation from the leadership of what is usually termed 'business unionism'; see Obika Gray, *Radicalism and Social Change in Jamaica* (Knoxville: University of Tennessee Press 1991), 58, 77, 94, 95.

2. See "Protests signal borderline: Seaga blames communists; Manley plays it cool", *Latin American Regional Reports Caribbean* RC-85-02, (22 February 1985): 2.

3. See Ellen Ray and Bill Schaaf, "Massive destabilization in Jamaica", *Covert Action Information Bulletin* no. 10 (August-September 1980): 12.

4. See NJM minutes, WPJ papers, "Contributions to rethinking", mimeo. 1987, .

5. Manning Marable, *African and Caribbean Politics: from Kwame Nkrumah to Maurice Bishop* (London: Verso Press 1987), 227.

6. Trevor Munroe, *Jamaican Politics: a Marxist Perspective in Transition* (Kingston: Heinemann/Lynn Reinner 1990), 83.

7. Elean Thomas, in WPJ papers,"Contribution to rethinking", Appendix, 6.

8. George Louison, "Interview with George Louison", *Intercontinental Press* 22, no. 7, 16 April 1984, 214.

9. Louison, "Interview with George Louison".

10. Ellen Ray and Bill Schaap, "US crushes Caribbean jewel", *Covert Action Information Bulletin* no. 20 (Winter 1984): 3.

11. On various aspects of the 'traditional' political culture of the English-speaking Caribbean, see Archie Singham, *The Hero and the Crowd* (New Haven: Yale University Press 1985); Carl Stone, *Democracy and Clientelism in Jamaica* (New Brunswick: Transaction Books 1980); Gordon Lewis, *The Growth of the Modern West Indies* (London: MacGibbon and Kee 1968); Ivar Oxaal, *Race and Revolutionary Consciousness* (Cambridge, Mass.: Schenkman Publishing Co., 1971).

12. Regis Debray, *Revolution in the Revolution* (New York: Monthly Review Press 1967); Che Guevera, *Guerilla Warfare* (Lincoln: University of Nebraska Press 1985).

13. People's National Congress, *Report of the Third Biennial Congress of the People's National Congress* Vol. 1 (Georgetown: GNNL 22-26 August 1979), 38, 40, 48-53, 101.

14. From the author's personal observation in attendance at various PNC meetings and conferences, statements like these were frequently made by PNC leadership cadres in addressing their members.

15. See Ivar Oxaal, *Race and Revolutionary Consciousness*, 21, 23, 60; Franklyn Harvey, *Rise and Fall of Party Politics in Trinidad and Tobago* (Toronto: The New Beginning Movement 1974), 16, 41-45; NJAC, *Conventional Politics or Revolution*" (Belmont, n.d.), 31-36.

16. Bill Reviere, "Ideology, mass work and political behaviour in the Commonwealth Caribbean: an exploratory study of Dominica", paper presented at ISER/Department of Economics-sponsored symposium in commemoration of the 20th Anniversary of the 1970 February Revolution in Trinidad and Tobago, held at UWI, St Augustine, 19-21 April 1990, 6.

17. Manning Marable, *African and Caribbean Politics*, 174.

18. People's Progressive Party, *Report of the Central Committee to the 22nd Congress of the People's Progressive Party*, Annandale, 3-5 August 1985, 117-126.

19. For example in the PPP Central Committee up to 1989 less than 5 percent of members could be said to comprise the poorer classes of workers and farmers, while the parliamentary list of the party for the 1992 elections comprised only about 10 percent of such lower class members; yet this record is very favourable compared to the working class representation in the leadership hierarchy of other Left (not to mention the Right) political organizations throughout the Caribbean.

20. *Report of the Central Committee to the 22nd Congress of the PPP*, 112.

21. "At the crossroads – the emergence and potential of the ULF", *Caribbean Dialogue* 2, nos. 3 & 4 (April-May 1977).

22. *Report of the Central Committee to the 22nd Congress of the PPP*, 112.

23. "Race and class in the struggle for parliamentary power", *Caribbean Dialogue* 3, no. 2 (February-March 1977): 25.

24. A breakdown of the racial-cum-class composition of the ULF in 1976 was as follows:

Race	Industry	Percent
East Indian	Sugar workers	60
African	Petroleum	25
Differentiated	Commercial etc.	15

Source: Figures drawn from *Caribbean Dialogue* 2, no. 1 (January 1976): 2.

25. *Caribbean Dialogue* 3, no. 2 (February-March 1977): 25.

26. *Caribbean Dialogue* 3, no. 2 (February-March 1977): 27.

27. Some examples of these private politized police in the English-speaking Caribbean were what were infamously known as the "mongoose gang" of Eric Gairy in Grenada, the 'thug armies' led by Rabbi Washington and used by Forbes Burnham in Guyana, and the private neighbourhood garrison thugs used mainly by the JLP particularly at election time in Jamaica, during the 1970s.

28. "Post-independence struggles and the emergence of the USA", *Caribbean Dialogue* 2, nos. 5 & 4 (1976): 12.

29. See R.T. Smith, *British Guiana* (London: Oxford University Press 1962).

30. See Leo Despres, *Cultural Pluralism and Nationalist Politics in British Guiana* (Chicago: Rand McNally 1967).

31. See Cheddi Jagan, *The West on Trial* (Berlin: Seven Seas Books 1972), 160; Philip Reno, *The Ordeal of British Guiana* (New York: Monthly Review Press 1964); R.T. Smith, *British Guiana*; see also, Peoples' Progressive Party, "The great betrayal", (pamphlet) (Georgetown, September 1955).

32. See Richard Garnet, *Intervention and Revolution: America's Confrontation with Insurgent Movements Around the World* (New York: Meridian Press 1968), 283.

33. *Covert Action Information Bulletin* no. 20 (1984): 3-9.

34. Jesse Burnham, "Beware of my Brother Forbes", (PPP pamphlet), n.d.

35. Author's interview with Rory Westmaas, Georgetown, 1995.

36. See Brian Meeks, *Caribbean Revolutions and Revolutionary Theory: an Assessment of Cuba, Nicaragua and Grenada* (London: Macmillan Press 1993), 170, 171.

37. "Interview with George Louison", *Intercontinental Press* 22, no. 7 (16 April 1984): 214.

38. "Interview with George Louison" 211.

39. See Cheddi Jagan, "Primary interest is struggle", *The Daily Chronicle*, 22 December 1956, 7; also *New World Fort-*

nightly 15 April 1965, 20-25; *New World Fortnightly*, 1 June 1965, 7-8.

40. Don Robotham, "Letter of resignation from WPJ", 18 August 1988; also similar letters of resignation, from Lambert Brown, Douval Campbell, Barry Chevannes, Derek Gordon and Tony Harriott, dated 23 August 1988, among WPJ papers.

41. See People's National Congress, *Report of the Third Biennial Congress of the People's National Congress*, 56, 61.

42. People's Progressive Party, *Report of the Central Committee to the 22nd Congress of the PPP*, 119.

43. Trevor Munroe, *Report of the Central Committee of the Second Congress, Workers Party of Jamaica* (Kingston: WPJ 1981), 73.

44. According to WPJ statistics, the party in the space of about three years between the first and second congresses, had produced 623 pamphlets, 105 booklets and 5 books . . . and used up " 1,322 reams of paper and spent 26,761 man hours" on this propaganda project, WPJ, *Report to the Second Congress 1981*, 74.

45. NJAC, *People's Declaration of Policy For the Development of a New Trinidad and Tobago* (Port of Spain, n.d.,), iv.

46. From my personal observation as a temporary consultant to the Guyana Government on political education in 1975, and also from conversations with Elvin McDavid, chief executive officer of the PNC at the time, efforts made by the political education committee of the then ruling party to involve senior ministers in political education sessions were for a variety of reasons successfully rebuffed by these ministers themselves.

47. *Caribbean Dialogue* 2, nos. 3 & 4 (1976): 40.

48. Obika Gray, *Radicalism and Social Change*, 82.

49. WPJ papers, "Contribution to rethinking", 44.

50. WPJ papers, "Contribution to rethinking", 155.

51. See "ULF assembly?' *Caribbean Dialogue* 2, nos. 3 & 4 (April-May 1976): 32.

52. Obika Gray, *Radicalism and Social Change*, 181.

53. Lloyd Best, "Whither New World"? *New World Quarterly* 4, no. 1 (1968): 1 ff.

54. *Caribbean Dialogue* 3, no. 2 (February-March 1977): 23.

55. Ivar Oxaal, *Race and Revolutionary Consciousness*, 68.

56. Lloyd Best, "Whither New World?", 2.

57. Norman Girvan, "Chairman's report on the New World group Jamaica, for the period August 1967 to September 1968", *New World Quarterly* 4, no. 3 (1968): 1-4.

58. *Caribbean Dialogue* 3, no. 2 (1977): 23.

59. NACLA, *Report on the Americas* ((November-December 1984): 25.

60. NACLA, *Report on the Americas* ((November-December 1984): 25; *Caribbean Dialogue* 3, no. 1 (1977), back p.

61. *Caribbean Dialogue* 3, no. 2 (February-March 1977): back p.

62. Mohammed Insanally, "Political defection and political change in Guyana", mimeo. University of Guyana, 1972.

63. *Caribbean Dialogue* 3, no. 1 (January 1977): 17.

64. *Caribbean Dialogue* 3, no. 1 (January 1977): 16.

65. Carl Stone, "Understanding political tendencies in Jamaica", mimeo: Department of Government, University of the West Indies, Mona, 1983.

66. Stone, "Understanding political tendencies in Jamaica", 9.

67. Stone, "Understanding political tendencies in Jamaica", 13.

68. Stone, "Understanding political tendencies in Jamaica", 21.
69. "Lukewarm support for elections", *Caribbean Contact* (December 1984): 1.
70. "Lukewarm support for elections".
71. "Lukewarm support for elections", 11.
72. See *Latin American Regional Report Caribbean* RC-81-06, 17 July 1981, 2.

Chapter 7

1. Caribbean political processes, see my " Foreign influence, political conflicts and conflict resolution in the Caribbean", *Journal of Peace Research* 32 , no. 4 (November 1995).
2. See John M. Rothgeb, Jr. *Defining Power Influence and Force in the International System* (New York: St Martin's Press 1993).
3. See Carey Fraser, *Ambivalent Anti-Colonialism* (Westport: Greenwood Press 1994), 95.
4. Cited from Trevor Munroe, *Jamaican Politics: a Marxist Perspective in Transition.* (Kingston: Heinemann/Lynn Reinner 1990), 132.
5. Munroe, *Jamaican Politics*, 134.
6. See George Beckford, and Michael Witter, *Small Garden Bitter Weed: Struggle and Change in Jamaica* (London: Zed Press 1980), 63.
7. Trevor Munroe, *Jamaican Politics*, 1990, 132.
8. *Report of the British Guiana Constitutional Commission* (London: HMSO 1954), 135-138; Cheddi Jagan, *The West on Trial* (Berlin: Seven Seas Books), 160 ff.
9. *Report of the British Guiana Constitutional Commission*, 15
10. Fraser, *Ambivalent Anti-Colonialism*, 170
11. People's Progressive Party, *The Struggles of the PPP for Guyana's Independence*, Georgetown, May 1966, 24
12. See Ellen Ray and Bill Schaap, "US crushes Caribbean jewel", *Covert Action Information Bulletin* no.20 (Winter 1984): 4.
13. *Hearings Before the Select Committee to Study Government Operations with to Intelligence Activities and Covert Action in Chile* (Washington DC: United States Senate 1976).
14. See Ellen Ray and Bill Schaap, "US crushes Caribbean jewel".
15. George Black, " The American's man: a talk with Eric Gairy", NACLA, *Report on the Americas* (March-April 1985): 9.
16. Paul Seabury and Walter McDougal, *The Grenada Papers* (San Francisco: Institute for Contemporary Studies 1984), 282.
17. Author's separate interviews with Forbes Burnham in Belfield in 1982, and with Elvin McDavid in Georgetown in 1987.
18. See "Guyana: the faces behind the masks", *Covert Action Information Bulletin* no. 10 (August-September 1980): 24-25.
19. See Working People's Alliance, "Towards a revolutionary socialist Guyana". mimeo. Georgetown, 1979.
20. *Caribbean Dialogue* 2, nos. 5 & 6 (June/July 1976): 2-4.
21. *Caribbean Dialogue*, 2, no. 5 & 6 (June/July 1976): 2-4.
22. For varying figures on the amount of foreign dollars spent on the 80-day strike in Guyana in 1965 see Jenny Pearce, *Under the Eagle: US Intervention in Central America and the Caribbean* (Boston: South End Press 1981), 85; Richard Garnet, *Intervention and Revolution: America's Confrontation with Insurgent Movements around the World* (New York: Meridian 1968), 286; Cheddi Jagan, *The West on Trial*, 249-254.
23. Fraser, *Ambivalent Anti-Colonialism*, 199.
24. Jagan, *The West on Trial*, 248

25. NACLA, *Report on the Americas* (July-August 1985): 18

26. Jagan, *The West on Trial*, 249.

27. Jagan, *The West on Trial*, 253.

28. Richard Garnet, *Intervention and Revolution*, 282.

29. Jagan, *The West on Trial*, 254.

30. Garnet, *Intervention and Revolution*, 282.

31. *Caribbean Dialogue* 2, no. 2 (1976): 18.

32. *Caribbean Dialogue* 2, no. 2 (1976): 18.

33. *Caribbean Dialogue* 2, no. 2 (1976): 19.

34. Ellen Ray and Bill Schaap, "Massive destabilization in Jamaica: 1976 with a new twist", *Covert Action Information Bulletin* no.10 (August-September 1980): 12.

35. Ray and Schaap, "Massive destabilization in Jamaica", 16.

36. Bob Woodward, *Veil: the Secret Wars of the CIA 1981-1987* (New York: Pocket Books 1987), 585.

37. See *Caribbean Dialogue* 5, no. 2 (1977), back p.; NACLA, *Report on the Americas* (November-December 1984): 23.

38. NACLA, *Report on the Americas* (July-August 1985): 56.

39. NACLA, *Report on the Americas* (July-August 1985): 56.

40. The overwhelming bulk of the political detainees incarcerated by British military forces in the famous Sibley Hall detention centre on an island in the Mazaruni river during the 1963-64 disturbances was drawn from PPP leadership cadres.

41. NACLA, *Report on the Americas* (November-December 1984): 25.

42. NACLA, *Report on the Americas* (November-December 1984): 25.

43. NACLA, *Report on the Americas* (July-August 1985): 32.

44. NACLA, *Report on the Americas* (July-August 1985): 53

45. See Hilbourne Watson, "The Caribbean Basin Initiative", *Contemporary Marxism* 10, (1985): 1-37.

46. NACLA, *Report on the Americas* (July-August 1985).

47. See Jenny Pearce, *Under The Eagle* 187; Chris Searle, *Grenada: The Struggle Against Destabilization* (London: Writers and Readers 1983) 37.

48. NACLA, *Report on the Americas* (July-August 1985): 34.

49. NACLA, *Report on the Americas* (July-August 1985): 34.

50. NACLA, *Report on the Americas* (March-April 1985): 9.

51. Quoted from Carey Fraser, *Ambivalent Anti-Colonialism*, 95.

52. Fraser, *Ambivalent Anti-Colonialism*, 95

53. NACLA, *Report on the Americas* (July-August 1985): 25.

54. Ivelaw Griffith, "The quest for security in the Caribbean", PhD dissertation, City University of New York, 1990, 169, 170.

55 NACLA, *Report on the Americas* (November-December 1984): 30.

56. NACLA, *Report on the Americas* (March-April 1985): 9.

57. NACLA, *Report on the Americas* (March-April 1985): 9.

58. See John Walton, "Debt, protest and the state in Latin America", in *Power and Popular Protest: Latin American Social Movements*, edited by Susan Eckstein (Berkeley: University of California Press 1989).

Chapter 8

1. Antonio Gramsci, *Selections from the Prison Notebooks* (New York: International Publishers 1978), 322.

2. See Karl Marx and Frederick Engels, *The German Ideology* (New York: 1967), 13-14; and Karl Manheim, *Ideology and Utopia* (New York: 1936), 6-8.

3. See Carl Stone, "Decolonization and the Caribbean state system: the case

of Jamaica", Inter-American Politics Seminar Series, Center for Inter-American Relations, 5-6 May 1978; Hilbourne Watson, "Non-capitalist development and the Commonwealth Caribbean: a critique of its theoretical and prescriptive conditions", paper presented at Caribbean Studies Association, Annual Conference, St Thomas, Virgin Islands, 26-30 May 1981.

4. Trevor Munroe, *Social Classes and National Liberation in Jamaica* ; Richard Jacobs and Ian Jacobs, *Grenada: the Route to Revolution*, (Havana: Casa de Las Americas 1980); and George Beckford and Michael Witter, *Small Garden Bitter Weed: Struggle and Change in Jamaica* (London: Zed Press 1982).

5. C.Y. Thomas, "On formulating a marxist theory of regional integration", *Transition* 1, no. 1 (1978); also, C.Y. Thomas, "From colony to state capitalism in the Caribbean", *Transition* 5 (1982); Fitzroy Ambursley and Robin Cohen (eds.), *Crisis in the Caribbean* (New York, 1983); George Beckford, *Persistent Poverty*, (London: Oxford University Press 1972); and Jay R. Mandle, "Caribbean dependency and its alternatives", *Latin American Perspective* 42, 11, no. 3 (Summer 1984).

6. C.Y. Thomas, *Rise of the Authoritarian State in Peripheral Societies*, (New York: Monthly Review Press 1984); Walter Rodney, *History of the Guyanese Working People*, (Baltimore: Johns Hopkins University Press 1981).

7. See Samir Amin, *Unequal Development* (New York: 1976), 379.

8. Carl Stone, "Decolonization and the Caribbean state system", 14, 16.

9. Stone, "Decolonization and the Caribbean state system", 21.

10. Alec De Tocqueville, *The Old Regime and the French Revolution* (New York: 1955).

11. Lyford P. Edwards, *The National History of Revolution* (Chicago, 1970).

12. Jurgen Habermas, "Conservatism and Capitalist Crisis", *New Left Review* no. 115 (May-June 1979).

13. C.L.R. James, *Party Politics in the West Indies* (Port of Spain: Vedic Enterprises Ltd., 1962).

14. Gramsci, *Prison Notebooks*, 177.

15. Gramsci, *Prison Notebooks*, 376.

16. C.L.R. James, "Letters to Constance Henderson/Webb, 1939-1946", Schomburg Center.

17. cf. Trevor Munroe, *Jamaican Politics: a Marxist Perspective in Transition* (Kingston: Heinemann/Lynn Reinner 1990), 257-262.

18. Munroe, *Jamaican Politics*, 89-96.

19. See Walter Rodney, *Groundings With My Brothers* (London: Bogle L'Overture Publishers 1969).

20. See, for example, *Walter Rodney Speaks: the Making of an African Intellectual* (Trenton: African World Press 1990), 45, 84, and passim.

21. See John Hoffman, "Marxism, revolution, and democracy", *Revolutionary World* 46/48, (1982): 79.

22. See Anthony Brewer, *Marxist Theories of Imperialism: a Critical Survey* (London: Routledge and Kegan Paul 1980), 72, 76; C.Y. Thomas, *The Rise of the Authoritarian State*, 102-103; and Gordon K. Lewis, "Grenada 1983: the lessons for the Caribbean Left", paper presented at the Conference on the Grenada Revolution, 1979-1983, University of the West Indies, St Augustine, Trinidad, 24-25 May 1984, 14.

23. Ministry of Finance, Cooperative Republic of Guyana, *Privatization Policy Framework Paper*, June, 1993.

24. See Ira Kipnis, *The American Socialist Movement, 1897-1912* (New York: Greenwood Press 1968), 278-280.

25. See John Patrick Diggins, *The Rise and Fall of the American Left* (New York: W.W. Norton and Company 1992), 170.

26. See Timothy Wickham-Crowley, *Guerillas and Revolution in Latin America: a Comparative Study of Insurgents and Regimes Since 1956* (New Jersey: Princeton University Press 1992), 217, 218 and passim.

27. Rodney, *Groundings With My Brothers.*

28. See Steve Ellner, "Introduction: the changing status of the Latin American Left in the recent past", in *The Latin American Left: From the Fall of Allende to Perestroika* edited by Barry Carr and Steve Ellner (Boulder: Westview Press 1993), 13-15.

29. See my "The race-class problematic and Leftist political practice: Caribbean examples", paper presented to conference on "Black politics and theory in crisis", Columbia University, New York, Fall 1994.

30. *Intercontinental Press*, 1 April 1985, 179.

31. See Guenter Lewy, *The Cause That Failed: Communism in American Political Life* (New York: Oxford University Press 1990), 294-295.

32. Carl Stone, "Understanding political tendencies in contemporary Jamaica", Inaugural Lecture, Department of Government, University of the West Indies, Mona, 12 May 1983, 8-9, 22.

33. C.Y. Thomas, "Speech on Grenada", *Intercontinental Press*, 15 October 1985, 614 ff; also, C.Y. Thomas, *The Rise of the Authoritarian State.*

34. Don Robotham, Letter of resignation from WPJ", 18 August 1988.

35. Trevor Munroe, "Address to Second Sitting – Fourth Congress, Workers' Party of Jamaica", 27 January 1990, 2; also, Trevor Munroe, "Report . . . to 4th Congress of the WPJ, First Sitting", 9 September 1988, 8.

36. Gordon K. Lewis, "Grenada 1983", 13-14.

37. Lewis, "Grenada 1983", 13-14.

38. See my "Foreign influence, political conflicts and conflict resolution in the Caribbean", *Journal of Peace Research* 34, no. 4 (November 1995).

39. See Bob Woodward, *Veil*, 325.

40. See John Patrick Diggins, *The Rise and Fall of the American Left*, 342 ff.

Bibliography

Books

Albercrombie, Nicholas, et al., eds., *The Dominant Ideology Thesis*. London: Allen and Unwin 1980.

Ambursley, Fitzroy and Robin Cohen, eds., *Crisis in the Caribbean*. New York: Monthly Review Press 1983.

America's Watch, *Political Freedom in Guyana*. London, 1985.

Amin, Samir, *Delinking: Towards a Polycentric World*. London: Zed Press 1985.

Amin, Samir, *Empire of Chaos*. New York: Monthly Review Press 1992.

Amin, Samir, *Unequal Development*. New York: 1976.

Avebury, Lord, *Something to Remember*. London, 1980.

Ayearst, Morley, *The British West Indies: the Search for Self Government*. New York: New York University Press 1960.

Barnet, Richard, *Intervention and Revolution: America's Confrontation with Insurgents Around the World*. New York: Meridian Books 1968.

Beckford, George, *Persistent Poverty*. London: Oxford University Press 1972.

Beckford, George and Michael Witter, *Small Garden Bitter Weed: Struggle and Change in Jamaica*. London: Zed Press 1980.

Bocock, Robert, *Hegemony*. Sussex: Tavistock Publications 1986.

Brewer, Anthony, *Marxist Theories of Imperialism: a Critical Survey*. London: Routledge and Kegan Paul 1980.

Bryan, Anthony, et al., eds., *Peace, Development and Security in the Caribbean*. New York: St Martin Press 1990.

Chabal, P., *Amilcar Cabral: Revolutionary Leadership and People's War*. Cambridge: Cambridge University Press 1983.

Chase, Ashton, *A History of Trade Unionism in Guyana*. Georgetown: New Guyana Co. Ltd., 1964.

Chase, Ashton, *133 Days Towards Freedom*. Georgetown: New Guyana Company Ltd.,1954.

Chilcote, Ronald H., and Dale L. Johnson, *Theories of Development: Mode of Production or Dependency*. Beverly Hills: Sage Publications 1983.

Civil Liberties Action Council, *Memorandum by the Civil Liberties Council (CLAC) to the United Nations Human Rights Commission on Violations of Fundamental Rights in Guyana.* 19 June 1970.

Clapham, Christopher, *Third World Politics: an Introduction.* London: Croom Helm 1985.

Cruse, Harold, *The Crisis of the Negro Intellectual.* New York: William Morrow and Company 1967.

De Tocqueville, Alex, *The Old Regime and the French Revolution.* New York: 1955.

Debray, Régis, *Revolution in the Revolution.* New York: Monthly Review Press 1967.

Despres, Leo, *Cultural Pluralism and Nationalist Politics in British Guiana.* Chicago: Rand McNally 1967.

Diggins, John Patrick, *The Rise and Fall of the American Left.* New York: W. W. Norton and Company 1992.

Duffus Commission, *Grenada: Commission of Inquiry into the Breakdown of Law and Order and Police Brutality.* Kingston (27 February 1975).

Edwards, Lyford P., *The Natural History of Revolution.* Chicago, 1970.

Fanon, Frantz, *The Wretched of the Earth.* Middlesex: Penguin 1963.

Fraser, Carey, *Ambivalent Anti-Colonialism.* Westport: Greenwood Press 1994.

Frank, Andre Gunder, *Latin America: Underdevelopment or Revolution.* New York: Monthly Review Press 1970.

Garnet, Richard, *Intervention and Revolution: America's Confrontation with Insurgents Around the World.* New York: Meridian Books 1968.

Gilpin, Robert, *The Political Economy of International Relations.* London: Macmillan 1979.

Girvan, Norman, *Foreign Capital and Economic Underdevelopment in Jamaica.* Mona: ISER 1971.

Government of Great Britain, Colonial Office, *West India Royal Commission (The Moyne Report) Cmnd. 6607.* London: HMSO 1945.

Government of Trinidad and Tobago, *Report of the Commission of Inquiry into Subversive Activities in Trinidad and Tobago* House Paper no. 2 1965. Port of Spain: Government Printery 1968.

Gramsci, Antonio, *Selections from the Prison Notebooks.* New York: International Publishers 1978.

Gray, Obika, *Radicalism and Social Change in Jamaica.* Knoxville: University of Tennessee Press 1991.

Griffith, Ivelaw, ed., *Strategy and Security in the Caribbean.* New York: Praeger 1991.

Guevara, Che, *Guerilla Warfare.* Lincoln: University of Nebraska Press 1985.

Harris, Bonita, ed., *WPA Manifesto: Justice, Opportunity, Security for a Multiracial Guyana.* Georgetown: Guyana National Newspaper Ltd 1992.

Harris, Richard, *Marxism, Socialism, and Democracy in Latin America.* Boulder: Westview Press 1992.

Harvey, Franklyn, *Rise and Fall of Party Politics in Trinidad and Tobago.* Toronto: The New Beginning Movement 1974.

Henry, Zin, *Labour Relations and Industrial Conflict in Commonwealth Caribbean Countries.* Port of Spain: Columbus Publishers 1972.

Hintzen, Percy, *The Cost of Regime Survival.* Cambridge: Cambridge University Press 1989.

International Commission of Jurists, *Report of the British Guiana Commission of Inquiry: Racial Problems in the Public Service.* Geneva 1965.

Jacobs, Richard and Ian Jacobs, *Grenada: the Route to Revolution.* Havana: Casa de Las Americas 1980.

Jagan, Cheddi, *The Truth about Bauxite.* Georgetown, 1971.

Jagan, Cheddi, *The West Indian State.* Georgetown, 1972.

Jagan, Cheddi, *The West on Trial.* Berlin: Seven Seas Books 1972.

Jagan, Janet, *Army Intervention in the 1973 Elections in Guyana.* Georgetown: New Guyana Company Ltd., 1973.

James, C. L. R., *Party Politics in the West Indies.* Port of Spain: Vedic Enterprises Ltd., 1962.

Keith, Nelson and Novella Z. Keith, *The Social Origins of Democratic Socialism in Jamaica.* Philadelphia: Temple University Press 1992.

Keohane, Robert O., *After Hegemony, Cooperation and Discord in the World Economy.* Princeton: Princeton University Press 1984.

King, Sidney, *Next Witness.* Georgetown, n.d.

Kipnis, Ira, *The American Socialist Movement, 1897-1912.* New York: Greenwood 1968.

Knight, Franklyn W., *The Caribbean.* New York: Oxford University Press 1970.

Knowles, William H., *Trade Union Development and Industrial Relations in the British West Indies.* Berkeley: University of California Press 1959.

Kwayana, Esui, *The Bauxite Strike and the Old Politics.* Georgetown (mimeo) 1971.

Lewis, Gordon K., *The Growth of the Modern West Indies.* London: MacGibbon and Kee 1968.

Lewis, Rupert and Trevor Munroe, eds., *Government and Politics of the West Indies.* Kingston: Department of Government, University of the West Indies 1971.

Lewis, W. Arthur, *Labour in the West Indies: the Birth of a Workers Movement.* London: Fabian Society 1939.

Lewy, Guenter, *The Cause that Failed: Communism in American Political Life.* New York: Oxford University Press 1990.

McAffee, Cathy, *Storm Signals: Structural Adjustment and Development Alternatives in the Caribbean.* Boston: South End Press 1991.

MacEwan, Arthur, *Debt and Disorder: International Economic Instability and US Imperial Decline.* New York: Monthly Review Press 1990.

Mandle, Jay, *Patterns of Economic Development : an Interpretative Essay on Economic Change.* New York: Gordon and Breach Science Publishers 1982.

Manheim, Karl, *Ideology and Utopia.* New York: 1967.

Manley, Michael, *Budget Speech Debate.* Hansard 29 May 1974.

Manley, Michael, *Jamaica; Struggle in the Periphery.* London: Writers and Readers 1982.

Marable, Manning, *African and Caribbean Politics.* London: Verso Press 1987.

Mark, Francis, *The History of the Barbados Workers Union.* Bridgetown: Advocate Commercial Printing n.d.

Marx, Karl, *Critique of Hegel's Philosophy of Right.* Cambridge: Cambridge University Press 1977.

Marx, Karl and Frederick Engels, *The German Ideology*. New York: International
    Publishers 1967.
Meeks, Brian, *Caribbean Revolutions and Revolutionary Theory: an Assessment of Cuba,
    Nicaragua and Grenada*. London: Macmillan 1993.
Ministry of Finance, Co-operative Republic of Guyana, *Privatization Policy Framework
    Paper*. June 1993.
Moore, Brian L., *Race, Power and Social Segmentation in Colonial Society: Guyana After
    Slavery, 1838-1891*. New York: Gordon Breach Science Publishers 1987.
Munroe, Trevor, *Jamaican Politics: a Marxist Perspective in Transition*. Kingston:
    Heinemann/Lynn Reinner 1990.
Munroe, Trevor, *Report of the Central Committee to the Second Congress, Workers Party of
    Jamaica*. Kingston: WPJ 181.
Munroe, Trevor, *Programme: Workers Party of Jamaica*. Kingston, December 1978.
Munroe, Trevor, *Social Classes and National Liberation in Jamaica*.
NJAC, *An Analysis of the Economic System*. Port of Spain, October 1981.
NJAC, *Conventional Politics or Revolution*. Belmont n.d.
NJAC, *People's Declaration of Policy: for the Development of a New Trinidad and Tobago*.
    Port of Spain: n.d.
Oxaal, Ivar, *Race and Revolutionary Consciousness*. Cambridge, Mass.: Schenkman
    Publishing Co., 1987.
Oxaal, Ivar, *Report of the Demba Panel of Consultants on Community Attitudes and Their Effects
    on Industrial Relations*. Georgetown, 1966.
Padmore, George, *Pan Africanism or Communism*. New York: Doubleday 1972.
Payer, Cheryl, *The Debt Trap: the International Monetary Fund and the Third World*. New York:
    Monthly Review Press 1974.
Pearce, Jenny, *Under the Eagle: US Intervention in Central America and the Caribbean*.
    Boston: South End Press 1981.
People's National Congress, *Report of the Third Biennial Congress of the People's National
    Congress*. Vol. 1. Georgetown: Guyana National Newspapers Ltd., 22-26 August 1979.
People's Progressive Party, *For a National Front Government*. Georgetown, August
    1977.
People's Progressive Party, *History of the PPP*. Georgetown, 1963.
People's Progressive Party, *National Unity for Democracy, Peace and Social Progress, Report to
    the 22nd Congress*. 1985.
People's Progressive Party, *Political Programme: for Socialism in Guyana*. Georgetown, 1979.
People's Progressive Party, *Report of the Central Committee to the 22nd Congress of the
    People's Progressive Party*. Annandale 3-5 August 1985.
People's Progressive Party, *Strengthen the Party! Defend the Masses! Liberate Guyana!
    Report to the 21st Congress 30 July-2 August 1982*.
People's Progressive Party, *21 Years, 1950-1971*. Georgetown, n.d.
Post, Ken, *Arise Ye Starvelings*. The Hague: Martinus Nijhoff 1978.
Quamina, Odida, *Mine Workers of Guyana: the Making of a Working Class*. London:
    Humanities Press 1981.

Ramara, Kojo, *Central Committee Report to the Second Annual Convention of* YULIMO. mimeo n.d.

Reno, Philip, *The Ordeal of British Guiana*. New York: Monthly Review Press 1964.

Report of the British Guiana Constitutional Commission. London: HMSO 1954.

Report of the Inquiry into the Disturbances in British Guiana in February, 1962. London: HMSO 1962.

Robinson, William I., *A Faustian Bargain*. Boulder: Westview 1992.

Rodney, Walter, *A History of the Guyanese Working People*. Baltimore: Johns Hopkins University Press 1981.

Rodney, Walter, *Groundings with my Brothers*. London: Bogle L'Overture 1969.

Rodney, Walter, *People Power: No Dictator*. Georgetown: WPA Publications 1979.

Rothgeb, John M., *Defining Power Influence and Force in the International System*. New York: St Martins Press 1993.

Ryan, Selwyn, *Race and Nationalism in Trinidad and Tobago*. Toronto: Toronto University Press 1972.

Seabury, Paul and Walter McDougal, *The Grenada Papers*. San Francisco: Institute of Contemporary Studies 1984.

Searle, Chris, *Grenada: the Struggle Against Destabilization*. London: Writers and Readers 1983.

Singham, Archie, *The Hero and the Crowd*. New Haven: Yale University Press 1985 .

Smith, Raymond T., *British Guiana*. London: Oxford University Press 1962.

Staniland, Martin, *What is Political Economy?* New Haven: Yale University Press 1985.

Stone, Carl, *Democracy and Clientelism in Jamaica*. New Jersey: Transaction Books 1980.

Taylor, John G., *From Modernization to Modes of Production*. London: Macmillan 1979.

Thomas, C. Y., *The Poor and the Powerless: Economic Policy and Change in the Caribbean*. New York: Monthly Review Press 1988.

Thomas, C. Y., *The Rise of the Authoritarian State in Peripheral Societies*. New York: Monthly Review Press 1984.

Unger, Roberto Mangabeira, *False Necessity: an Anti-Necessitarian Theory in the Service of Radical Democracy*. Cambridge: Cambridge University Press 1987.

United States Senate, *Hearings Before the Select Committee to Study Government Operations with Respect to Intelligence Activities and Covert Action in Chile*. Washington, D.C., Government Printing Office 1976.

United States State Department, *Warsaw Pact Economic Aid Programs in Non-Communist LDCs: Holding Their Own in 1986*. Washington, D.C., 1988.

Wallerstein, Immanuel, *The Capitalist World Economy*. Cambridge: Cambridge University Press 1979.

Waters, Anita., *Race, Class and Political Symbols: Rastafari and Reggae in Jamaican Politics*. New Brunswick: Transaction Books 1989.

Woodward, Bob, *Veil: the Secret Wars of the CIA 1981-1987*. New York: Pocket Books 1987.

Workers' Party of Jamaica papers.

Working People's Alliance, *Argument for Unity against the Dictatorship*. Georgetown: 1983.

Working People's Alliance, *For a Revolutionary Socialist Guyana*. Georgetown: March 1979.

Working People's Alliance, "Manifesto: for the redemption reconstruction and rebirth of Guyana". Georgetown: mimeo n.d.

Wright, Eric Ohlin, *Classes*. London: Verso Press 1087.

Zaharuddin, M., *From Self Destruction to Self Reliance*. Georgetown: PNC Publication 1973.

Zimbalist, Andrew and John Weeks, *Panama at the Crossroads*. Berkeley: University of California Press 1991.

Articles

"ACLM: theses on liberation", *Caribbean Dialogue* 1, no. 3 (November-December 1975).

"At the crossroads – the emergence and potential of the ULF", *Caribbean Dialogue* 2 nos. 3 & 4 (April-May 1977).

Barriteau, Eudine, 'The 1984 general elections in Grenada", *Caricom Perspectives* 29 (January-February 1985).

Barros, Robert, 'The Left and democracy: recent debates in Latin America", *Telos* no. 68 (Summer 1986).

Best, Lloyd, "Outline of a model of pure plantation economy", *Social and Economic Studies* (September 1968).

Best, Lloyd, "The February Revolution in Trinidad and Tobago". In *Readings in Government and Politics of the West Indies*, Trevor Munroe and Rupert Lewis eds.: Department of Government, University of the West Indies Kingston: 1972.

Best, Lloyd, "Whither New World?", *New World Quarterly* 4, no. 1 (1986).

Bishop, Maurice, "In nobody's backyard". In *Maurice Bishop Speaks: the Grenada Revolution 1979-1983*, edited by Steve Clark. New York: Pathfinder Press 1983.

Black, George, 'The American's man: a talk with Eric Gairy", NACLA *Report on the Americas* (March-April 1985).

Brown, Ethelred Revd., "My recent visit to Jamaica", *The Ambassador* 2, no. 2 (1952-1953).

Burnham, Jesse, "Beware of my Brother Forbes". PPP pamphlet n.d.

"CCCs 'no' to Grenada's invasion", *Caribbean Contact* (November 1983).

"Dispute at Aroima", *Combat*, no. 2 (1992).

Duncan, Neville,"Political violence in the Caribbean". In *Strategy and Security in the Caribbean* edited by Ivelaw Griffith. New York: Praeger 1991.

Editorial, "Real threat to security of our region", *Caribbean Contact* (March 1981).

Ellner, Steve, "Introduction: the changing status of the Latin American Left in the recent past". In *The Latin American Left: From the Fall of Allende to Perestroika* edited by Barry Carr and Steve Ellner. Boulder: Westview Press 1993.

Farhi, Faridah, "State disintegration and urban-based revolutionary crisis: a comparative analysis of Iran and Nicaragua", *Comparative Political Studies* 21, no. 2 (July 1988).

"Fascism on the rise", *Caribbean Dialogue* 2, no. 2 (March 1976).

Frank, Andre Gunder and Maria Fuentes, "Civil democracy, social movements on recent world history". In *Transforming the Revolution: Social Movements in the World System*, edited by Samir Amin, et al. New York: Monthly Review Press 1990.

"GAWU recognized after a year of struggle at CRM", *Combat* no. 2 (1992).

Girvan, Norman, "Chairman's report on New World Group, Jamaica for period August 1967 to September 1968", *New World Quarterly* 4, no. 3 (1968).

Girvan, Norman, "After Rodney – the politics of student protest in Jamaica", *New World Quarterly* 4, no. 3 (1968).

Government of Trinidad and Tobago, "Industrial Stabilization Act 1985", *Laws of Trinidad and Tobago* Act no. 8. Port of Spain: Government Printer 1965.

Griffith, Ivelaw, 'The quest for security in the Caribbean". PhD dissertation, City University of New York 1990.

Guyana Chronicle (3 September 1977).

Guyana Chronicle (5 September 1977).

Guyana Chronicle (22 October 1977).

"Guyana: the faces behind the masks", *Covert Action Information Bulletin* no.10 (August-September 1980).

Guyana Trade Union Congress, "Minutes of a meeting of the Political Committee of the Guyana Trades Union Congress". (19 March 1985).

Habermas, Jurgen, "Conservatism and capitalist crisis", *New Left Review* no. 115 (May-June 1979).

Henry, Paget, "Political accumulation and authoritarianism in the Caribbean: the case of Antigua", *Social and Economic Studies* 4, no. 1 (March 1991).

"Highlights of the Jamaica Progressive League's history", *Souvenir Journal, Second Anniversary Celebration of Jamaica Independence* (August 1962).

Hill, Robert, 'Walter Rodney: a brief biography". Introduction to *Walter Rodney Speaks.* Trenton: African World Press 1990.

Hoffman, John,"Marxism, revolution and democracy", *Revolutionary World* 46/48 (1982).

Insanally, Mohammed, "Political defection and political change in Guyana". Mimeo. University of Guyana 1972.

Intercontinental Press (1 April 1985).

Jagan, Cheddi, "Imperialist intrigue in the Caribbean'", *Thunder* (January-March 1976).

Jagan, Cheddi, "Primary interest is struggle", *The Daily Chronicle* (22 December 1956).

"Jagan on critical support", *Caribbean Dialogue* 1, no. 3, (November-December 1975).

"Jamaica: state of emergency", *Caribbean Dialogue* 2, nos. 5 & 6 (June-July 1976).

James, C. L. R.,"Letters to Constance Henderson/Webb"

Joseph, Samuel, "Barbadian socialism, social democracy, or partnership with imperialism", MONALI, *Workers Unite: Against Imperialism* 1, no. 2 (April-June 1976).

Keith, Sherry and Robert Girling, 'This hypocrisy about Cuba in Africa", *Caribbean Contact* (July 1981).

Keohane, Robert O.,"The theory of hegemonic stability and change in international economic regimes". In *Change in the International System* edited by Ole Holsti. Boulder: Westview Press 1980.

King, Sydney, "Observation on Jagan's Congress Speech on the 'political situation' ". University of Puerto Rico 1956.

La Guerre, John Gaffar, "Socialism in Trinidad and Tobago", *Caribbean Issues* 4, no. 2 (August 1978).

Latin America Regional Reports, Caribbean, RC 81-06 (17 July 1981).

Latin America Regional Reports, Caribbean, RC 81-07, 21 August 1981.

Lewis, Gordon K., "Grenada 1983: the lessons for the Caribbean Left". Paper presented at the Conference on the Grenada Revolution, 1979-1983, University of the West Indies, St Augustine, Trinidad, 24-25 May 1984.

Louison, George, "Interview with George Louison", *Intercontinental Press* 22 no. 7 (16 April 1984).

"Lukewarm support for elections", *Caribbean Contact* (December 1984).

Lutchman, H. A., "Patronage in colonial society", *Caribbean Quarterly* 16, no. 2 (1970).

Lewis, Michael, "Letter from prison", *Caribbean Dialogue* 3, no. 1 (January 1977).

Mandle, Jay, "Caribbean dependency and its alternatives", *Latin American Perspective* 42, 11, no. 3 (Summer 1984).

"Manley reveals Rightist plot", *Caribbean Dialogue* 2, nos. 5 & 6 (June-July 1976)

"Manley stays on as PNP turns Right", *Latin America Regional Report: Caribbean* RC 81-08 (September 1981).

Mars, Perry, "Foreign influence, political conflicts and conflict resolution in the Caribbean", *Journal of Peace Research* 34, no. 4 (November 1995).

Mars, Perry, "The Guyana 1985 elections in retrospect", *Bulletin of Eastern Caribbean Studies* 13, no. 4 (September-October 1987).

Mars, Perry, "The race-class problematic and Leftist political practice: Caribbean examples". Paper presented to conference on "Black Politics and Theory in Crisis. Columbia University, New York, Fall 1994.

Mintz, Sydney, "The question of Caribbean peasantries: a comment", *Caribbean Studies* 1, no. 3 (1961).

Munroe, Trevor, "Address to second sitting – fourth congress, Worker's Party of Jamaica". (27 January 1990).

Munroe, Trevor, "Report . . . to fourth congress of the WPJ first sitting". (9 September 1988).

NACLA, *Report on the Americas* (November-December 1984).

NACLA, *Report on the Americas* (March-April 1985).

NACLA, *Report on the Americas* (July-August 1985).

NACLA, "Soviet collapse not so relevant", *Report on the Americas* 35, no. 5 (May 1992).

"PPP supports mixed economy, free press", *Starbroek News* (23 March 1990).

People's Progressive Party, "The great betrayal". Pamphlet. Georgetown (September 1955).

Phillips, Dion, "Caribbean militarism: a response to a crisis", *Contemporary Marxism* no.10 (1985).

"Potentials and pitfalls of co-ops", *Caribbean Dialogue* 2 no.5 & 6 (June-July 1976).

Poulantzas, Nicos and Ralph Miliband, *"The problem of the capitalist state"*. In *Ideology in Social Science, Readings in Critical Social Theory*, edited by Robin Blackburn, Bungay, 1972.

"The Prophet", *New World* (Guyana) 30 April 1965.

"Protests signals borderline: Seaga blames communists; Manley plays it cool", *Latin American Regional Reports Caribbean* RC 85-02 (22 February 1985).

"The question of socialist strategy", *Caribbean Dialogue* 2, no. 2 (March 1976).

"Race and class in the struggle for parliamentary power", *Caribbean Dialogue* 3 no. 2 (February-March 1977).

Ray, Ellen and Bill Schaaf, "Massive destabilization in Jamaica", *Covert Action Information Bulletin* no. 10 (August-September 1980).

Ray, Ellen and Bill Schaaf, "US crushes Caribbean jewel", *Covert Action Information Bulletin* no. 20 (Winter 1984).

Riviere, Bill, "Ideology, mass work and political behaviour in the Commonwealth Caribbean: an exploratory study of Dominica". Paper presented to ISER/Depart. of Economics-sponsored symposium in commemoration of the 20th anniversary of the 1970 February Revolution in Trinidad and Tobago, University of the West Indies, St Augustine 19-21 April 1990.

Robotham, Don,"Letter of resignation from WPJ" (18 August 1988).

Runciman, W. G., "The 'triumph' of capitalism as a topic in the theory of social selection", *New Left Review* no. 210 (March-April 1995).

Ryan, Selwyn,"Analysis of Trinidad and Tobago elections", *Caricom Perspectives* (January-March 1987).

"Seaga stands to benefit from split in Jamaica Left", *Latin America Regional Report: Caribbean* RC-08 (October 1982).

Starboek News, 24 May 1989.

"State repression and political prisoners", *Caribbean Dialogue* 3, no. 1 (January 1977).

Stone, Carl, "Ideology, public opinion and the media in Jamaica", *Caribbean Issues* 14 no. 2 (August 1978).

Stone, Carl "Decolonization and the Caribbean state system: the case of Jamaica". Inter-American Politics Seminar Series, Center for Inter-American Relations, 5-6 May 1978.

Stone, Carl, "Understanding political tendencies in Jamaica". Mimeo. Department of Government University of the West Indies Mona 1983.

"Supplementary memorandum of the Jamaica Progressive League to the West India Royal Commission, 1938". Papers of Egbert Ethelred Brown. Schomberg Center, New York.

"There are many roads to socialism – Dr Jagan", *Starbroek News* 3 March 1990 and 11 April 1990.

Thomas, C. Y., "Comments on the Grenada crisis of 1983", *Intercontinental Press* (15 October 1985).

Thomas, C. Y., "On formulating a Marxist theory of regional integration", *Transition* 1, no.1 (1978).

Thomas, C. Y., "Perspectives on the future of the state in the Caribbean". Mimeo. Department of Economics, University of the West Indies, Mona, May 1995.

Thomas, C. Y., "Speech on Grenada", *Intercontinental Press* (15 October 1985).

Thomas, C. Y., "State capitalism in Guyana: an assessment of Burham's cooperative republic". In *Crisis in the Caribbean* edited by Fitzroy Ambursley and Robin Cohen. New York: Monthly Review Press 1983.

Thomas, C. Y., "The non-capitalist path as theory and practice of decolonization and socialist transformation", *Latin American Perspective* 5, no. 2 (Spring 1978).

Thomas, Elean. In WPJ papers, "Contribution to Rethinking".

"Tim Hector victorious at last", *Caribbean Contact* (February 1990).

"ULF assembly"? *Caribbean Dialogue* 2 nos. 3 & 4 (April-May 1976).

"US invades Grenada . . . Nicaragua next?", *Covert Action Information Bulletin* no. 29 (Winter 1984).

"US invasion of Grenada", *Intercontinental Press* 21, no. 22 (14 November 1983).

Walton, John, "Debt, protest and the state in Latin America". In *Power and Popular Protest: Latin American Social Movements* edited by Susan Eckstein. Berkeley: University of California Press 1989.

Watson, Hilbourne,"The Caribbean Basin Initiative and Caribbean development: a critical analysis", *Contemporary Marxism* no. 10 (1987).

Watson, Hilbourne, "Non-capitalist development and the Commonwealth Caribbean: a critique of its theoretical and prescriptive conditions". Paper presented at Caribbean Studies Association, Annual Conference, St Thomas, Virgin Islands, 26-30 May 1981.

Wheeler, Tim,"Jonestown and the CIA", *Daily World* (23 July 1981).

Williams, Dessima, "Grenada: from parliamentary rule to people's power". In *Democracy in the Caribbean* edited by Carlene Edie. Westport: Praeger 1994.

Working People's Alliance, "A new political system". Georgetown: mimeo n.d.

Working People's Alliance, "Draft programme for the Democratic Republic". Georgetown: mimeo n.d.

Working People's Alliance, Letter to Presidential Secretariat (3 January 1990).

Working People's Alliance, Press Release, " PNC unleashes savagery". (18 September 1981).

Working People's Alliance, "Text of election broadcast", Guyana Broadcasting Service (23 November 1985).

Index

distinguished from, 148; and state power, 37. *See also* Caribbean Left
Lenin, Vladimir, 60, 153
Leninism, 52, 59, 112, 114, 159, 162
Lewis, Gordon, 162
Liberalism, 10, 154, 155
Liberation, 120
Liberation Theology, 51, 155
Lopez, Nico, 120
Louison, George, 111, 125
LP (Liberation Party), 81, 98, 185n.62
LSW, 116
Lumpen proletariat, 22, 153
Luxemberg, Rosa, 154

Maha Sabha, 92
Majority rule principle, 32
Manheim, Karl, 147
Manley, Michael: and anti-imperialism, 54; and bauxite industry nationalization, 55; and democracy, 163; and democratic socialism, 84; and destabilization, 98, 139, 170; and foreign intervention, 135; and ideological pluralism, 88; occupation of, 108; and political violence, 97, 134; and race, 75; on tribalistic struggle, 34; and United States' destabilization of PNP, 4; and United States military aid, 141; and Westminster democracy, 119; and WPJ, 93
Manley, Norman, 131, 132, 133, 144-145
Manpower Citizens Association (MPCA), 46, 132, 135, 181n.37, 181n.38
Mao Zedong, 58, 153
Maoism, 52, 59, 185n.62
MAP, 51
Maraj, Bhadase, 117
Markist, 154
Marx, Karl, 60, 87, 147, 153, 154
Marxism: banning of Marxist literature, 95; and capitalism, 148; and Caribbean Left classification, 10-11; and Caribbean Left's leaders, 42, 149; and Caribbean Left's self-concept, 9; and class/race dynamics, 73; and democracy, 87; forms of, 52; and ideology, 149, 155; impact of, 161-164, 171-173; and imperialism, 63;

and labour movements, 48; and middle class intellectuals, 160; and mixed economy approach, 71; and Modern World Systems theory, 13; and political economy approach, 5; and political education, 119; and Radical Left movements, 56, 58; and Reformist Left movements, 55, 112; study of, 48
Marxism-Leninism: and Caribbean Left's development, 154, 155; and Caribbean Left's rightward shift, 10; and Caribbean Left's self-concept, 9; and political education, 120, 121; and PPP, 114; and Radical Left movements, 58; and Revolutionary Left movements, 58-60; Thomas on, 161; and WPA, 85, 136
Mass media: and authoritarianism, 67, 68; and destabilization, 35; middle class use of, 29; and mobilization strategies, 91. *See also* Press
Masses: alienation of, 5, 106, 122-127, 137; and Bishop, 137; and black consciousness, 57; Caribbean Left's neglect of, 8; and class relations, 32; commitment of, 162; and communism, 91; conservatism of, 126; and debt crisis, 17; escapist behavior of, 160; and ideological hegemony, 14; and ideology, 106, 109; and IMF structural adjustment, 146; independent action of, 109; and intellectuals, 14; and Left and Right political forces, 12; and Marxism-Leninism, 161; and middle class leadership, 7, 105-106; and mobilization strategies, 173; and New World Group, 50; and organic leadership, 114-115; political awareness of, 2; and political education, 119-122; political participation of, 31; and political violence, 98, 158, 160; and Radical Left movements, 56; and Reform Left movements' class alliances, 55; revolutionary potential of, 6; and vanguardist politics, 112-113; and Westminster democracy, 66. *See also* Elite – mass gap; Subordinate classes; Working class
MBPM (Maurice Bishop Patriotic Movement): and electoral participation, 88,